NEW FRONTIERS IN HISTORY

series editors
Mark Greengrass
Department of History, Sheffield University

John Stevenson
Worcester College, Oxford

This important series reflects the substantial expansion that has occurred in the scope of history syllabuses. As new subject areas have emerged and syllabuses have come to focus more upon methods of historical enquiry and knowledge of source materials, a growing need has arisen for correspondingly broad-ranging textbooks.

New Frontiers in History provides up-to-date overviews of key topics in British, European and world history, together with accompanying source material and appendices. Authors focus upon subjects where revisionist work is being undertaken, providing a fresh viewpoint which will be welcomed by students and sixth-formers. The series also explores established topics which have attracted much conflicting analysis and require a synthesis of the state of the debate.

Published titles

David Andress   French society in revolution 1789–1799
Jeremy Black   The politics of Britain
Paul Bookbinder   Weimar Germany
Michael Braddick   The nerves of state: taxation and the financing of the English state, 1558–1714
Michael Broers   Europe after Napoleon
David Brooks   The age of upheaval: Edwardian politics, 1899–1914
Carl Chinn   Poverty amidst prosperity
Conan Fischer   The rise of the Nazis
T. A. Jenkins   Parliament, party and politics in Victorian Britain
Neville Kirk   Change, continuity and class: Labour in British society, 1850–1920
Keith Laybourn   The General Strike of 1926
Frank McDonough   Neville Chamberlain, appeasement and the British road to war
Evan Mawdsley   The Stalin years, 1929–1953
Alan O'Day   Irish Home Rule 1867–1921
Panikos Panayi   Immigration, racism and ethnicity 1815–1945
Daniel Szechi   The Jacobites
David Taylor   The New Police
John Whittam   Fascist Italy

Forthcoming titles

Ciaran Brady   The unplanned conquest: social changes and political conflict in sixteenth-century Ireland
John Childs   The army, state and society 1500–1800
Barry Coward   The Cromwellian protectorate
Simon Ditchfield   The Jesuits in early modern Europe
Bruce Gordon   The Swiss Reformation
Susan-Mary Grant   The American Civil War and Reconstruction
Tony Kushner   The Holocaust and its aftermath
Alan Marshall   The age of faction
Keith Mason   Slavery and emancipation
Alexandra Walsham   Persecution and toleration in England, 1530–1660

British politics
in an age of reform

Michael J. Turner

Manchester University Press
Manchester and New York

Published by Manchester University Press
Oxford Road, Manchester M13 9NR, UK
and Room 400, 175 Fifth Avenue, New York, NY 10010, USA
www.manchesteruniversitypress.co.uk

Distributed exclusively in the USA by
Palgrave, 175 Fifth Avenue, New York NY 10010, USA

Distributed exclusively in Canada by
UBC Press, University of British Columbia, 2029 West Mall,
Vancouver, BC, Canada V6T 1Z2

British Library Cataloguing-in-Publication Data
A catalogue record for this book is available from the British Library

Library of Congress Cataloging-in-Publication Data
A catalog record for this book is available from the Library of Congress

ISBN 0 7190 5186 X paperback

First edition published 1999 by Manchester University Press

First digital, on-demand edition produced by Lightning Source 2005

Contents

Contents

Acknowledgements

I would like to thank the editors of the *New Frontiers* series, and everyone at Manchester University Press who helped with the publication of this volume. I am also grateful to those colleagues in the History Department at Reading University who took on a few more students than usual so that I could concentrate on writing.

Any errors or shortcomings in the book are entirely my own responsibility.

My wife and family have offered invaluable encouragement, and this work is dedicated to them.

MJT

Abbreviations

The following journal titles have been abbreviated in the end notes and the bibliographical essay:

AmHR   *American Historical Review*
EcHR   *Economic History Review*
EHR   *English Historical Review*
HJ   *Historical Journal* (formerly *Cambridge Historical Journal*)
HR   *Historical Research* (formerly *Bulletin of the Institute of Historical Research*)
HSANZ   *Historical Studies of Australia and New Zealand*
IRSH   *International Review of Social History*
JBS   *Journal of British Studies*
JHI   *Journal of the History of Ideas*
JMH   *Journal of Modern History*
NH   *Northern History*
P&P   *Past and Present*
PH   *Parliamentary History*
SH   *Social History*
TRHS   *Transactions of the Royal Historical Society*
VS   *Victorian Studies*

Note on party names and ministerial changes

Party names

The 'Whig' and 'Tory' party denominations arose during the political and religious struggles of the seventeenth century. They were originally insults: Whigs were militant Scottish Presbyterians, Tories were Irish robbers. Party labels had less currency after the Hanoverian accession of 1714, and many former Tories were excluded from public life because of their supposed hostility towards the ruling dynasty. The use and meaning of the terms changed during the late eighteenth century. They were widely employed at the 1807 general election, by which time it was generally understood that Whigs were advocates of civil and religious liberty, and that Tories were defenders of court, Church and established institutions. This distinction involved a serious clash of opinion on the salient issues of the time, notably Catholic emancipation, parliamentary and economical reform, the royal prerogative, ministerial conduct and public order.

Governments 1760–1832

The following administrations (overleaf), generally known by the name of the chief minister, held office between George III's accession (1760) and the passing of the Great Reform Act (1832).

Party names and ministerial changes

1757–62	Duke of Newcastle
May 1762	Earl of Bute
April 1763	George Grenville
July 1765	Marquess of Rockingham
July 1766	Earl of Chatham (Pitt the Elder)
October 1768	Duke of Grafton
January 1770	Lord North
March 1782	Marquess of Rockingham
July 1782	Earl of Shelburne
April 1783	Duke of Portland (Fox–North coalition)
December 1783	William Pitt (Pitt the Younger)
March 1801	Henry Addington
May 1804	William Pitt
February 1806	Lord William Wyndham Grenville ('Ministry of All the Talents')
March 1807	Duke of Portland
October 1809	Spencer Perceval
June 1812	Lord Liverpool
April 1827	George Canning
August 1827	Viscount Goderich
January 1828	Duke of Wellington
November 1830	Earl Grey

Introduction

This is a study of British politics during the late eighteenth and early nineteenth centuries, with special focus on the years between the fall of Lord North in 1782 and the passing of the Great Reform Act in 1832. It seeks to describe and explain the events, ideas, policies, reactions and motives that made this 'an age of reform'. Though such characterisations will always have their detractors, and though we must recognise at the outset that not all contemporaries were conscious of living through 'an age of reform', it is hoped that the concept will be found useful as both a descriptive and an analytical tool. Who wanted reforms, and why, and the arguments and tactics employed against reform are matters that will feature prominently in what follows. But attention will also be given to the accidental, unconscious and ineffective, in addition to what was intended, conscious and successful, for politics in the 'age of reform' did not proceed in unbroken lines of development. Controversy, obstruction and conflict typify this period alongside the implementation of particular reforms. Old and new political practices co-existed. There was continuity as well as change, a love for tradition as well as a longing for progress.

What have been the 'new frontiers' in the writing of late eighteenth- and early nineteenth-century British political history? Where is new research going? Clearly, the frontiers have never been fixed. They constantly shift as historians adopt new approaches or focus upon previously obscure topics. Some have emphasised change, while others insist that much did not change. Some investigate agency, others structure. Historians who write 'history from below', seeking to raise the political activity and aspirations of common people from unmerited neglect, are countered by those who see in the politics of unreformed Britain only the operation of networks of power and patronage controlled from above. Since there is no such thing as definitive history, and no historian can presume to have the last word on any given subject, new research will repeatedly alter, complement, or even invalidate previous findings. Conclusions often differ because of personal, political, social and other influences: historians cannot detach themselves completely from their own surroundings.

Among the most significant revisions which have affected modern interpretation of late eighteenth- and early nineteenth-century British politics are those associated with L. B. Namier, E. P. Thompson and J. C. D. Clark. The work of their supporters and opponents has also enriched historical debate, and the controversies generated by these three scholars are worthy of brief discussion because they encompass some of the historical problems with which the present study is most concerned.

Lewis Namier, who began his research in the 1920s and reached the height of his fame and influence in the 1950s, questioned older assumptions about the unreformed political order. Historians after 1832 had seen little merit in the pre-1832 system. Nineteenth-century Whig historians had looked back on the Great Reform Act as a symbol of inevitable progress and the consummation of an alliance between the Whigs and the people, who joined together to reform a crumbling, outmoded, disreputable system. They traced reform as an idea and a movement back to the early years of George III's reign, and considered the eventual passing of a reform act a crowning triumph for the Whig political creed. 'Whig history' focused on the development of parliamentary government and judged eighteenth-century politics in the light of subsequent events. Since the Victorian system of government was superior and desirable, it was thought, politicians in previous generations must have consciously tried to promote or obstruct progress towards the ideal.

Namier countered this orthodoxy. He built up a full command of contemporary source materials and focused attention upon the workings of the unreformed parliament, insisting that parliament could best be understood through the personalities and mentalities of its members. Namier argued that political principles counted for little in the unreformed system, that much of what eighteenth-century politicians did was irrational, and that history does not proceed in an orderly and logical fashion. He defended the pre-1832 system. It suited the political needs of its era, Namier claimed, and should not be judged according to modern ideas of representation: as political circumstances and opinions changed, so did the composition of the House of Commons. Namier investigated the use of secret service money and concluded that the old electoral system was not as corrupt as was often supposed. He also denied that party was important in the unreformed system. Parliamentary government and the familiar two-party framework did not replace royal government until the late nineteenth century, he thought, and George III's reign was a period of transition during which a mixture of groups and interests (including a large number of 'independents') operated. Allegiances constantly shifted, and the basic division was not between formed parties but between allies and opponents of court and ministry.

One of the core assumptions of Whig historians was that George III broke with existing constitutional practice and tried to reassert royal power. The Whigs therefore rallied to defend the constitution, demanding that measures should be taken permanently to limit the influence of the court. Namier attacked this interpretation. He maintained that George III respected the established constitution, that plenty of contemporaries noted this, and that there was no organised Whig opposition to the court.

Critics of Namier who wrote when the 'Namier school' was in its heyday[1] offered much unfavourable comment. They pointed out that when analysis is focused only upon a short period, as in Namier's microscopic research into the early 1760s, the historian loses sight of the bigger picture. They argued that ideas were more important than he allowed, and that his personal dislike for intellectuals and belief in the irrationality of human nature prompted him to suppose, wrongly, that motive forces in history are not conscious or reasonable.

There were more detailed criticisms. Herbert Butterfield noted that contemporaries who initially found nothing inappropriate about George III's actions subsequently changed their minds. They came to consider his political ambitions improper and arbitrary. They denied that his conduct accorded with the established constitution. This was a modern-looking political system in the sense that the dominance of Whig families before George III's accession in 1760 had involved government by ministries based on party principle. When George III tried to free himself from restraints, Whigs were bound to claim that he was overthrowing a settled and recognised system of government. Namierite history, thought Butterfield, placed too much emphasis on chance and inconsistency. Serious political issues were at stake after 1760, and there was a genuine conflict of ideas. Clear purpose and principle moved the king, his allies and his enemies, and his chief opponents in the Rockingham Whig connection evolved an early form of party. They had conscious political goals. George III said he wanted to destroy party, indeed, and he would hardly have considered this necessary unless it really existed.

Though George III might not have acted against the letter of the constitution, suggested W. R. Fryer, he did break with established practice. His predecessor, George II, had not enjoyed a free choice of ministers, for example, and by trying to secure this freedom George III attempted something unusual. Fryer accepted that George III's infringement of settled conventions might not always have been conscious or intended. But many specific examples could not be excused on such grounds, for the king was well aware of what he was doing. According to Fryer, Namierites tended to ignore some basic realities of late eighteenth-century politics. Certain standards of behaviour were appropriate to the times, and of key importance was the fact that ministers had to be able to manage the House of Commons. Therefore George III could never expect an entirely free choice of ministers. The Commons imposed upon the king certain unwritten rules over and above the limitations imposed by law. Sometimes George III evaded these, as when he appointed ministers who did not have a Commons majority, dismissed those who had parliament's backing, took advice from men who were not ministers, or tried to frustrate and divide cabinets, normally by favouring some of their members over the rest. George III wanted more say on matters of personnel and policy.

This involved him in conflict with parliament, for some of parliament's powers were designed to check executive influence.

George III's actions were sometimes defensive rather than aggressive. As Fryer noted, it had long been accepted that a cabinet could not discuss important matters without the king's permission. When in office, however, the Rockingham Whigs offered collective advice without notifying George III in advance, and Pitt the Younger and his Tory successors subsequently carried this practice further. Ministers were clearly encroaching upon the rights of the crown. Hence George III's insistence, especially after 1801, that ministers should pledge before accepting office that they would not recommend Catholic emancipation (the king's bugbear). But the decline in royal political power between the early part of George III's reign and the passing of the Great Reform Act in 1832 could not be reversed, even if remnants of the crown's former influence survived (as in Brighton and Windsor at election time, because of special local circumstances, and in the political creed of politicians such as Peel, who held that the first duty of a public servant was to the crown and that it was important for a minister to have the monarch's confidence).

While Namier was interested mainly in the 'structure of politics', a different set of preoccupations shaped Edward Thompson's *The Making of the English Working Class*, originally published in 1963 (Thompson added a new postscript in 1968, in order to answer some of his critics, and there was a new preface when the book was reissued in 1980). Thompson's central thesis is that between 1780 and 1832, working people came to feel an identity of interests among themselves and against their rulers and employers. By 1832 the most significant factor in politics was the presence of the working class. Thompson supported this assertion by linking the popular traditions of the eighteenth century with the radicalism of the 1790s, by examining the impact on labouring folk of the industrial revolution and new work disciplines, by exploring the changing nature and influence of religion, and by investigating wartime luddism and the upsurge in radicalism after 1815 and their association with political theory and class consciousness in the 1820s and 1830s. Thompson was most interested in the 'agency of working people', in their conscious efforts to shape politics, society and economy. He viewed class not as a structure or category, but as something that *happens* in human relationships. Common experiences and shared interests had created class consciousness by 1832, Thompson argued, and this was expressed in traditions, values, ideas and institutions.

Some reviewers in the 1960s rejected Thompson's notion of a continuous underground tradition linking the agitation of the 1790s with the upsurge in radicalism after the French wars. They questioned his argument about the connection between constitutional and violent protest. Thompson responded[2] by claiming that underground activity and insurrectionary plotting were even more mature than he had previously thought, that conspirators of the early 1800s later joined in luddism and the postwar radical agitation, and that the same people could and did engage in both constitutional and violent activity, depending on prevalent circumstances. Thompson stressed continuity of protest at the local level. This was a matter of sympathy and co-ordination as well as direct participation: even if many workers in disturbed districts did not join in machine-breaking, Thompson suggested, we cannot ignore their radicalism, their refusal to inform on offenders, and their collections in aid of captured luddites. When critics argued that Thompson exaggerated the size and scope of popular movements because this assisted him to impose his notion of class, Thompson pointed to clear signs of 'a rising standard of popular political expectation' and insisted that his opponents were looking for the wrong kind of proof for the existence of class. According to Thompson, class and class consciousness are cultural formations and cannot easily be measured. The 'making of the working class' was just that – a *making*, a process.

Thompson was accused of being more sentimental than analytical, more emotional than factual. Critics complained that there was little evidence to substantiate some of his assertions. He in turn condemned their 'modish agnosticism' and called for an exercise of 'the historical imagination'. In 1980 Thompson confirmed that all the research conducted and published since 1963 had not led him to alter his opinions about the wartime revolutionary underground nor the political aspects of luddism. He continued to argue against both the positivist accounts of historians who stress only 'modernisation', and Marxist historians who regard class as a definable 'thing' (so that the class consciousness it ought to have can be deduced from this definition). In the 1980s and 1990s some commentators argued that class terminology was not used by many early nineteenth-century radicals.[3] The latter tended to use more inclusive, participatory language. They spoke of 'the people' rather than of classes, though it should be remembered that the precise meaning of terms is not always easy to determine, and that political rhetoric and symbols were flexible tools whose message and purpose were hotly contested.

Thompson remained a champion of 'history from below'. He disliked concepts of paternalism because he found that these offered a model of society only as it was seen from above. Political and social relations between the high and low in eighteenth- and early nineteenth-century England were not static or settled, he thought, but dynamic.

Dynamism was minimised in Jonathan Clark's *English Society 1688–1832*, published in 1985. Clark asserted that society was still agrarian, traditionalist, deferential, pious and hierarchical in the century and a half before the Great Reform Act, and that the real challenge to the established order came not from social and economic change but from religious heterodoxy and radical political ideas. Unreformed England, contended Clark, was a 'confessional state' in which religion dominated, and the old order collapsed when the bulwarks of orthodox Anglican Christianity were removed. Protestant Dissenters and Catholics were granted civil rights by the repeal of the Test and Corporation Acts in 1828 and the passing of Catholic emancipation in 1829. Seriously breached in this manner, and abandoned by some of its former defenders, the established constitution could not survive. Parliamentary reform in 1832 marked its final destruction.

Clark presented his case in 1985 in a highly confrontational fashion. He rejected the work of historians who assumed that social and economic pressures undermined the old order. He disparaged researchers of liberal or socialist sympathies as intolerably teleological and deterministic in historical method. By focusing narrowly on ideological struggles in unreformed England, however, Clark exposed his own biases and enabled his critics to argue that eighteenth-century society was rather more complex than he appreciated.[4]

Particular parts of Clark's analysis are questionable, notably his treatment of radicalism and his ideas about the end of the old order between 1828 and 1832. Many historians have seen radicalism not as a united movement, but as an internally divided one. Radicalism was a discontinuous and at times disorderly mixture of motives and aims. Agitation and mobilisation covered a range of issues, including parliamentary reform, social improvement, the slave trade, local government, economic policy and the privileges of the Church. Yet Clark finds radicalism more coherent than this, for he sees its source and core as heterodox Dissent. It is true that many reformers were Dissenters. Indeed, it was assumed at the time that there was a link between Dissent and radicalism. But plenty of reformers were not Dissenters, and anti-establishment opinion could easily have developed from political rather than religious premises. In addition, much agitation was not lasting, widespread or ideological in character. It had immediate causes: material hardship and high taxes, perhaps, or revelations of political corruption. Clark stresses the Church–Dissent rivalry and the conflict between the old order and reform, but many people found themselves in the broad centre of contemporary opinion rather than at the extremes, and united action by Anglicans and Dissenters, conservatives and liberals, on a range of economic, social and cultural issues, was not uncommon.

As for the end of the old order, Clark emphasises the opinions and conduct of ultra Tories, who were so outraged when a Tory ministry passed Catholic emancipation that they turned against it and thereby tipped the political balance in favour of reform. This addresses only one of the many causes which led to parliamentary reform in 1832. Amazingly, Clark ignores the important role of extra-parliamentary pressure, as well as the full range of personal and political influences shaping the conduct of those at court and in parliament at this time. Some ultra Tories were not in fact prepared to accept parliamentary reform, and others may have voted for reform because of the resentment they and their rural supporters felt against recent agricultural and financial policies, not because of Catholic emancipation.

It should be clear from the above that Namier, Thompson and Clark all had their own agendas, and that these influenced their interpretations and conclusions. The present study is not offered as an exemplar of any particular school or method, and the foregoing discussion is intended only to indicate some of the 'new frontiers' – and the controversies surrounding them – which have influenced twentieth-century historical scholarship. Nobody who seeks to understand more about British politics between the 1780s and 1830s can afford to ignore the arguments to which revisionist work has given rise, nor the specific developments which historians are still seeking to explain. Since the 1960s there has been a burgeoning of interest in the growth of popular pressure for reform, and in the responses of elite politicians. Attention has been paid to the nature of radicalism, and how it related to the expansion of political activity and development of the political press. The level of participation in the unreformed electoral system has become a major debating point, and it is clear that non-voters as well as voters evinced political commitment and consciousness in the late eighteenth and early nineteenth centuries. Among the significant pre-occupations of the 1980s and 1990s is the 'linguistic turn', the attempt to recreate the intellectual framework upon which political vocabulary and programmes rested. This relates closely to the contested meanings of particular words and symbols. Meanwhile older concerns are continually revisited: whether Fox was moved more by principle or by personal ambition; the strengths and weaknesses of Pittite government; the evolution of party, authority of parliament, development of the cabinet and powers of the crown; the impact of revolution and war on domestic politics; the concept of 'liberal' Toryism under Lord Liverpool; the motives behind and actual effects of parliamentary reform in 1832; the role of popular pressure during the reform crisis of 1830 to 1832.

All of the problems listed above are addressed in what follows. Each chapter offers a mixture of detailed narrative and lucid explanation, and broader themes are investigated alongside specific events. Readers will find that contemporaries (high and low) have been allowed to speak for themselves. Extensive use has also been made of work published in recent decades, and the need for synthesis as well as analysis has been recognised. End notes have been kept to a minimum, and apologies are offered to those historians who receive inadequate credit in the text. The bibliographical essay appended to this study mentions some of the works which have done most to shape opinion of the 'age of reform'. The specified books, articles and essays represent a solid bedrock of knowledge and insight upon which future labourers must seek to build.

Notes

1 This discussion of Namier is based mainly on H. R. Winkler, 'Sir Lewis Namier', *JMH*, 35, 1963, pp. 1–19; H. Butterfield, 'George III and the constitution', *History*, 43, 1958, pp. 14–33; W. R. Fryer, 'The study of British politics between the Revolution and the Reform Act', *Renaissance and Modern Studies*, 1, 1957, pp. 91–114, and 'King George III: his political character and conduct, 1760–84. A new Whig interpretation', *Renaissance and Modern Studies*, 6, 1962, pp. 68–101.

2 For what follows see especially Thompson's postscript of 1968 and preface of 1980, and E. J. Yeo, 'E. P. Thompson: witness against the beast', in W. Lamont (ed.), *Historical Controversies and Historians*, London, 1998, pp. 215–24.

3 For example, G. Stedman Jones, *Languages of Class. Studies in English Working Class History 1832–1982*, Cambridge, 1983; P. Joyce, *Visions of the People. Industrial England and the Question of Class 1840–1914*, Cambridge, 1991.

4 One of the most useful extended reviews of Clark's work is J. Innes, 'Jonathan Clark, social history and England's ancien regime', *P&P*, 115, 1987, pp. 165–200.

1

Crown and politicians

Introduction

The early part of George III's reign saw intense political instability. The king's own conduct and principles contributed to rising controversy in these years, as did personal rivalries among political leaders, conflicts of opinion on vital public issues, and the suspicions generated by new motives and goals. Brief, unstable ministries in the 1760s gave way after 1770 to a period of ascendancy for Lord North, the first man to satisfy two vital qualifications for political success: royal approval and a parliamentary majority. North was a talented political manager, but he proved unequal to the pressures of the American war of independence and was brought down in 1782. Meanwhile the largest and most influential group in opposition, the Rockingham Whigs, had evolved a coherent party doctrine which justified organised resistance to king and ministers. This doctrine clashed with the political creed of George III, and added extraordinary bitterness to the crises of 1782 to 1784. There followed a period of stable and constructive government under William Pitt the Younger, who enjoyed royal approval, parliamentary ascendancy and substantial support in the nation. His resignation in 1801, however, suggested that the relationship between crown and ministers was still evolving, and that there was no settled balance of power. The long French war and continuing growth of pressure from without added to the tension of the 1790s and early 1800s, and ensured that there could be no quick return to the prudent courses charted by Pitt during the 1780s.

Seeds of controversy in high politics

George III, who became king in 1760 at the age of twenty-two, was idealistic and conscientious, but politically inexperienced. His initial purposes were to end the Seven Years' War (1756–63) and to promote his favourite, the Earl of Bute, to high office. These aims were part of a much wider programme, for George III believed that his grandfather and predecessor, George II (who reigned from 1727 to 1760), had allowed the political authority of the crown to be undermined by great aristocratic families, whose selfish and corrupt leaders had eroded royal power and limited the monarch's independence. George III wanted to restore to the crown an unfettered use of royal prerogatives, and he considered this a God-given duty. The cardinal requirement was for the king to have full control over the selection and appointment of ministers, but at first it was not easy to find a combination of men who would agree to work together, who enjoyed uninterrupted royal approval, and who could transact business successfully in parliament.

In the 1760s there was a series of short-lived ministries under Bute, George Grenville, the Marquess of Rockingham, the Earl of Chatham (Pitt the Elder) and the Duke of Grafton. In pursuit of political peace and competent government, George III needed a strong prime minister with whom he could work to promote these ends and maintain an appropriate balance between crown and parliament. All efforts in this direction were unavailing, partly because of serious personality clashes. The king disliked Grenville's dictatorial manner, for example, and resented Rockingham Whig attempts to impose conditions as the price of their service. Most of the established political families refused to work with Bute, whom they resented as an agent of the court, while relations between Chathamites and Rockingham Whigs deteriorated to the point of open hostility by 1770. The main political groupings also disagreed with each other about how to deal with rebellion in America, misgovernment in India, domestic unrest and radicalism (particularly that associated with 'friend to liberty' John Wilkes), and the rise of influential extra-parliamentary interests (most notably in trade and finance). The Grenvillites were inflexible and conservative, whereas some Rockingham Whigs favoured moderate reforms. The latter eventually declared themselves for American independence and, at home, economical reform (public retrenchment to curtail executive patronage and weaken the influence of the crown).

Though organised political parties had still to develop, parliamentary 'connections' gathered behind particular individuals or families, and these began to associate themselves more closely with certain measures and ideas. Cabinets tended to be coalitions, however, and George III normally preferred minor changes of personnel to a general replacement of one set of ministers by another. This was an age in which royal approval remained a principal requirement for longevity in office. Ministers were accountable to parliament, but the fact that they were the king's appointments carried weight. A large number of 'independent' MPs in the House of Commons tended to vote with ministers while they had royal backing and made no mistakes. The government's majority in the House of Lords would also be secure in these circumstances. The development of party sentiment began to affect allegiances and voting patterns in due course, but as yet party remained rudimentary.

The expansion of political participation

Political awareness and activity were no longer the preserve of a wealthy landed elite. Excitement at election times, grievances about the nature of the representative system, the growing interest in and access to political news, development of the press and other forms of communication, and the responses generated by economic problems and parliamentary battles meant that political participation and debate were less exclusive and restricted than in previous decades.

The career of Wilkes was a catalyst for the rise of metropolitan radicalism. Though Wilkes was more an ambitious publicity-seeker than a genuine reformer, he rose to become a popular figurehead and critic of the establishment who brought into focus some of the issues about which contemporaries were most concerned: the use of general warrants (authorising the arrest of

suspects without specifically naming the individuals concerned), ideas of individual liberty, freedom of the press,
corporate privileges, the reporting of parliamentary debates and
the propriety of ministerial conduct. Radicals drawn from the
middling class of lesser merchants, traders and artisans in the
City of London, prompted by economic concerns and social
unease, hailed Wilkes as their champion, and the Bill of Rights
Society was established in 1769 to support the cause of liberty
and pay off his debts (indebtedness was used against Wilkes by
political opponents, but his followers held that the debts of the
people's champion were a public responsibility).[1] These radicals
initially failed to extend their influence outside London because
wider interest in parliamentary reform, one of their central
goals, was lacking.

Another influential pressure group, the City merchants,
gained political successes by focusing their meetings, petitions
and propaganda on specific complaints. In 1766, backed by
agitation in Manchester, Liverpool, Bristol, Glasgow and other
commercial centres, City merchants secured the repeal of the
1765 Stamp Act. This had been passed by Grenville in an
attempt to raise revenue in the colonies, but it had prompted
Americans to suspend importation and consumption of British
goods. Merchants at home, fearing for their profits, managed to
persuade the Rockingham government of 1765 to 1766 to
remove the offending statute.

The existence of a politicised public was confirmed at times of
unusual excitement. Demonstrations could be pro- as well as
anti-establishment. In April 1775, when George III issued the
proclamation of rebellion (confirming that American colonists
were now at war with the imperial authority), many towns
organised loyal addresses. Rather different was the general
sense of frustration at the end of the 1770s. The American war
was going badly and in many regions there was agitation for
peace and reforms. This drew strength from metropolitan radicalism, but particularly from discontent in the provinces. The
lead was taken by the Yorkshire Association under Christopher
Wyvill, a conservative landowner and parson who advocated
economical and parliamentary reform. Associations were
formed in other counties to join in the demand for reforms, and
this was one of the rare occasions during the eighteenth century

when an organised and substantial protest movement arose outside London. Meanwhile in Ireland there were calls for self-government, in parliament opposition leaders increased the pressure on North's ministry, and the Rockingham Whigs attempted to secure outdoor support for their own scheme of economical reform. There were 'No Popery' riots in Scotland in 1779 after North proposed mild relief for Catholics, and anti-Catholic fury was seen in London in June 1780 during the Gordon Riots (named after the leader of the Protestant Association, Lord George Gordon). By the early 1780s, mismanagement of the American war provided a focus for people with economic, social and political complaints.

Popular agitation rested on rapidly developing resources, which widened the arena for collective action. The expansion of the press increased the availability of political information. There was growing demand for news and comment: newspaper sales tended to be higher when parliament was in session, and more pamphlets were published and reviewed during the session than over the summer recess. The abandonment of general warrants in the 1760s and relaxation of restrictions on reporting Commons debates in the 1770s extended press freedoms, and in British law there was no pre-publication censorship. Not only was there a demand to be catered for, but the ability and inclination to meet this demand increased. Newspaper readership was much greater than sales figures suggest, and for each copy there were many readers, or many to whom it was read. The idea spread that a free press would ensure responsible government, and though politicians complained about the dishonesty and low character of those who peddled political news and opinion, it was clear that newspapers, pamphlets, books and other printed matter were becoming vital tools for informing a politically interested public. As well as stamped material (stamp duty had to be paid on legal and other documents and newspapers of a prescribed size), there was also much that was unstamped, and during elections or periods of intense political controversy hundreds of squibs, handbills, songs and cartoons would be put into circulation. The political print, in particular, became a form of mass communication. Pictures and caricatures could be understood even by the uneducated, and were often to be seen in public places.

The dissemination of news and opinion was furthered by the rise of the coffee house and political club. London's coffee houses became centres for conversation and business, and provision of newspapers was one of their regular services. There were about 200 coffee houses in the metropolis by 1780, at least 300 by 1820, and some were frequented by political leaders or used as meeting places for clubs and places from which to solicit patronage. The fact that most people who wanted political information could obtain it without difficulty is underlined by the availability of newspapers in many inns, shops and other places of popular resort, and by the spread of subscription reading-rooms. Press activity and club life were not confined to London, moreover. Manchester, Bristol, Liverpool and other thriving provincial towns also had newspapers, debating societies, coffee houses and taverns, all assisting in the formation of local political cultures.[2]

The increase in political consciousness facilitated a more critical examination of government and representation. The role of the crown, conduct of ministers, functions of parliament and nature of organised opposition were often discussed, but most attention was given to the electoral system. In time, a growing number of people concluded that the legislature was not sufficiently responsive to public opinion. Parliamentary reform was regarded as the panacea, and it was assumed that government would be cheaper, disinterested and more efficient if the basis of representation was widened. Parliamentary boroughs were concentrated in the south and south-west of England. Taking the United Kingdom as a whole, in the late eighteenth century the vote was restricted to about 3 per cent of adult males. Few boroughs had more than a thousand electors. Many were pocket boroughs, controlled by government or a patron, or rotten boroughs, where electorates were tiny and borough owners supreme. Boroughs varied in size and voting rights. The main franchises related to ownership of land (burgage boroughs), membership of a town corporation, which was often self-elected and non-resident (corporation boroughs), possession of the 'freedom' of a town by inheritance, marriage, apprenticeship or purchase (freeman boroughs), headship of a household with a fireplace and six months' residence (pot-walloper boroughs), and payment of local rates (scot and lot boroughs). In the counties, the vote had been enjoyed since the fifteenth century by 40s freeholders, a relatively low qualification by George III's reign because of changed currency values. Freeholds included land, offices in Church and state, and money incomes. Great landed families dominated county elections, though, and a county's representation was often shared in order to avoid costly and troublesome contests. Only two of the eighty-five counties were contested at the 1780 general election.

Most borough and county electorates were amenable to patronage, intimidation, bribery and other forms of control, and electoral purity became a primary goal of the nascent reform movement of this period. The work of J. A. Phillips and Frank O'Gorman, however, has indicated that the unreformed electorate cannot be regarded only as narrow, mercenary and deferential. In some regions there were high levels of partisanship, participation and politicisation, and elections provided opportunities for voters and non-voters alike to express opinions and negotiate with politicians. O'Gorman also insists that a genuine sense of party not only arose in high politics (that is, among the privileged elite), but can also be discerned at local level.[3]

A fusion of high and low politics

The remarkable expansion of popular political activity towards the end of the eighteenth century created a potential for the merging of high and low (non-elite) politics, a conjunction that would be strikingly promoted by the French Revolution. But this trend had become clear before 1789, particularly when opponents of the court appealed for extra-parliamentary support in pursuit of their political goals. George III came to the throne seeking to promote a new reign of virtue. He viewed the old Whig grandees as architects of a corrupt political system, wanted to remove them from positions of power, and expected merit and purity in politics rather than venality and faction. He held that politicians should be eager to serve their king and nation, and should make no conditions about measures or personnel. For public as well as self-interested reasons, however, many of the leading politicians of the day refused to accept his interpretation of appropriate political conduct. Whenever George III tried to enforce compliance, he united his enemies and made them even more determined to frustrate his designs. These struggles were almost inevitable in view of the confusion over the precise nature of the crown's constitutional function. There was uncertainty because the constitution rested on custom and practice as well as statute. Since the Glorious Revolution of 1688 there had been unambiguous restraints on the crown's political role, but some questions had never been settled. Even while he was George III's chief minister, North reminded the king that the decisions of the House of Commons could not be disregarded. Yet this opinion, pervasive as it was by the 1770s, did not fix the boundary of the king's rights. In practice those rights could be what the king chose to make them. Labouring under a deep sense of responsibility as head of state and the fount of executive power, George III tried to do what he thought his grandfather had failed to do. Under the guidance of constitutional conventions, he wanted to use the powers of the crown to their fullest extent in order to promote the public interest.

To George III and his adherents, this activity represented a legitimate attempt to reverse an improper monopolisation of power during previous decades by great Whig families. To the latter, however, George III's creed posed an ominous threat to the constitution. The orthodox Whig view, or 'Rockingham legend', was that George III and his allies broke with established constitutional practice by seeking to increase the powers of the crown. As this ideology evolved, party spirit became increasingly important, with the Rockingham Whigs its main exponents. Their chief propagandist, Edmund Burke (Rockingham's secretary), complained in his *Thoughts on the Causes of the Present Discontents* (1770) of a dangerous growth in royal influence. He argued that power was exercised by persons around the king who were not ministers and not accountable to parliament, and that sound government would be impossible until this secret influence was broken. The Rockingham Whigs took up the great commission by forming a party, defined by Burke as a body of men who united to serve the nation by their joint endeavours, according to a principle upon which they were all agreed. The Rockingham theory represented a clear and coherent plan for future conduct, and when North fell in 1782 Rockingham leaders demanded that the secret system should be dismantled and ministerial personnel completely changed.

The Rockingham 'connection' was the precursor of nineteenth-century political parties. Rockingham Whigs had a unifying idea and a distinctive identity, and strong provincial ties added to their animosity towards crown and ministry. They had numerical strength and recognised leaders. They developed early party methods such as confidence motions and whipping, established opposition clubs, and used newspapers to influence outdoor opinion. Indeed, the Rockingham Whigs made concerted efforts to attract extra-parliamentary support and involved themselves in several petitioning campaigns, though their cautious, patrician view of popular political participation always held them back. They were prepared to co-operate with public opinion only on their own terms, suspecting that, once mobilised, this opinion would be impossible to control.[4]

Some Rockingham Whigs tried to take advantage of the wave of extra-parliamentary protest in 1779 and 1780, hoping to attach popular pressure to their anti-court agenda and demands for economical reform. North survived, however, for three main reasons. Encouraging news came from America of successful operations by British forces; the Gordon Riots created a reaction against popular political participation; and the Commons resolution of April 1780 moved by opposition MP John Dunning, that 'the influence of the crown has increased, is increasing, and ought to be diminished', made parliament seem less subservient and corrupt than had been claimed, and prompted some reformers to abandon their agitation. Wyvill could not keep his movement united, and Rockingham leaders were not prepared to go further than the Dunning motion at this time (they favoured economical reform, but were uneasy about Wyvill's commitment to parliamentary reform). This annoyed Burke, who wanted to co-ordinate opposition efforts in parliament with Wyvill's activity out of doors. Burke was convinced that no party would be able to carry substantial improvements without the backing of 'respectable' opinion.[5]

The crises of 1782 to 1784

By the early 1780s, with hope of victory in America fast receding, the parliamentary opposition stepped up its efforts against

North and took full advantage of the war's unpopularity out of doors. People had lost all patience with the financial burdens, economic problems and military failure associated with North's regime, and he repeatedly asked George III to let him resign. North realised that he had lost the essential backing of independent backbenchers in the Commons, who were no longer prepared to support him or the war, and that no minister could serve a king who wanted to continue the war when the Commons majority wanted to end it. The Rockingham Whigs declared that North had forfeited the confidence of parliament, and George III's reluctance to accept this situation was strengthened by his knowledge that North's departure would force him to admit Rockingham Whigs to a share of power. They in turn insisted that if they were to take office there would have to be a complete change of ministers, no royal veto on American independence, and economical reform. In addition, the Marquess of Rockingham expected to have a decisive say in new appointments. George III rejected these conditions. When North resigned in March 1782, however, the king had no choice but to call on the Rockingham Whigs, because in prevalent circumstances it seemed that no government could stand without their co-operation.

The new administration was a coalition. Rockingham became first lord of the treasury (the office normally held by the prime minister). The most talented and ambitious member of Rockingham's connection, Charles James Fox, became secretary of state for foreign affairs, and Burke was given an office outside the cabinet. Their partners in government were led by the Earl of Shelburne, who became secretary of state for home and colonial affairs. Shelburne was a highly intelligent politician, but devious, and the Rockingham Whigs did not trust him. Many of his followers were former Chathamites. He enjoyed the king's favour, respected the political role of the crown, and favoured non-party government (a basic Chathamite principle). Personal and ideological differences between the Rockingham and Shelburne wings of the ministry meant that it was never a united entity.

George III hoped that the coalition would only be temporary. He made clear his preference for Shelburne and contempt for Fox, who had long been irritating the king with insulting speeches about excessive royal influence. George III was also offended by Fox's lifestyle. Fox was a gambler and libertine, and his friendship with the king's wayward son George, Prince of Wales, caused enormous annoyance at court. In recent years Fox had identified himself closely with reform causes, partly the consequence of his return as MP for Westminster in 1780, for that large scot and lot borough was unusually influenced by popular opinion. By the time of North's resignation, Fox was known as an outspoken critic of court and government, and the advocate of parliamentary supremacy.

Though the Rockingham Whigs disliked Shelburne and knew that he was a royal favourite, they expected to dominate the government. George III had been forced to give up his chosen minister, North, and the war policy, and his appointment of the Rockingham Whigs, who had their own legislative programme, also indicated the crown's vulnerability at this juncture. Furthermore, Shelburne lacked influential spokesmen in the Commons while the Rockingham Whigs had Fox and Burke. Shelburne's position might have been stronger had he been able to rely on the outstanding young politician of the day, William Pitt. The second son of Chatham, trained by his father specifically for a public career, Pitt the Younger's early speeches in the Commons marked him out as a political prodigy, and he was thought to have the talents needed to uphold Chathamite ideas on government against the Rockingham Whigs. When Shelburne proposed to bring Pitt into office in the spring of 1782, the Rockingham Whigs ruled him out on account of his youth and inexperience, though it may have been Pitt's choice to remain on the back benches, for this preserved his independence and raised the value of his adherence.

One of the few issues on which both wings of the Rockingham–Shelburne government came to an agreement was Irish policy. Demands for a measure of autonomy were growing within Ireland,[6] and anxiety about Irish defence had prompted the rise of a volunteer movement during the American war, a conflict in which France and Spain interfered as allies of the Americans. In 1782 the ministry decided to grant Ireland a measure of legislative and judicial independence. The Dublin parliament would control Ireland's internal affairs, while defence, trade and foreign policy would continue to be

21

regulated by the imperial parliament in London. Ministers were hoping for Irish goodwill, and Rockingham and his friends were ready to make concessions because they had extensive estates in Ireland and were allies of the Irish leader Henry Grattan and commander of the volunteers Lord Charlemont. But the precise relationship between Ireland and the imperial power, and the means of co-ordinating the decisions of the two parliaments, were left for future agreement. The government's cautious approach added to the friction, and some Irish spokesmen declared that the new independence did not go far enough. They demanded parliamentary reform, to check electoral corruption and make the crown-appointed Irish executive more accountable to the Dublin parliament. Unrest in Ireland continued for other reasons, not least because the Catholic middle classes and peasantry resented their political, social and economic subjection to Anglo-Irish Protestant landowners.

On parliamentary reform there was no agreement in cabinet, and Rockingham's disapproval ensured that the matter was not taken up as a government question. It was Pitt who advanced the cause from the back benches in the Commons, after discussions with Shelburne, Wyvill and others. In the Commons on 7 May 1782 Pitt called for a committee to consider the state of the representative system. He had no detailed plan of reform in mind, but sought rather to promote discussion about the duration of parliaments, powers of the crown, rotten boroughs, distribution of seats and purity of elections. Pitt did not wish to innovate. His goal was to restore the constitution by eliminating obvious anomalies. Though his motion was defeated, the narrowness of the margin (only twenty votes) encouraged reformers in parliament and out of doors to feel confident about future efforts.

Both wings of the Rockingham–Shelburne ministry favoured administrative and financial improvements, though for different reasons. The Rockingham Whigs saw economical reform as a means of limiting royal influence, while Shelburne's concern was efficient government. There were inquiries into the public accounts, extending work done in this field by North, and efforts to prevent abuses in government departments. Salaries continued to replace fees in some departments, though many pensions and sinecures remained intact because they were considered indispensable to the operation of government. The disfranchisement of revenue officers and exclusion from parliament of government contractors were designed to curb executive power, though it seems that the number of revenue officers entitled to vote in parliamentary elections was over-estimated, and that the measures of this period did not remove a single borough from government control.[7] Burke's civil list reform addressed the question of royal influence and expenditure. George III's civil list allowance was fixed at £900,000 a year, but Burke's determination to restrict bribery and corruption led him to ignore the king's need to make occasional payments which did not fit into the categories prescribed by statute. Grants had to be sought to cover specific charges, and Burke's measure was soon revealed to be virtually useless. He had mistakenly assumed that the civil list was a major source of official patronage, and though he thought he was striking at the king's capacity to manipulate people and events, the result was that the civil list could not meet its proper purposes.

George III disliked these economical reforms, but prevalent circumstances meant that the tide could not be stemmed. Paradoxically, in time the crown became less vulnerable to accusations about corrupt influence because it was clearly impossible for the king to control MPs, borough patrons or voters in the way Rockingham Whigs had claimed. Moreover, reorganisation of the civil list may not have greatly reduced royal power, and for E. A. Reitan the question of influence is less significant than the civil list's changing constitutional status. Parliament had now established its right to regulate royal finances.[8]

The decisive division in the cabinet related to peace terms with America and France. Fox believed that a quick peace with America would improve Britain's position in talks with the French. He favoured prompt recognition of American independence, but Shelburne maintained that the Americans should have control only over internal affairs, and that autonomy should be conceded on the understanding that America's commercial and foreign policies would accord with those of Britain. To encourage the Americans to accept this form of independence, Shelburne was prepared to give up far more territory than Fox. Ministers argued at length about the peace proposals, and Fox thought of resigning if he could not prevail. Then, on 1 July 1782, the Marquess of Rockingham died of influenza. This created a ministerial crisis, because Fox and his allies insisted that the Duke of Portland, a senior peer in the Rockingham connection, should succeed as prime minister. The attempt to force Portland on George III failed, however, and the king invited Shelburne to take the premiership. While George III asserted that it was the crown's right and duty to appoint ministers, Fox developed a new doctrine, that ministers should name their own leader and decide on appointments and policy without interference from the king.

Shelburne's promotion led to Fox's resignation, but other Rockingham Whigs stayed in the cabinet and assumed that Shelburne would not depart from agreed lines of policy. They lamented Fox's rashness and petulance. On 9 July Fox told the Commons that he had resigned from the government on matters of principle and policy, but his arguments were rejected by Henry Conway, one of the Rockingham Whigs who remained in place under Shelburne. Burke supported Fox, while Pitt stated that Fox's resignation owed more to personal scheming than principle: Fox claimed that Shelburne planned to abandon measures agreed in cabinet under Rockingham, yet he had not waited to find out if this was true. Fox's resignation increased the instability in high politics at this time. John Derry regards it as a 'grievous miscalculation' on Fox's part, and Leslie Mitchell agrees that Fox lost the argument and a great deal of parliamentary support.[9] Fox always maintained that he had good reasons for resigning. Shelburne was the ally of the court, Fox stressed, and his appointment as first lord of the treasury confirmed the existence of sinister royal influence. George III's reluctance to accept the Rockingham Whigs in office, moreover, amounted to a repudiation of constitutional liberty and the authority of parliament. Fox's conduct rested unequivocally upon these beliefs, and he was disappointed when other Rockingham Whigs did not follow him into opposition.

Pitt was brought into Shelburne's ministry as chancellor of the exchequer, and he helped the prime minister to negotiate with other groups in an attempt to construct a firm majority in the Commons, where the largest connections at this time were those that followed Shelburne (about 140 MPs), Fox (about 90) and

North (about 120). Among the independents there were plenty of men who habitually supported the king's ministers, or who saw Shelburne as the best hope for political stability, peace and retrenchment, but Shelburne still needed to win over some Foxites or Northites in order to stay in power. He sought to bring them in without their chiefs, demonstrating the old Chathamite aversion to bargains with organised parties. Meanwhile George III insisted that Fox must be kept out of office, and urged North to use his influence to improve the new government's position in parliament.

Shelburne proposed a number of administrative, commercial and financial improvements, and repeated his commitment to a reform of the representative system. He favoured an increase in the number of county MPs, who were generally considered to be independent in character and whose electorates were larger and less amenable to bribery than those of boroughs. Wyvill's movement organised meetings and petitions, and Pitt's discussions with leading reformers continued into 1783. Shelburne's programme did not appeal to the conservative followers of North, however, and he could not be sure of decisive support out of doors. The ministry's problems mounted because Shelburne could not persuade the Americans to accept the type of independence he was offering, and his peace plan was strongly condemned in parliament. Shelburne intended that the new relationship with America should be part of a global strategy for increasing British wealth and influence, but the Americans did not wish to pursue a foreign policy shaped by their former imperial masters. To complete the peace treaties as he wanted, Shelburne needed commercial agreements with America. He found that MPs, merchants, manufacturers and other interests in Britain did not understand or share his commitment to freer trade.

Shelburne realised that he could not carry on without additional support (see Document 1). Some of North's friends were approached. But they refused to join the government without their leader, and Pitt objected to a union with North, the minister who had lost America and thrown away the gains made by Chatham during the Seven Years' War. Talks with Fox also collapsed because Fox would not agree to serve under Shelburne. Finally two defeats on the peace terms prompted

Shelburne's resignation, on 24 February 1783. To his surprise, and to the disgust of George III, Fox and North had agreed to combine to bring the ministry down.

Though Fox and North had been staunch enemies since the mid-1770s, their alliance was not as bizarre as has sometimes been imagined. Fox knew that if he joined Shelburne he would be unable to dominate in cabinet. North, on the other hand, might allow Fox to lead in return for the rewards of office. Fox's readiness to accommodate Northites in this respect made coalition possible, though North had other reasons for siding with Fox rather than with Shelburne. North saw that stable government was impossible without some parliamentary re-alignment, and he feared that a common interest in reforms would eventually draw Fox and Shelburne together. Then North's connection might be decimated at a future general election if Shelburne and Fox, in office together, stirred reform opinion in the nation and took full advantage of executive influence in many constituencies. For both Fox and North, therefore, coalition was the best option. The main drawback was that their union was interpreted very unfavourably at court and by influential sections of parliamentary and public opinion. George III considered the conduct of Fox and North disgraceful, and in view of the fact that Fox had been one of North's bitterest critics in recent years, the king was sure that the new alliance would soon fall apart. Fox's critics accused him of inconsistency and lack of principle, but he maintained that the coalition was a necessary and appropriate device for defeating Shelburne and defending parliament against the crown.

Tension mounted because the king refused to summon Portland, nominal leader of the Fox–North coalition, until April 1783. George III was deeply annoyed by Shelburne's resignation, and by the coalition's effort to exert control over appointments and measures. The king was determined not to yield to Fox's interpretation of relations between crown and ministry, and he tried to persuade others (including Pitt) to take over as prime minister and save monarchy and nation from extreme danger. Finally, George III accepted that he had no choice but to make Portland first lord of the treasury. Fox and North became secretaries of state. The resentful king withheld all tokens of favour from the new administration, and searched for allies who would assist the crown to stifle it. Fox and North did not have an easy time in office in 1783. Apart from George III and the parliamentary opposition, they had also to contend with unresolved problems relating to the peace, economical reform, the representative system, the conduct and debts of the Prince of Wales, Ireland and India.

Ministers proceeded to pass the peace terms they had previously obstructed, claiming that it was now impossible to alter them. The acceptance of terms so recently rejected provoked further charges of inconsistency and cynical ambition. No attempt was made to append to the peace settlement the commercial and political arrangements proposed by Shelburne. Economical reform did continue, though in a gradual and un-controversial fashion. Fox and North wanted more co-ordination in government, for this would both limit the king's practical role and restrict departmental autonomy (an obstacle to order and efficiency). Ministers had to be wary of court reaction, however, and knew that most MPs and peers would not welcome too hasty or excessive a change. In addition, Northites were less favourable to economical reform than were followers of Fox, and the unity of the cabinet had to be preserved at all costs. The approach remained cautious. Salaries continued to replace fees, and abuses were removed slowly as offices became vacant. As part of Fox's agreement with North and his followers, it had been decided that parliamentary reform would not be a government policy. When Pitt proposed a measure from the opposition benches, Fox did not offer strong support and many Rockingham Whigs abstained. Pitt aimed to check bribery at elections, disfranchise corrupt boroughs and add their voters to county electorates, and increase the representation of the counties and London. Northites and the court interest opposed this moderate scheme, and it was heavily defeated in the Commons in May 1783. It had not attracted a great deal of outdoor support, though Pitt had at least kept the issue alive and made plain his continuing attachment to the cause of parliamentary reform.

Relations between George III and the Prince of Wales had been strained for many years, and the king was incensed by his son's political intrigues and profligate behaviour. When the ministry (despite North's misgivings) attended to the prince's debts and financial establishment, this destroyed any remote chance that George III would come to accept the Fox–North coalition in office. Parliament approved an annual allowance for the Prince of Wales. This was to be taken from the civil list, which subjected the king to further financial restraint. Parliament also made a special grant to cover the prince's debts. George III was outraged, revelations about the prince's extravagance caused indignation out of doors, and economy-minded MPs made plain their reluctance to sanction any more grants of this kind. Now and in the future, Fox lost more than he gained by his association with the heir to the throne.

On Ireland the ministry lacked initiative and preferred to wait on events. The respective rights and responsibilities of the Dublin and imperial parliaments therefore remained unclear. If little was done for Ireland, ministers could not avoid taking action on India. Financial problems, wars and disrupted trade, and the failure of previous reforms to stabilise East India Company (EIC) politics meant that government had to act. Parliamentary committees had for several years been investigating Indian affairs. Burke, back in office with the Fox–North coalition, had involved himself enthusiastically in these inquiries, and he was now an acknowledged expert on India. He decided that British and Indian interests would best be served if the authority and operations of the EIC were thoroughly reorganised. Regulation was deemed necessary because of British reliance on Indian revenues, the EIC's importance to public credit and finance, and general concern about peace, stability and efficient administration. But Burke and Fox wanted to make sure that Indian reform would not increase executive power and crown patronage. The India bill introduced in November 1783 was designed to implement the following plan: control of the EIC's territorial possessions would be given to a board of seven commissioners, named in the bill, who could be dismissed only by the king with parliament's approval. Vacancies would be filled, and a new board appointed after four years, by the king. The EIC's commercial affairs would be overseen by nine assistant commissioners, chosen from among its larger shareholders. The first nine were also named in the India bill, with subsequent appointments to be made after shareholder elections. The principal effect of the plan, therefore, would be to take power from the old ruling faction in the EIC and give it not to the executive, but to a board which would remain relatively unaffected by parliamentary politics.

There were loud objections to these proposals (as North had predicted), partly because commissioners at home could not be expected to deal effectively with affairs in distant India. The EIC mobilised support in defence of its rights. Extra-parliamentary excitement grew, controversy was carried on in newspaper, pamphlet and satirical print, and opponents of the Fox–North coalition focused attention on the method of appointing commissioners. Determined to avoid any increase in royal power, members of the government had apparently concocted a scheme to accumulate patronage for themselves. The commissioners named in the India bill were all supporters of Fox and North. George III had denied the ministers royal patronage, but Fox knew that the vast Indian patronage would more than make up for this. Though Fox told the Commons that the India bill was premised on necessity rather than choice, Pitt accused the government of an attempt to subvert the constitution and violate chartered privileges and property rights. He urged parliament and public to resist Foxite tyranny.

The ministerial majority in the Commons was sufficiently secure for the India bill to be passed without difficulty, but Fox overestimated the chance of success in the Lords and reckoned without the intervention of George III. The king had appointed the coalition in the spring only because he could persuade no other combination of political leaders to take office. Now, in November, the struggle over the India bill created an opportunity to oust Fox and North. The king was able to enlist the support of several influential figures: Lord Thurlow, who had been lord chancellor from 1778 to 1783 and wanted to return to office; Henry Dundas, a former Northite who had served under Shelburne in 1782; and John Robinson and Charles Jenkinson, experienced patronage managers who had risen to prominence during the 1770s. Pitt, who had wisely refused to accept the premiership after Shelburne's resignation because he preferred to wait for more favourable circumstances, now agreed to unite and lead the disaffected elements. He offered a viable alternative to the Fox–North coalition. Ambitious, talented and proud, Pitt had for several years been widely regarded as the coming man, and he decided at the end of 1783 that the time was right for him to make his move.

As Robinson assessed the likely consequences of a change of ministry and general election, George III made it known (through Thurlow and Pitt's cousin, Earl Temple) that he would consider anyone voting for the India bill in the House of Lords to be his enemy. The measure was defeated, and the king dismissed the coalition on 18 December. Pitt became first lord of the treasury at the head of an administration which consisted of veteran aristocratic politicians and, in minor posts, new men. Most commentators expected this government to fall within weeks, knowing that Fox and North still commanded a Commons majority. Certainly, the early weeks were difficult for Pitt and his colleagues. Temple resigned from the cabinet almost at once, fearing impeachment for his role in the defeat of the India bill. Government business was obstructed, and the Commons majority registered strong protests against the fall of Fox and North and the appointment of Pitt. It was un-constitutional, claimed adherents of the Fox–North coalition, for the king's opinions on any measure to be reported and used as they had been when the India bill went before the Lords.

George III was unmoved. Though Foxites would never tire of accusing him of an assault upon parliamentary independence, the king was convinced that his actions were justified: if passed, the India bill would have facilitated a gross abuse of power, and it was Fox rather than the king who had tried to upset the delicate balance between royal influence and the rights of parliament. Many MPs came to share this view, and there was plenty of support for it out of doors, where opponents of the India bill regarded Fox as a more dangerous corrupter than George III could ever be. The controversy raged on. In parlia-ment Pitt began to rally independent backbenchers and attract deserters from North. Pitt presented himself as an untarnished, patriotic, non-party leader. His contacts with reformers won him outdoor support, and royal approval was an essential asset. Pitt survived early Commons defeats and refused to resign even though government measures were continually blocked. In time there were more desertions to him, and his opponents became frustrated and divided. Pitt and his colleagues may have envisaged a quick dissolution and general election, but it soon became clear that they needed supplies. When the Commons postponed consideration of the land tax, dissolution had to be put off. Delay did not harm the ministry, for Robinson and the government's electoral managers were preparing the ground in many constituencies, making deals and organising voters, and it was important to hold the election at the right moment for optimum effect.

As self-appointed defender of the rights of the Commons (see Document 2), Fox attacked Pitt and preached legislative independence more boldly than ever before, urging that parliament must resist improper use of the royal prerogative. A vital principle was at stake, said Fox, but he was also worried about what would happen if there was a quick dissolution. In the prevalent political climate an election could only help Pitt, Fox thought, because executive influence and popular turmoil would sway the results in many constituencies. Over two hundred petitions were organised in towns and counties during these months, supporting king and ministers and condemning the actions of the Fox–North coalition. Fox's arguments against Pitt and George III had limited appeal when they were able to pose as saviours of the constitution. In contrast, Fox was assailed for the dishonourable alliance with his former enemy North, for contesting the king's right freely to select and appoint ministers, and for his attempt to engross Indian patronage. Meanwhile Pitt introduced an alternative Indian reform. He proposed to entrust political and military matters to a board of control appointed by the crown, and to leave most Indian patronage in the hands of EIC directors. The measure was defeated in the Commons by just eight votes, testimony to Pitt's successful erosion of the Fox–North majority. Furthermore, George III and Pitt were confident enough to reject suggestions that a more broadly based cabinet should be put together. Fox and Portland wanted Pitt to resign as the preliminary to their participation, but Pitt refused to take second place in any reconstructed ministry, and there was no possibility that George III would accept a Foxite interpretation of the dismissal of the previous ministry.

The failure of these talks forced MPs and voters to take sides, and by March 1784 Pitt had convinced many observers that his survival in office offered the best hope for stable and competent administration. Parliament was dissolved on 25 March, though it still had three years to run. At the ensuing general election over a hundred Foxites lost their seats. Pitt gained a large majority, and George III was vindicated. Historians have argued at length about the principal reasons for this. Some attribute the government's electoral success to the familiar favours, bargains and bribes long identified with executive patronage and constituency manipulation, while others stress popular opinion and voter choice.[10] A full explanation would have to include all these ingredients, along with pro-court propaganda, Pitt's known sympathy for reforms and his desire to place nation above faction, continuing resentment against Fox's India bill, and the support given to government by the EIC and other private interests (they reckoned that Pitt would respect their privileges, whereas his opponents had not).

Pittite government

Though there were early defeats for Pitt's administration in the new parliament, ministers were gradually able to build up a commanding position by convincing parliamentary and public opinion of their competence and probity. After all the stresses of recent years there was urgent need for political peace and sound government, and Pitt was taken to represent these goals more faithfully than his political enemies. In time, his influence in parliament and over the cabinet increased, but he was wise enough to make a tactical retreat when he could not get his own way. Pitt evolved a pragmatic, flexible approach, realising that his policies needed a wide basis of support if they were to work as intended, and therefore that cabinet colleagues, the Commons majority, and George III had to be persuaded of their usefulness or necessity. With Pitt, the king at last had a prime minister on whom he could fully rely. Though they were never personally close, they had a high regard for each other. Pitt respected the crown's political role and knew he could not impose his will at court, but as his administrative talents and parliamentary authority developed, and as the extent and complexity of government business increased, Pitt's hold on office became firmer and he enjoyed more advantages in his dealings with the king. George III was willing to trust him from the outset, because he knew that Pitt would observe established constitutional conventions as they were understood at court, and that Pitt's fall would mean the return of the factious Foxites.

As Pitt's influence grew, Fox's began to decline, and parliamentary opposition became weaker during the 1780s. Ian Christie points out that it was never a united force, for though many Northites refused to support Pitt, they also failed to join with the followers of Fox and Portland.[11] Fox was determined to uphold principles and vindicate past conduct, but proscription from office was a difficult burden for his party and Fox frequently failed to provide effective leadership. Burke complained about his lengthy periods of inactivity. This problem, combined with personality clashes and the misguided belief that the opposition would benefit from its close tie to the Prince of Wales, brought serious divisions after 1783 and prepared the way for open schism in Whig ranks in the early 1790s.

Pitt was serious and aloof while Fox devoted himself to friendship and pleasure, and this contrast in their characters made the political divide even more stark. Pitt's ascendancy rested partly on Fox's humiliation and defeat, and Fox resolved that viable constitutional government would be impossible unless the wrongs committed by Pitt and his master George III were reversed. From 1783 this goal shaped Fox's thought and action, and it was married to the old Rockingham legend about excessive royal influence. The legend remained a constant theme in opposition politics and would continue to serve a purpose even after the deaths of Pitt and Fox in 1806.

After the 1784 election Pitt set about providing efficient and vigorous government, promoting political stability and carrying useful reforms in as non-partisan a manner as possible. He never built up a parliamentary party to assist in the accomplishment of his political goals, preferring to rely on patriotic appeal and commitment to the public interest. Fox was a party man because he saw party as the essential bulwark against the crown. Pitt preferred to call himself an 'independent' Whig, though it has recently been argued that he was not as uninvolved in parliamentary management as is often thought.[12]

In office Pitt attended to the outstanding problems of the day with great ingenuity. The India Act of 1784, based on his previously defeated bill, established a board of control to supervise EIC affairs. The company would still direct commerce and, subject to royal approval, control patronage and appointments, but it could not make military alliances or involve itself in Indian politics. When established, the board of control consisted of six privy councillors, two of whom were members of the cabinet, and the long-term significance of Pitt's reform (which owed much to the advice of Dundas, Jenkinson and Robinson) was that ministers of the crown would now be dominant partners in the relationship between government and EIC. The framework established in 1784 for regulating Indian administration and trade lasted into the 1850s.

Pitt's talent was demonstrated most convincingly by his fiscal and commercial policies. His general purposes were to increase trade with Europe and compensate for the loss of the American colonies, to promote economic progress after a long and expensive war, and to restore confidence in the system of public finance after several years of political unrest. During the 1780s these goals began to seem attainable, and Pitt deserves some of the credit for this, but much was beyond his direct control, and objections from parliament and from cabinet colleagues who did not share his liberal economic ideas imposed a limit on what Pitt tried to do. New taxes were very unpopular in the nation, moreover. Some of them adversely affected certain industries, and were withdrawn soon after their introduction. Nevertheless, on the whole Pitt's record was one of modest success. Reorganisation of public finance began with the budgets of 1784 to 1787. Pitt tried to increase government revenue through taxes and loans, but he saw that permanent improvement depended on two related operations: he had to lower the national debt and extend trade.

The debt had been doubled by the American war, its interest charges were the largest single item of public expenditure, and government ran up an annual deficit which added to the debt on which charges had to be paid. Pitt established a sinking fund in 1786 in order gradually to pay off the debt. He predicted that a budget surplus would make available £1 million·a year for the fund. This would be used to buy government stock, interest on which could be used to buy more stock so that compound interest would be applied to reduce the debt. Pitt also decreed that his sinking fund, unlike earlier such funds, would be devoted exclusively to debt reduction and not used to meet temporary financial needs. Though the notion of a sinking fund was not new, therefore, Pitt envisaged that his fund would work in a new way. The fund was reorganised in 1792 and in its new form survived until the 1820s. Initially it restored financial confidence, reassured the state's creditors that their money was safe, and indicated a determination to solve revenue problems and check the growth of debt. But Pitt's policy did not succeed as he intended. It required an excess of revenue over expenditure. This was achieved during the 1780s, owing to higher customs yields, but the war against France after 1793 forced up government spending and made balanced budgets impossible. Pitt did not suspend the sinking fund because he expected the war to be short. Money was borrowed at high interest to service the debt at a lower rate of interest, and this provoked enormous controversy throughout the war and into the period after 1815. There was no permanent reduction of debt or restoration of the public finances.

In pursuit of more revenue, and seeking to augment national prosperity, Pitt facilitated freer trade along the lines outlined in Adam Smith's *Inquiry into the Nature and Causes of the Wealth of Nations* (1776). In 1784 Pitt simplified and consolidated customs and excise, lowering duties to stimulate consumption and combat smuggling. In order to provide manufacturers with cheaper raw materials and a larger market for their finished products, tariffs were reduced and in some cases removed. In 1785 Pitt proposed a plan to increase trade between Britain and Ireland. He hoped not only to assist Ireland's economic development and extend British trade generally, but to foster a community of interest between the Dublin and imperial parliaments, still urgently necessary following the grant of legislative independence to Ireland in 1782. But there was intense opposition to Pitt's Irish commercial propositions. In the Commons Fox denounced them for offering too much to Ireland. He said they amounted to a surrender of British commerce and navigation. There was also protest from industrialists and merchants in the Midlands, Lancashire and the West Riding, who formed a Great Chamber of Manufacturers to resist Pitt's plan. They pointed out that Irish labour costs were much lower than those in Britain: in free competition buyers would tend to abandon British for cheaper Irish products. It was also claimed that to admit Ireland to external trade would be to ruin British merchants, who operated within established regulations affecting imports, exports and the carrying trade. Disputes in parliament and out of doors prompted Pitt to amend his plan in May 1785, but Irish leaders rejected his modifications and the whole project had to be withdrawn in August.[13] This was Pitt's most serious defeat in the early years of his premiership.

Pitt recovered quickly, and regained the initiative in commercial matters with the Anglo-French commercial treaty of 1786. This time Pitt consulted manufacturing and trading interests in advance. He found that most of them expected profitable business from a system of freer trade with France. Foxites exploited traditional anti-French sentiment to cause difficulties for Pitt in parliament, but he won the necessary divisions. The treaty provided for the lowering of duties on a range of products, and henceforth Britain's trade with France was to proceed on the principle of reciprocity. In the Commons Pitt stressed that manufacturers had not mobilised opinion against the treaty, which indicated that they recognised its benefits. He extolled relative commerce, the exchange of staples for staples, and trusted that there could be no reasonable objection to arrangements which would open France to British exports by allowing French goods easier access to Britain. Pitt's victory was of limited practical significance, however, because Anglo-French trade would soon be disrupted by the French Revolution and subsequent wars.

Though most of Pitt's attention before the war was given to financial, economic and administrative problems, he also maintained his reputation as a moderate parliamentary reformer during the 1780s, even if, as with Irish trade, he had to accept that he could not carry a Commons majority with him. On parliamentary reform there were added complications, notably George III's disapproval and a lack of unanimity among cabinet colleagues. Pitt persuaded the king to allow him to introduce a reform bill, but this was not a government measure. Pitt knew that George III would not promote its passage, though the king accepted that Pitt's previous commitments made some gesture necessary, and promised not to intervene. In the spring of 1785

Pitt proposed that thirty-six rotten boroughs should be disfranchised, the relevant patrons compensated for their loss, and the seats transferred to London, Westminster and the counties. He also wanted to extend the county franchise to 40s copyholders and some leaseholders. This mild scheme, involving no fundamental constitutional innovations, gratified reformers who had supported Pitt in parliament and out of doors. Pitt told the Commons that moderate reform would bring parliament and public closer together, and that throughout history the representative system had evolved gradually as social and political conditions changed. The system was flexible. This was its greatest recommendation, said Pitt, and his reform was merely designed to root this flexibility in settled principles. He saw no reason why the seats of decayed boroughs should not be transferred to towns which had grown in wealth and population. But many MPs, including government supporters, disliked Pitt's measure. North pointed to a lack of interest in the nation. Fox claimed that the people deserved and expected more than Pitt was prepared to offer, and he rejected the idea that owners of corrupt boroughs should be compensated. But then Fox declared that Northite objections to reform should be given fair consideration. Fox's incoherence was further underlined when, despite his criticisms, he voted in favour of Pitt's measure. Clearly, Fox experienced a conflict of motives at this time. He had to demonstrate consistency as an advocate of parliamentary reform, while offering opposition to Pitt as prime minister and maintaining the alliance with North.

Pitt was defeated by 248 to 174 votes in the Commons on 18 April 1785 when he sought leave to introduce his reform bill. The majority against reform was considerably lower than it had been in 1783, but Pitt was a realist and he decided to defer further efforts indefinitely. Most reformers out of doors understood why he was reluctant to press the matter. Despite the continuing efforts of Wyvill and others, indeed, extra-parliamentary pressure for electoral reform seemed to be dwindling. In a time of stable government and an improving economic situation this was not surprising, though it is also possible that contemporaries did not consider the representative system to be as flawed as later commentators claimed. As well as bribery, intimidation and deference, relations between patrons and voters were shaped by persuasion and mutual dependence. Many boroughs were quite open in this respect, and even when seats were uncontested there was vigorous canvassing and electoral negotiation, if only to prevent a future rupture between voters and their landlords or employers. Paul Kelly has examined the complexities of this negotiation and found that relations between elector and elected were far from settled.[14]

Pitt carried forward economical reform and administrative reorganisation with great assurance. Burke and Fox had desired above all to restrict the crown's political influence, but Pitt approached these matters in a more dispassionate and thorough manner. He examined public expenditure as a whole, seeking significant savings, and continued the gradual abolition of sinecures and introduction of salaries to replace fees. Government departments and their tasks were reformed, officials were subjected to new standards of proficiency, and unnecessary offices were suppressed. Pitt also reorganised the civil list and management of crown lands and woods (given up by George III in 1760). With a growing band of trusted and competent senior assistants the prime minister set about raising the reputation of public men. His measures won the approval of economy-minded MPs and the nation's taxpayers, and were of lasting constitutional importance. The assault on sinecures, unnecessary offices and tainted officialdom did not begin with Pitt, but he made a political virtue of his desire to improve and reform government. One result of his activity was that former methods and tools of corruption gradually disappeared. The abolition of hundreds of revenue offices, for example, meant that these could no longer be used by government as political bribes or rewards. The drive for efficiency undermined old patronage networks. In a wider sense, the powers of the crown quickly waned. Though Fox's claim that the Commons should make and unmake ministries had been discredited in 1783 and 1784, in practice this was happening long before George III's death in 1820. Royal patronage was no longer sufficient to support a prime minister who did not have parliament's backing.

Efficiency and probity were not ends in themselves. Philip Harling has convincingly argued that the underlying purpose was to justify aristocratic rule at a time when popular attacks on

'Old Corruption' were weakening the authority of the governing elite. Therefore tax reforms, retrenchment, administrative improvements, eradication of abuses and other efforts to purify government can all be regarded as responses to external pressure. Pitt and his successors tried to convince parliament and people that the state was being reformed, and that inefficiency and corruption no longer prevailed, in order to make aristocratic rule less objectionable. 'Old Corruption' was, as Harling puts it, 'a parasitical system ... through which the elite fed its insatiable appetite for power and money at the people's expense', and it rested on sinecures, contracts, pensions, offices, rotten boroughs and economic policies designed to benefit vested interests (finance, agriculture, shipping). But gradually the elite sanitised government. It was Pitt who showed the way. By the 1830s the critique of 'Old Corruption' had lost much of its popular appeal, and Harling rejects the view of W. D. Rubinstein that this corruption still existed 'in actual fact as well as in radical rhetoric'.[15]

If Harling is right about the long-term effect of reforms implemented by Pitt and his immediate successors, nevertheless the extent of the changes introduced before 1801 should not be exaggerated. As premier, Pitt proceeded slowly, and improvements in one department were not necessarily possible or useful in another. Reform was uneven. It probably owed less to direct administrative reorganisation, moreover, than to financial policies, especially the imposition of new taxes, the need to improve collection of existing taxes, and a more thorough supervision of accounting and expenditure. Cautious and pragmatic as ever, Pitt was careful not to go too far too quickly. He had no desire to help his political opponents by provoking resistance and controversy. Therefore there was no rapid change to payment by salary instead of fees, for those affected would expect compensation. Many of Pitt's supporters still thought of public office as property, and he had to respect their views. Though some sinecures were abolished by legislation, Pitt preferred a piecemeal method. He kept a record of unnecessary sinecures, and as their holders died he quietly refrained from appointing successors. Pitt's caution led many opposition MPs and reformers out of doors to question his much-vaunted thoroughness and efficiency, and arguments have persisted among modern historians. While admitting Pitt's respect for traditional approaches, W. R. Ward regards him as a 'new broom' who laid the foundations for modern tax procedure, but J. R. Breihan asserts that Pitt's reputation for probity was far more significant than his actual achievements in financial and administrative reform. Many improvements were slowed down or abandoned because Pitt's approach remained essentially conservative.[16] In addition, critics of the government might have agreed that Pitt was not corrupt while doubting the probity of his allies and colleagues. During Pitt's second period as prime minister, from 1804 to 1806, his long-time deputy, Henry Dundas, now Viscount Melville, first lord of the admiralty, resigned when threatened with impeachment as a result of financial irregularities in his department. The Melville affair provoked renewed attacks on 'Old Corruption', and many commentators complained that Pitt had not carried economical reform far enough when prime minister between 1783 and 1801.

It is likely that gradual and moderate Pittite transformation (political, constitutional, economic, commercial, financial) would have continued through the 1790s had it not been for the French war. The constructive approach of the 1780s was abandoned during the war because needs and priorities changed. The cost of government soared, and many of Pitt's previous measures had been premised on a healthy budget surplus and careful control over expenditure.

By 1793 Pitt had demonstrated his worth as prime minister, provided nearly a decade of stable government, and promoted economic progress and financial recovery. He presided over a regime that seemed less factious and corrupt than its predecessors. These developments owed something to Pitt's ideas about how the premiership and cabinet should operate. The formation, organisation and disciplines of party did not figure among his priorities. Instead, Pitt preferred to pick out ambitious and talented individuals, who in view of his parliamentary ascendancy were naturally drawn to the government side. He appointed them to positions of responsibility, and instilled in them his code of administrative pride and efficiency. Eschewing party, Pitt remained a distant figure even to allies, and he tended not to confide in them until he considered the time right. This increased his influence over the ministry. Such was his prestige and control, in fact, that little was done by government without his knowledge or consent. The departmental autonomy known under North was passing away, and collective ministerial responsibility began to develop as both an idea and a practice. The cabinet's identity and activity were moulded from above, not determined (as Foxites desired) by the House of Commons. Under Pitt, the cabinet came to be a place where he tested his ideas rather than the place where policy was decided. By the 1790s he was framing policy outside cabinet, often in a triumvirate with Dundas and William Wyndham Grenville (the son of George Grenville and Pitt's cousin, raised to the peerage in 1790, foreign secretary from 1791).

Cabinet government, collective responsibility and the office of prime minister were still evolving, however, and Pitt knew that if he chose or was forced to resign, the cabinet would not inevitably break up. It could easily continue with a new premier who was acceptable to George III. Furthermore, shared ministerial responsibility was limited to important financial measures and foreign policy (and it would become much clearer after 1832). Nor could Pitt determine cabinet personnel. Thurlow, the king's choice as lord chancellor, temporarily sided with the Foxite opposition during the regency crisis of 1788 to 1789 (see below), and Pitt could not remove him because he retained royal favour. Only later, in 1792 when Thurlow refused to support government financial policies, could Pitt force him to resign. Under normal circumstances Pitt could not remove any minister with whom he had a disagreement. Some questions were left open, notably parliamentary reform, religious toleration and the slave trade, and on these there was no insistence on cabinet unanimity. Though Pitt's personal ascendancy, along with administrative and financial reforms, brought a clearer pattern to government activity, some departmental autonomy also survived.

Pitt's ministry built up considerable support in parliament and the nation. The propertied ranks valued political stability and social order, reformers approved of Pitt's progressive policies, and commercial interests welcomed his promotion of freer trade and financial confidence. Pitt needed this bedrock of support, for though his mother was a Grenville he had no close links with any other great political clan. Therefore he had to cultivate support in the City and elsewhere. Careful disposal of peerages and honours, gifts denied to Pitt's predecessors by George III, was crucial. Pitt's promotions to the House of Lords eventually altered the balance of power there and considerably strengthened the government's hand against the old Whig aristocracy.[17] For this Pitt required George III's co-operation, another reminder that one of the essential fixtures in the framework of Pittite government was royal approval. This prop was in danger of crumbling only once before 1801, during the regency crisis. In November 1788 George III began to show signs of mental collapse (now thought to be a symptom of porphyria, an inherited disease affecting the body's metabolism). There was a recovery in February 1789, but had the king's incapacity been permanent, Pitt would have been obliged to accept a regency under the Prince of Wales, and the prince would almost certainly have installed a Foxite administration. This made the crisis particularly lively. Pitt argued that regency powers should be defined by parliament. The prince's role could thereby be explicitly limited. In response Fox claimed that the Prince of Wales, his political ally, had an inherent right immediately to assume all the powers which George III could no longer exercise.

There was growing excitement as newspapers, pamphlets and other printed matter commented on the issues at stake. Government and opposition both published a mass of propaganda. Public meetings were organised, addresses sent to parliament, and preparations began in many constituencies in case there was a dissolution. Foxites welcomed the chance to revive the struggles of 1783 and 1784. Then the key issue had been the extent of the royal prerogative; now the question was who should exercise it. Only by advocating unlimited regency could Fox avoid the need to compromise with the victors of 1783 and 1784. In addition, he would not have to rely on a Commons which he always maintained had been improperly elected. Fox's conduct was consistent, therefore, even if the case for an unlimited regency was constitutionally dubious and contradicted his earlier championship of parliamentary sovereignty. Once again, he was accused by critics of cynical opportunism and abandonment of principle, and when George III recovered it was clear that Fox had gambled too heavily on the king's permanent incapacity.

The crisis ended and there were spontaneous celebrations all over the country. Fox's reputation was seriously damaged, and opposition leaders blamed each other for their defeat. Portland mistrusted the prince and had persistently advised caution. Burke was angered by Fox's failure to consult others during the crisis, complained about the lack of co-ordination in opposition activity, and resented the growing influence of Richard B. Sheridan, the playwright and Whig propagandist. An intimate of the prince who wanted office and emolument for himself, Sheridan had proposed that a new coalition ministry should be formed by opposition leaders in unison with some of Pitt's colleagues. This in turn annoyed Fox and Portland, who wanted no contact with these enemies of the constitution. Nor was the selfish and impatient prince the easiest person to deal with.

After the regency crisis, it appeared that the opposition was on the point of fragmentation, and this situation was hardly remedied by proceedings against Warren Hastings, former governor-general of Bengal, between 1788 and 1795. Controversy over India attracted Fox because he wanted to vindicate his India bill of 1783 and draw attention back to his dismissal from office. Hastings became a convenient focus for condemnation, a symbol of the corruption, war, misgovernment and instability which Pitt's ministry and the ruling faction of the EIC had allegedly allowed to continue in India. But the Hastings affair, which failed to result in conviction, proved an enormous drain on Foxite resources and energy, and the breach between Burke and Fox grew wider.

The weakening of opposition through the 1780s, and Whig divisions induced by revolution and war in Europe, greatly enhanced Pitt's political ascendancy. The continuing importance of royal favour was demonstrated in 1801, however, when a combination of difficult circumstances forced Pitt to resign. During the 1790s the ministry noted with alarm the civil disorder and plotting of revolutionary separatists in Ireland. Then the Irish rebellion of 1798 and attendant French invasion, together with unresolved problems relating to the co-ordination of policies favoured by the Dublin and imperial parliaments, prompted Pitt to propose a legislative union. He saw this as a wartime necessity, a means of promoting effective administration and social peace in Ireland, and a useful settlement of outstanding Anglo-Irish disagreements. In order to win Irish Catholic approval for union, it was suggested that the combining of the two parliaments at Westminster would be followed by Catholic emancipation. Pitt found to his cost, however, that the cabinet was divided on this matter, and that parliamentary and public opinion was hostile. To these disadvantages was added the opposition of the king.

George III maintained that he could not accept Catholic emancipation. To do so would be to break his coronation oath, by which he was bound to defend the Established Church. The king and most of his subjects believed that the Church would be endangered by emancipation, and that Pitt's project would effectively destroy the political and religious settlement achieved after the Glorious Revolution. The king had other reasons for resisting. He was not satisfied with the ministry's conduct of the war against France, and he suspected that Pitt, Dundas and Grenville had come to regard themselves as indispensable. Had the cabinet been united behind Pitt on emancipation, George III would have had less room to manoeuvre. But by the end of January 1801 the king knew that Henry Addington, speaker of the Commons since 1789, was willing to serve as prime minister if Pitt resigned, and that some of the cabinet would stay on under a new premier. Pitt tried to persuade the king of the necessity of emancipation, and to force ministers into line, yet he also discussed matters at length with Addington, and seems not to have been reluctant to leave office. The loss of royal support was crucial, and Pitt's health and confidence were also fading. Exhausted after dealing with finance, administration and war for so many years, and unable to persuade the king to accept a policy to which he felt committed, Pitt resigned after seventeen years as prime minister. In accounting for this decision Pitt pointed to the king's conduct: George III had refused to prevent his name from being used to influence opinions on emancipation. Here were reminders of 1783 and Fox's India bill, and Pitt resigned not simply because he was resisted on emancipation, but because on this issue the king was taking advice from others.

John Ehrman thinks that Pitt's illness and exhaustion were far less significant in 1801 than the cabinet's internal divisions and its failure to formulate a successful war strategy. Pitt wanted peace and could not honourably resign at a time of mounting pressure. Therefore he decided to give way to a prearranged successor who would be better able to make peace with France (and Pitt always intended to guide Addington from outside the government). Emancipation was not just an excuse for resignation. Pitt was eager to preserve accepted constitutional practice, especially the offering of advice to the monarch by the prime minister. His departure was a protest against court intrigue and George III's conversations with persons other than the responsible leader of the cabinet. While the king insisted that he must adhere to his coronation oath, Pitt upheld ministerial competence. In addition, Pitt could not separate emancipation from his public reputation. Surrender would have damaged his prestige, but resignation did not. In response to another of George III's temporary mental breakdowns, Pitt then agreed never to raise the emancipation issue again because he did not wish to disturb the king further, nor to rule out a possible return to office.

Hence Pitt preserved his good name and principles intact in 1801, as Ehrman makes clear, while George III had demonstrated again that no ministry could survive unless it retained royal confidence. The latter point is stressed by Charles Fedorak, who denies that Pitt was firmly committed to emancipation or constitutionally obliged to resign. An alternative interpretation is that emancipation *was* Pitt's main concern, that he considered it just and necessary, and that resignation was the direct result of his failure to carry it. This is the line taken by Richard Willis.[18]

Political change and the 'influence of the crown'

Royal confidence was a considerable asset to Addington, who also benefited because his ministry's opponents were deeply divided on questions of war and peace. There was more scope for royal involvement when high politics were in a state of flux, but George III could not retain Addington (whom he valued as a barrier against Catholic relief and opposition Whigs) once the prime minister found that he had lost control of the House of Commons. Opinion quickly turned against the Addington government after its early successes, notably the settlement of peace terms with France (the Treaty of Amiens was signed in March 1802) and its fiscal retrenchment. The resumption of war in May 1803, an increase in taxation, and accusations about Britain's lack of military preparedness combined to weaken Addington's position, and in the spring of 1804 his parliamentary opponents voted together to bring him down. Pitt returned to the premiership. George III continued vigorously to exercise royal powers, though, and Pitt had to respect the king's views on men and measures. Fox was excluded in 1804. Though Pitt made token efforts to form a coalition government, there was no question of him disputing George III's free choice of ministers, and Pitt had already agreed that Catholic relief would not be taken up as a government question.

Pitt preferred not to have Foxites in his cabinet anyway, but this proscription annoyed Pitt's former associate Lord Grenville, and pushed Grenville and Fox closer together. Grenville had refused to abandon the Catholic cause, and in 1804 he chose not to join Pitt's new administration. Grenville had been calling for the establishment of a broad coalition ministry, to include all the leading politicians of the day, and he regarded this comprehensive alliance as essential for political stability and success in war. Having co-operated with Foxites in opposition, moreover, and sharing their commitment to Catholic emancipation, Grenvillites decided that it would be dishonourable to join Pitt in office.

Pitt's return to the premiership gave new life to the Rockingham legend about pernicious royal influence. Indeed, during Pitt's administration of 1804 to 1806 royal favour became especially important because the cabinet was divided and its Commons majority insecure. Pitt repeatedly insisted that he would not resign while he had the king's approval, and this position was generally respected in parliament and out of doors. But the ministry was unsuccessful in war (the only notable victory of this period came at Trafalgar, in October 1805), and could not promote political stability nor provide effective government. Pitt tried to strengthen his cabinet and offered a place to Lord Moira, an ally of the Prince of Wales, but George III disapproved of Moira and suggested instead that Pitt should approach Addington. The latter still enjoyed royal favour, was raised to the peerage as Viscount Sidmouth, and joined Pitt's ministry in January 1805. Sidmouth argued with Pitt on policy and patronage matters, however, and resigned after only five months. Pitt then contacted Grenville and Fox, realising that his ministry might collapse without additional support. Again the king made clear his aversion to the leaders of the opposition. George III did not want them in office. He objected to their factious conduct and declared that public men should be uniting to win the war, not reviving controversial issues like Catholic emancipation. The government carried on in a state of drift and confusion. Finally the prime minister's health gave way and a tired, disillusioned Pitt died in January 1806.

There was no restoration of stable government at home, and no decisive breakthrough in the war against Napoleon (who had assumed power in France in 1799). In these circumstances the importance of good relations between crown and politicians was accentuated. Political leaders recognised that royal preferences were still important, and sometimes decisive. Nevertheless, George III had to accept what could not be changed. None of Pitt's associates had the talent or stature to succeed their departed chief as prime minister in 1806. The king had to appoint Grenville as premier, which meant readmitting Fox and his followers to high office. The new administration, known as the 'Ministry of All the Talents', might have lasted had Fox survived. He proved to be the most energetic and influential member of the cabinet. Fox held it together, and he did his utmost to avoid alienating the king: the Talents pressed Prussia to evacuate Hanover, of which George III was elector, and included Sidmouth, a royal favourite. But Fox died in September 1806 and the cabinet never recovered. Foxites now looked to Charles Grey (2nd Earl Grey from November 1807) as their leader, and Grey and Grenville made the mistake of taking up Catholic relief as a cabinet question. Bitter controversy ensued. Pittites and Addingtonians joined the king to resist the government's relief bill, and the Talents were forced to resign in March 1807. By this time Portland, Lord Hawkesbury and the Earl of Eldon, all of whom had served previously under Pitt and Addington, had expressed a willingness to take office and shield the king from further vexation on the Catholic issue.

Grey and Grenville were glad to leave office in 1807, for their cabinet had become deeply divided. It had lost parliamentary and public support, its shambolic defence policy was heavily criticised, and there was no coherent war strategy. The king's opposition to Catholic relief offered a perfect excuse to resign: it enabled Grey and Grenville to focus attention on royal power and gloss over the shortcomings of the Talents ministry. The fall of the Talents was another defining moment in the development of Whig identity. Foxites and Grenvillites now had exclusive use of the Whig name, and their commitment to Catholic emancipation and restriction of the royal prerogative became clearer than ever before.

From 1807, respect for the king's views on Catholic emancipation was a test for appointment to the cabinet. Ministries might include supporters of emancipation, but the issue could never be taken up as government policy. It was an open question, and the prime minister had to be a known opponent of concessions to Catholics. Portland was premier from 1807 to 1809, Spencer Perceval from 1809 to 1812, and Lord Liverpool (formerly Lord Hawkesbury) from 1812 to 1827, and they and their administrations studiously preserved the required neutrality on Catholic emancipation.

A stronger sense of party developed during the early 1800s, with wider and more regular use of the Whig and Tory labels. These came to denote differences of opinion on royal influence, Catholic emancipation and the king's treatment of the Talents. At the 1807 general election, party names and affiliations influenced politicians and public alike. The Portland ministry won a large majority and wiped out the electoral gains made by the Talents in 1806. As in 1784, George III and his allies had successfully upheld the king's right to have a say on government policy and personnel.

The political situation changed in 1810, however, when George III suffered another mental collapse. This time he showed no signs of recovering as he had in the past. The prime minister, Perceval, proposed a limited regency along the lines defined by Pitt in 1788. Whigs repeated Fox's arguments from that time, that the Prince of Wales should be regent by hereditary right and that parliament could not properly impose restrictions. Grenville was led by prevalent circumstances to oppose a regency measure not unlike the one he had supported in 1788. The government's majority was secure, and the regency bill passed in 1811 limited the prince's powers for one year. Leaders of the opposition expected him to reward their past services with office as soon as the limitations expired, but the prince regent eventually decided that old friendships mattered less than the need for a vigorous prosecution of the war and for resistance to Catholic emancipation. Meanwhile Grenvillites and Foxites quarrelled about individual claims for places in a new cabinet, should one be formed, and Grey decided that he could not take office when the Whig alliance was so divided and unruly. Negotiations continued, but it became clear that the prince would not exert himself to form an exclusively Whig ministry, and Grey and Grenville were not prepared to join a coalition government with Tories who would outnumber and overrule them. There was no change of ministers when limits on the regent's power lapsed in February 1812.

Liverpool succeeded Perceval as prime minister in June 1812 and most of Perceval's cabinet remained in place, but there was further negotiation and intrigue before this arrangement was confirmed. As before, the regent was probably not genuine in his overtures to Grenville and Grey, and they knew this, again refusing to join a ministry they would not be able to control. The Whigs' political association with the Prince of Wales no longer counted for anything, and Liverpool's appointment was a symptom of this rather than a cause.

The prince succeeded as George IV in 1820, a grossly over-weight, temperamental, lazy, self-indulgent man in his late fifties. He never grew out of the bad habits of his youth. Indeed, in adulthood they burst forth in all their stark ugliness, and as regent and king the fourth George was generally ridiculed and detested. His inattention to government business and lack of political expertise passed the initiative to ministers who could command a majority in parliament. Royal support, though still important, was a declining asset relative to other political advantages, and the administrative and financial reforms of preceding decades meant that government policy and personnel had passed beyond the crown's direct control. Liverpool and his colleagues normally dealt with the crown from a position of strength. They benefited, moreover, from the obvious inability (and unwillingness) of Whig leaders to form an alternative administration. Royal powers had continued to wane since Pitt's day, and the crown's political function would soon be rather more formal than active. George IV occasionally stirred himself to cause as much trouble as possible for ministers when they refused to yield to his wishes. Though his threats, complaints and plots exasperated Liverpool and the cabinet, they did not change the fact that George IV's freedom of choice on men and measures was more restricted than George III's had been. There were periods when Liverpool's ministry lost royal favour, but it did not fall and was not forced to resign.

The most serious conflict between the crown and Liverpool's administration occurred at the beginning of George IV's reign, when the king demanded a divorce from his estranged wife, Caroline. The two had separated acrimoniously many years before, and Caroline lived abroad. In 1820 ministers advised against divorce, because it would necessitate a public inquiry. King and queen were both known for their promiscuity and decadence, and a messy scandal could only benefit critics of crown and government. Ministers were unable to persuade Caroline to remain abroad, however, and she returned to claim her rights as queen. Under pressure from the parliamentary opposition, and uneasy about growing excitement out of doors, Liverpool and his colleagues would have preferred not to press ahead with divorce proceedings, but the king's insistence forced them to act. A bill of 'pains and penalties' was introduced to deprive Caroline of her title and privileges. It was narrowly passed by the House of Lords. The ministers had little chance of carrying it through the Commons, though, and they abandoned the measure in November 1820. An irate George IV tried and failed to replace Liverpool's administration. This affair suggests that even when there was a complete breakdown in relations between king and ministers, by itself royal disapproval was not enough to bring a government down.

Development of the cabinet system, collective responsibility and office of prime minister continued in these years, and it is significant that Liverpool could write in 1823 that his colleagues would all resign if he was dismissed by the king. Soon it would be an agreed constitutional convention that the forced departure of a prime minister meant a change of government. Collective responsibility meant that individual ministers were not expected to repudiate an agreed policy. There was also strong reaction whenever the monarch took advice from persons other than members of the cabinet, and advice tended increasingly to be channelled through the prime minister. When George IV tried to consult ministers separately, or made suggestions about their departmental business and patronage, they reminded him that his opinions ought to be expressed first to the premier. As Arthur Aspinall has demonstrated, the balance of power between crown and ministers was by now shifting perceptibly in favour of the latter.[19]

During the 1820s, ministerial ascendancy still depended on successful management of parliament, especially the Commons. This task was becoming more difficult because of continuing efforts to keep down the cost and increase the efficiency of government. Executive patronage, exercised more by ministers than by the king, had been shrinking for some time. Pitt and his successors had no choice but to respect and respond to the anti-corruption proclivities of the age, in order to raise government's reputation in parliament and nation. Sinecures, parliamentary seats, offices, contracts, pensions and other elements of executive largesse were all affected. This interfered with ministers' ability to control parliament, and after 1812 Liverpool's cabinet would sometimes be forced to retreat in response to a determined demonstration of independence by a majority of MPs. Executive power, also known as the 'influence of the crown', continued to stimulate controversy long after the days of Pitt and Fox.[20]

Conclusion

The politics of the late eighteenth century were shaped by several new and unsettling developments. Problems had to be addressed within a continually changing political structure, owing in particular to the quickening development of radicalism and extra-parliamentary protest, the outbreak of revolution and war in Europe, the rise of party, and a prolonged struggle between crown and politicians over patronage and influence.

The motives and conduct of George III have prompted considerable historiographical debate. Whig historians of the nineteenth century treated the Rockingham legend as a true account of George III's politics, as do their modern sympathisers, but several commentators have challenged this Whig orthodoxy. Years of research led Lewis Namier not to accept the Rockingham legend, but to argue that the idea of a corrupt king seeking to subvert the constitution and manipulate people and events is totally invalid. John Brooke rejects the premise behind the Dunning motion of 1780 and suggests that what were really increasing were the pretensions of the House of Commons. Ian Christie argues that opposition MPs assumed rather than demonstrated that royal power was expanding. There was much exaggeration, and neither the number of placemen in the Commons nor the number of parliamentary seats under government control increased between 1760 and 1780.[21]

The struggles inspired by George III and his allies and opponents created long periods of political confusion. In 1782 and 1783 there were four changes of government within twenty months. More instability followed between 1801 and 1812, when the ministerial alliance and support base built up under Pitt during the 1780s and 1790s fell apart. There were five changes of government in just over ten years. Factional contests, unresolved domestic issues and a lack of success in the French war created opportunities for decisive royal interventions, and the course of public affairs continued to be shaped in part by George III's approval and disapproval of particular men and measures. By the 1820s, however, the 'influence of the crown' was in irreversible decline. George IV lacked his father's energy, determination and political talent, but decline was not simply a matter of personal ineptitude. Economical reforms implemented by Pitt and his successors in office had reduced executive largesse and increased parliament's independence. The Whig opposition had also pressed for more limits on royal influence and government patronage. In 1809, for example, a measure to prevent the sale of parliamentary seats was proposed by Whig MP John Curwen. Together with other administrative reforms of the period, this limited the number of seats a government could reserve for its regular supporters.

The 'influence of the crown' was becoming far less significant by 1820. Party, public opinion and ministerial responsibility were taking the place of influence in politics, and its scope was narrowing as the independence and power of the House of Commons expanded. The old balance between crown, Lords and Commons, writes J. A. W. Gunn, became a balance within the Commons, which was seen to contain all the elements of the old familiar political system: crown (the executive power, that is, ministers and their supporters), Lords (followers and relatives of peers), and Commons (MPs who were independent of executive and aristocratic control).[22] Even in the 1760s, though, George III had realised that he could not maintain in office an administration which lacked a Commons majority. In addition, North in 1782 and Shelburne in 1783 had both resigned in the context of rapidly developing ideas about parliamentary accountability. Royal favour alone was not enough. To survive, a government needed a reliable majority in parliament.

Notes

1   J. Saintsbury, 'John Wilkes, debt, and patriotism', *JBS*, 34, 1995, pp. 165–95.

2   On this expansion of political consciousness, see J. Brewer, *Party Ideology and Popular Politics at the Accession of George III*, Cambridge, 1976, pp. 139–60, 163–200, 219–39, and 'English radicalism in the age of George III', in J. G. A. Pocock (ed.), *Three British Revolutions 1641, 1688, 1776*, Princeton, 1980, pp. 323–67; I. R. Christie, *Myth and Reality in Late Eighteenth-Century British Politics, and Other Papers*, London, 1970, pp. 311–33; H. Barker, 'Catering for provincial tastes? Newspapers, readership and profit in late eighteenth-century England', *HR*, 69, 1996, pp. 42–61; E. Nicholson, 'Consumers and spectators: the public of the political print in eighteenth-century England', *History*, 81, 1996, pp. 5–21; A. Aspinall, 'The reporting and publishing of House of Commons debates, 1771–1834', in R. Pares and A. J. P. Taylor (eds), *Essays Presented to Sir Lewis Namier*, London, 1956, pp. 227–57; D. T. Andrew, 'Popular culture and public debate: London 1780', *HJ*, 39, 1996, pp. 405–23; M. Thale, 'London debating societies in the 1790s', *HJ*, 32, 1989, pp. 57–86.

3   J. A. Phillips, 'The structure of electoral politics in unreformed England', *JBS*, 19, 1979, pp. 76–100, and *Electoral Behaviour in Unreformed England: Plumpers, Splitters and Straights*, Princeton, 1982; F. O'Gorman, *Voters, Patrons and Parties. The Unreformed Electoral System of Hanoverian England 1734–1832*, Oxford, 1989, chs 5, 6, and 'Campaign rituals and ceremonies: the social meaning of elections in England 1780–1860', *P&P*, 135, 1992, pp. 79–115.

4   The Rockingham legend and party identity are examined in Christie, *Myth and Reality*, pp. 27–54; Brewer, *Party Ideology and Popular Politics*, pp. 77–95, and 'Rockingham, Burke and Whig political

argument', *HJ*, 18, 1975, pp. 188–201; F. O'Gorman, 'Party in the later eighteenth century', in J. Cannon (ed.), *The Whig Ascendancy: Colloquies on Hanoverian England*, London, 1981, pp. 77–99; S. Farrell, 'Division lists and the nature of the Rockingham Whig party in the House of Lords 1760–85', *PH*, 13, 1994, pp. 170–89.

5   H. Butterfield, 'The Yorkshire Association and the crisis of 1779–80', *TRHS*, 4th series, 29, 1947, pp. 69–91; I. R. Christie, 'The Yorkshire Association 1780–84: a study in political organisation', *HJ*, 3, 1960, pp. 144–61.

6   In 1720, the parliament at Westminster had assumed the power to legislate for Ireland.

7   B. Kemp, 'Crewe's Act 1782', *EHR*, 68, 1953, pp. 258–63.

8   E. A. Reitan, 'The civil list in eighteenth-century British politics: parliamentary supremacy versus the independence of the crown', *HJ*, 9, 1966, pp. 318–37.

9   J. Derry, *Politics in the Age of Fox, Pitt and Liverpool*, Basingstoke, 1990, p. 38; L. G. Mitchell, *Charles James Fox*, Oxford, 1992, p. 51.

10   Electoral corruption is highlighted in W. T. Laprade, 'William Pitt and Westminster elections', *AmHR*, 18, 1913, pp. 253–74, and 'Public opinion and the general election of 1784', *EHR*, 31, 1916, pp. 224–37; C. E. Fryer, 'The general election of 1784', *History*, 9, 1925, pp. 221–3. See also W. T. Laprade (ed.), *Parliamentary Papers of John Robinson 1774–84*, London, 1922, pp. 65–132. Public support is stressed in M. D. George, 'Fox's martyrs: the general election of 1784', *TRHS*, 4th series, 21, 1939, pp. 133–68; P. Kelly, 'Radicalism and public opinion in the general election of 1784', *HR*, 45, 1972, pp. 73–88, and 'British politics 1783–4: the emergence and triumph of the Younger Pitt's administration', *HR*, 54, 1981, pp. 62–78.

11   I. R. Christie, 'The anatomy of the opposition in the parliament of 1784', *PH*, 9, 1990, pp. 50–77.

12   M. Duffy, 'The Younger Pitt and the House of Commons', *History*, 83, 1998, pp. 217–24.

13   J. Kelly, *Prelude to Union: Anglo-Irish Politics in the 1780s*, Cork, 1992.

14   P. Kelly, 'Constituents' instructions to Members of Parliament in the eighteenth century', in C. Jones (ed.), *Party and Management in Parliament 1660–1784*, Leicester, 1984, pp. 169–89.

15   W. D. Rubinstein, 'The end of "Old Corruption" in Britain 1780–1860', *P&P*, 101, 1983, pp. 55–86; P. Harling, 'Rethinking "Old Corruption"', *P&P*, 147, 1995, pp. 127–58, and *The Waning of 'Old Corruption'. The Politics of Economical Reform in Britain 1779–1846*, Oxford, 1996.

16   W. R. Ward, 'The administration of the window and assessed taxes 1698–1798', *EHR*, 67, 1952, pp. 522–42; J. R. Breihan, 'William Pitt and the commission on fees 1785–1801', *HJ*, 27, 1984, pp. 59–81.

17   M. W. McCahill, 'Peerage creations and the changing character of the British nobility 1750–1850', *EHR*, 96, 1981, pp. 259–84, suggests that distinguished public service began to replace land as the main qualification for titles.

18   J. Ehrman, *The Younger Pitt. The Consuming Struggle*, London, 1996, ch. 15; C. J. Fedorak, 'Catholic emancipation and the resignation of William Pitt in 1801', *Albion*, 24, 1992, pp. 49–64; R. E. Willis, 'William Pitt's resignation in 1801: re-examination and document', *HR*, 44, 1971, pp. 239–57.

19   A. Aspinall, 'The cabinet council 1783–1835', *Proceedings of the British Academy*, 38, 1952, pp. 145–252.

20   J. R. Dinwiddy, 'The "influence of the crown" in the early nineteenth century: a note on the opposition case', *PH*, 4, 1985, pp. 189–200; Harling, *Waning of 'Old Corruption'*, chs 4, 5; A. S. Foord, 'The waning of the "influence of the crown"', *EHR*, 62, 1947, pp. 484–507.

21   L. B. Namier, 'King George III: a study of personality', in his *Personalities and Powers*, London, 1955, pp. 39–58; J. Brooke, *King George III*, London, 1972, pp. 217–18; I. R. Christie, 'Economical reform and "the influence of the crown", 1780', *HJ*, 12, 1956, pp. 144–54, and 'George III and the historians, thirty years on', *History*, 71, 1986, pp. 205–21. See also H. Butterfield, *George III and the Historians*, rev. edn, London, 1988; R. Pares, *George III and the Politicians*, Oxford, 1953.

22   J. A. W. Gunn, 'Influence, parties and the constitution: changing attitudes 1783–1832', *HJ*, 17, 1974, pp. 301–28.

2

Revolution and war

Introduction

The French Revolution and subsequent wars dramatically affected British politics. There was a rapid and lasting polarisation of opinion as politicians and public disagreed about how to respond to events abroad. Britain joined the war against revolutionary France in 1793. In 1794 the Whig opposition finally disintegrated. Pitt's government concentrated on the war effort and introduced coercive measures to deal with radicalism and disorder at home. The conduct of the war, its economic consequences, and domestic repression were all condemned in parliament and out of doors, but the government was secure. The pressures of the time turned many contemporaries against change and innovation, and reform proposals were soundly defeated in parliament. Pitt's following fragmented after 1801, however, and there was another period of political instability. Whigs were briefly in office from 1806 to 1807. Then government was dominated by former allies and followers of Pitt. Out of doors, radicalism continued to develop. Campaigners pressed for a more representative legislature, and for more efficient and honest government. The French Revolution inspired new organisations and ideas, and local political struggles also contributed to the agitation of these years, accelerating the expansion of popular politics. Radical resources and tactics evolved quickly, and though the state's response was severe, radicalism survived and at the end of the war was thriving. But in this era of revolution and war, popular radicalism was more than matched by an upsurge in loyalism. Popular mobilisation took conservative as well as radical forms, and the loyalist reaction probably did more than state repression to restrain extra-parliamentary protest.

Price, Burke, Paine and the ideological ferment of the 1790s

The French Revolution began in June 1789, and in Britain there was much discussion about its meaning and implications. The revolution changed course several times, and British reactions changed too. There was great sympathy for the initial attempt to establish a constitutional monarchy, but then violence broke out in France, revolutionary fervour spread, new political theories were implemented, and the French Revolution fostered republicanism and war. These developments gained a rather less favourable reception in Britain, though opinions continued to be deeply divided.

On 4 November 1789 Dr Richard Price, the Unitarian minister and friend of Shelburne who had been a prominent advocate of American independence, addressed the London Revolution Society on the similarities between Britain's Glorious Revolution of 1688 and recent events in France. In his 'Discourse on the Love of our Country', Price spoke of improvements left unfinished by Britain's revolutionary settlement, called for religious toleration and parliamentary reform, and argued that the Glorious Revolution had established three fundamental rights which properly resided in the people: the rights to frame a system of government, choose rulers and dismiss them for misconduct. Price's radical interpretation of the Glorious Revolution was widely publicised. It drew forth an impassioned rebuttal from Burke, who was already uneasy about Foxite endorsement of events in France, and who believed that British society and government would be endangered if people followed the lead of such reckless spokesmen as Fox and Price.

Burke's *Reflections on the Revolution in France* appeared in November 1790. This book asserted that reforms could be safe and useful only when they accorded with a nation's traditions, and that experience mattered more than theory. Burke insisted that events in France had been misunderstood in Britain. Far from following the pattern of the Glorious Revolution, the methods and goals of French leaders represented its antithesis. Britain had experienced peaceful transition, but France was falling into chaos. French revolutionaries had no respect for the past. They were out to destroy social and political hierarchy in order to impose an artificial equality which could only lead to oppression and degradation. Burke warned reform groups in Britain against following the French example and condemned Price's version of British history (see Document 3). There was no right to choose governors, cashier them, or frame a system of government at will, Burke wrote, and the British public neither wanted nor exercised these powers. Instead, there was profound respect for custom, prescription and the hereditary principle. Rights were known to depend on uninterrupted use and the wisdom of past generations, whose binding compacts were transmitted to the present as an inviolable inheritance. The French were trying to build everything anew, Burke stressed, but Britons would be wise to recognise the past as their infallible guide.

Burke had already clashed openly with Fox on these points, and publication of the *Reflections* soon resulted in a schism which proved to be permanent. From the outset, Foxites ridiculed Burke's pessimistic predictions about events in France, and most of the early published responses to Burke were hostile. But he maintained that the correct understanding of the Glorious Revolution was being undermined by radicals, Dissenters, Price and even Fox, and that favourable comparisons between 1688 and the French Revolution were extremely harmful. As time passed and the French Revolution became more violent and unstable, Burke's arguments were seen to be upheld by events. As a result he was able to pose as a more faithful guardian of the Whig tradition than the Foxites, and to carry an influential section of opposition politicians with him over to the government's side.

The ideas of Price and Burke were widely debated. Many writers engaged in the controversy, which in turn contributed to the rise of reform and anti-reform associations and added to political tension in the nation. Argument about events in France, and their bearing on British politics and society, increased further with the publication of Thomas Paine's *Rights of Man* (part one in March 1791, part two in February 1792). Paine was a former excise officer, dismissed for demanding higher pay, who had emigrated to America in 1774. He became secretary to the first American committee on foreign affairs, and sided with the rebels during the American war of independence. Paine's *Common Sense* (1776) had established his reputation as a revolutionary thinker and the principal theorist of the American struggle, for it maintained that any necessary means should be employed to defend fundamental rights. In 1787 Paine returned to Europe. He attached himself to progressive movements and participated in the early stages of the French Revolution. His *Rights of Man* was a response to Burke, a vindication of revolutionary precepts, and an exaltation of democratic government.

Paine rejected Burke's arguments about prescription and the hereditary principle (see Document 4). The Glorious Revolution had not entitled one generation to bind posterity, for every generation was competent to decide how government should be organised. Laws, governors, customs and rights survived only because they were acceptable to the living, Paine explained, and the true basis of authority was consent rather than prescription. Burke assumed that rights established at fixed points in history gained their legitimacy from uninterrupted use, but Paine insisted that humans were born with inherent natural rights. Civil rights, pertaining to membership of a society, grew out of these natural rights, and government was established when natural rights were collected together. These convictions led Paine to conclude that the British system of government had arisen over the people instead of from the people: it was not based on consent. In contrast French revolutionaries recognised the true nature of rights. They were now establishing government by consent, and had cast aside political oppression and social discrimination in favour of equality, justice, freedom of conscience and a broad suffrage.

Paine's irreverent comments offended people of influence and property, who were quick to point to the destructive tendency of his principles. Indeed, he went too far even for many reformers. They did not press their own ideas to his democratic and republican conclusions, and some still thought of parliamentary reform in the context of constitutional balance and electoral purity. Moderate reformers held that political rights should be reserved for men who had the rank, character, wealth and education to exercise them responsibly. More advanced radicals, however, welcomed the *Rights of Man*. They could understand Paine's principles, and his work inspired them to organise petitions, attend meetings, discuss public issues and make contact with reform societies in other towns and regions with even greater eagerness. Paine's ideology became a favoured creed of artisan radicals. These men of skill and small means, who were self-reliant, literate and politically conscious, resented their lack of influence and had no confidence in aristocratic government and an unrepresentative parliament.

Paine's work rapidly sold tens of thousands of copies in cheap editions. Some London and provincial radical societies reprinted and circulated short extracts. This diffusion of anti-establishment propaganda alarmed the government and made Paine a marked man. At the end of 1792 he fled to France and was convicted of sedition in his absence. By this time Europe was at war. Revolutionary violence had increased in France during the September Massacres, and the French had invaded the Netherlands (a direct threat to British trade and security). Then the revolutionary regime in Paris issued the Declaration of Fraternity, a promise to assist any nation which rose to release itself from despotism. Hopes for the survival of the French monarchy faded, and Louis XVI was executed in January 1793. Britain joined the war against France in February.

The ideological ferment provoked most notably by Price, Burke and Paine would shape political discourse and activity for many years. Price's interpretation of the Glorious Revolution prompted many reformers to argue that the constitution must be restored to its former unadulterated condition, and that the work left undone since 1688 should now be completed. Paine promoted a new and distinctive tendency in British politics. Now the case for reform could be made more forcefully than before, with natural rights arguments rather than appeals to an old constitution corrupted in the distant past. Meanwhile Burke supplied emotional and intellectual foundations for conservative resistance to rapid or excessive change, and in doing so he encouraged a realignment in parliamentary and extra-parliamentary politics.

High politics

The early stages of the French Revolution stimulated a variety of responses among Britain's political elite. George III, who was enjoying a new wave of popularity after the regency crisis, disliked political instability in a neighbouring kingdom, but he regarded limitation of the French king's powers as an appropriate punishment for the latter's previous alliance with American rebels. The cautious Pitt was determined not to commit himself to a particular course of action until it became clear how events in France were going to unfold. Pitt hoped that reforms in France would increase the benefits of the Anglo-French commercial treaty and strengthen European peace, but his main priorities were still domestic (effective administration and balanced budgets), and Pitt predicted that the problem of how to respond to the French Revolution would be more perplexing for the opposition than for the government.

Whig divisions were exacerbated by the Hastings trial and the growing tension between Fox and Burke. As B. W. Hill has shown, Burke was increasingly devoted to cardinal principles which mattered little to Fox and his followers, leading Burke to believe that they did not have the necessary virtue or consistency to serve the public interest.[1] Fox's union with conservative Whig peers led by Portland was also becoming more fragile, and Pitt was right to think that conflicting responses to events in France would eventually break up the Whig opposition.

Foxites welcomed what they took to be a French version of the Glorious Revolution, and argued that the destruction of monarchical despotism would enable France at last to enjoy genuine freedom and progress. Fox warmly praised the draft of a new French constitution. He assumed that his friends among the liberal French aristocracy were true Whigs and would act like it, and that in France, as in Britain, the main obstacle to liberty and stability was an over-mighty king. The French Revolution would subject monarchy to constitutional limitations, would end traditional Anglo-French rivalry (because French policy would no longer be shaped by Bourbon ambitions), and would establish civil and religious liberty in France. French leaders, thought Fox, were doing what Britain's political elite was failing to do, a fact proved by the defeat in parliament of efforts to repeal the Test and Corporation Acts in 1787, 1789 and 1790 (these measures dated from the seventeenth century and excluded from many public offices anyone who did not receive Anglican communion). The Foxite analysis was not shared by more conservative Whigs. Burke's *Reflections* led to an open breach, though the publication was more the occasion rather than the cause, for tension had been building up for many months. Fox, Sheridan and the Prince of Wales all rejected Burke's propositions, but Burke gained a hearing from the friends of Portland, particularly Lord Loughborough, William Windham and Earl Fitzwilliam. Portland dithered: he did not wish to break up the Whig opposition, and his suspicion of Pitt still outweighed his unease about France. But the split between Burke and Fox eventually forced Portland to take sides, especially when the French Revolution took the violent paths anticipated by Burke and when Britain entered the European war against France.

Fox had initially hoped that the difficulty created by Burke would only be temporary, but the Commons debate on army estimates in February 1790 was an unmistakable presage. While Fox called for a reduction in military expenditure, on the grounds that Britain no longer had to worry about French enmity, Burke warned that French goodwill could not be taken for granted and that a malevolent democratic spirit was taking control of the reform process in France. Sheridan called Burke a friend of despotism, and to cheers from the government benches Burke declared that his political connection with Sheridan was now at an end. The *Reflections* were published eight months later, and Burke finally broke with Fox on 6 May 1791, during a Commons debate on the government of Canada, which was about to be reorganised. Burke stressed that all such reforms should be rooted in tradition, and he urged MPs to repudiate the French way of proceeding. Fox maintained that the French Revolution would prove to be a great catalyst for the advancement of humankind, and asserted that natural rights, which Burke had ridiculed, were the basis of every rational constitution. They arose from an original compact between government and people, and took the form of inherent freedoms which no prescription or accident could alter. Fox hoped that his friendship with Burke would survive their disagreement, but

Burke could not forgive Fox for what he saw as a gross dereliction of duty. Those who wanted disorder and upheaval in Britain would assume from Fox's words that he was with them, complained Burke, when his chief duty was to restrain them. Though some Foxites were pleased to be rid of Burke, Fox knew that the Portland Whigs were beginning to reassess their position, and in August 1791 Burke published his *Appeal from the New to the Old Whigs*, inviting opposition MPs to desert Fox and join the defenders of tradition, stability and order.

Pitt's ministry benefited from these developments, and made tentative contact with Burke during 1791. But Pitt did not fully agree with Burke's ideas, and Pitt's strict neutrality and refusal to make unqualified statements about the French Revolution annoyed Burke. Pitt and his cabinet colleagues remained detached but alert, and in this they had the backing of George III, who wanted no British intervention in French politics (even if the status and privileges of a brother monarch were at stake).

In view of the need to limit political instability at home in this difficult period, Pitt turned against movements for reform (see Document 5). The majority of MPs took a similar line, as became clear in March 1790 when Irish MP Henry Flood introduced a proposal for parliamentary reform. Flood's plan had three main parts: the enfranchisement of all resident householders paying 50s a year in tax, the removal of one seat from every decayed borough (most boroughs had two seats), and an addition of one hundred seats to the county representation. Fox spoke in favour of reform, but he saw clearly that public support was lacking (despite the efforts of Wyvill). Pitt, Burke and Windham all opposed Flood's plan. Significantly, Windham stressed that reform must wait for calmer times, and referred explicitly to the disturbing changes being attempted in France. Pitt argued that reforms should be discussed only when the time was right and if they addressed obvious abuses. He did not think that Flood's plan met either condition, and in the event Flood's motion was not even pressed to a division.

The 1790 general election brought no significant change in the relative strengths of government and opposition in the Commons. G. M. Ditchfield's study of MPs' voting patterns in these years has highlighted both a growing sense of party and the influence of outdoor opinion. There was some consistency in voting. Most opposition MPs voted for repeal of the Test and Corporation Acts, but few Pittites did, and supporters of repeal included most MPs for boroughs with relatively wide franchises. This could indicate Dissenting influence there, general commitment to reforms, or both. Repealers tended also to vote for parliamentary reform, but not abolition of the slave trade, so Ditchfield's correlation has its limits.[2] Opposition unity, moreover, was becoming less rather than more secure, and further difficulties were posed by the rise of extra-parliamentary reform societies and the question of whether or not to co-operate with them. Some Foxite MPs, most notably Charles Grey, were among the founders and leaders of one such body, the Society of the Friends of the People. Fox did not join this society. By giving it his blessing, however, he greatly annoyed Portland's group.

Portland Whigs disliked outdoor agitation and were not committed to parliamentary reform. These aristocratic patrons had no desire to lose the seats they controlled, and much preferred the old Rockingham policy of economical reform. The Portland group sought to prevent those elected to the Commons from being corrupted once they got there, not to reform the electoral system itself. Fox's sympathies were with reformers among his own following, and they believed that the mobilisation out of doors offered them a chance to enlarge their support base and erode the popularity gained by Pitt and George III during the regency crisis. Foxites should place themselves at the head of reform opinion in the nation, it was also suggested, in order to ensure that radicals would not be led astray by extremists. But Fox knew that if he openly sided with reformers in parliament and out of doors, this would further alienate the Portland Whigs. Fox was anxious to keep together the progressive and conservative wings of the Whig opposition, and he tried to avoid making a choice between them for as long as possible.

Grey forced Fox's hand, giving notice of a reform motion in the Commons on 30 April 1792. This pleased many Foxites, because they were not prepared to take direction from Portland and the Whig grandees, and wanted Fox to commit himself unequivocally to reform. George Tierney of the Friends of the People suspected that some of the grandees favoured an understanding with Pitt rather than continued opposition in union with Fox. Reform proposals in the Commons would force them to make up their minds, Tierney thought, and leave the parliamentary opposition stronger and more united. In April 1792 Fox sided with Grey, while Pitt attacked the Friends and insisted that reform would harm the peace and safety of the nation. Taunted with reminders that he had advocated reform during the 1780s, Pitt pointed out that circumstances had completely changed since then. Over subsequent months he and his cabinet colleagues discussed ways of detaching discontented Portland Whigs from the opposition and bringing them over to the government's side. Meanwhile there was growing concern about the spread of disorder, the rise of a powerful and organised reform movement, and the broad distribution of radical literature (especially Paine's work in cheap editions). Furthermore, the French Revolution, a source of inspiration for many reformers in Britain, was taking a more extreme course than many observers had envisaged. In May 1792 the government issued a proclamation against seditious publications and meetings. Pitt consulted Portland about this in advance, another sign of the cabinet's eagerness to divide its parliamentary opponents. Portland approved of the proclamation, but Fox denied that there was sedition in Britain, and asserted that the main threat to liberty and order came not from radical societies but from religious intolerance and resistance to reform.

Though for several years Pitt had been reluctant to involve his ministry in controversies at home and in France's internal problems, by the end of 1792 he realised that revolutionary fervour in France was out of control. Pitt was also disturbed by the military successes of French revolutionary armies against Austria and Prussia. The execution of Louis XVI made a rapid restoration of European peace unlikely. In February 1793 Britain went to war with France in order to protect British trade and interests abroad, restore a balance of power in Europe, restrain the ambitions of the new French regime, and combat the spread of dangerous principles. Pitt's government actively sought public support for war and for new measures to suppress agitation at home. Ministers were assisted in this by an upsurge in popular loyalism and the formation of hundreds of conservative associations. Anti-French and anti-reform sentiment grew because of changing opinions about the French Revolution, fear of France as an expansionist military power, unease about domestic radicalism and protest, and concern for the safety of property and established institutions.

By now the parliamentary opposition was rapidly falling apart. Fox would not change his earlier assumptions about the French Revolution. It represented a wonderful new birth for liberty, he believed, and if it had become violent, this was only because France was threatened by the European monarchies. The latter should not have meddled in the revolution, which would resume a moderate course if the French were left alone. Fox insisted that Britain should not join the European war in the cause of absolutist reaction, but Burke's apocalyptic interpretation of the French Revolution gained ground and Fox's position was increasingly questioned. Fox's judgement was flawed because from the outset he had tried to tie the revolution to his own political goals, and he never doubted that it would assist the Whig cause in Britain. Fox drew false parallels between events in France and the Glorious Revolution, believing that the need to limit royal power was the crucial motive in both cases. Fox lost support in parliament and out of doors, however, and Portland Whigs were infuriated when he advocated formal recognition of the French republic and declared himself ready to press for parliamentary reform. The outbreak of war between Britain and France gave Portland and his friends further cause to reconsider their position. Then, in May 1793, Grey followed up his reform speech of April 1792 by moving for a committee to consider reform petitions.

Grey insisted that parliament should be made more representative and that electoral anomalies must be removed, but Pitt argued that reform proposals at this juncture could do no good, since they would only encourage the disloyal to challenge government and the social order. In Britain there were radicals who sought to introduce French principles, said Pitt, and parliament should not give the slightest countenance to their designs. Pitt declared that he was not prepared to endanger the blessings of the constitution by entertaining a vain hope of improving it. Fox accused Pitt of inconsistency and error, welcomed Grey's motion, and scorned the use of French examples to discredit it. French excesses were irrelevant to discussion of reform in Britain, Fox maintained, and without reform the Commons could not perform its proper functions, the representation of the people and curbing of executive power. Fox's arguments made little difference. Grey's motion was heavily defeated, having attracted limited support from opposition MPs. Less than a third of them voted with Grey and, as before with Flood's proposal, one of the speakers against reform was William Windham, an ally of Portland. These circumstances encouraged Pitt and Dundas to think again of a coalition with Portland Whigs. Not only would this divide the opposition and weaken Fox, but in a time of disturbing developments at home and abroad it would give the ministry a valuable addition of influence and debating talent, and enable it to face the future with greater confidence.

Burke had long been advocating the formation of a new government of national unity, and as Pitt moved to take advantage of the rupture between Foxites and the followers of Portland, the prime minister found that the latter agreed with court, cabinet, the parliamentary majority and respectable opinion out of doors that war against France was necessary and justifiable. Though Portland again refused to break with Fox and destroy what was left of the Whig party, his friends began to ally with Pitt as individuals. Finally Portland agreed that if the war was going to be vigorously conducted, and radicalism contained at home, conservative Whigs would have to co-operate with Pitt. Portland became home secretary in July 1794, Windham secretary at war, and Pitt's cabinet of ten was expanded to thirteen. Burke accepted a government pension. Pitt was determined that the union with Portland Whigs should last. Though much policy would continue to be decided by an inner core of ministers (Pitt, Grenville and Dundas), six of the thirteen cabinet posts were now held by men who had opposed Pitt before 1793, and despite minor disagreements this coalition government was genuinely united in the cause of preserving British institutions from internal and external threats.

The opposition split of 1794 substantially reduced Fox's influence and following. In subsequent years his party could do little more than condemn the ministers' conduct of the war and the measures proposed to quell popular agitation. Fox denounced Pitt for fighting the war as an ideological conflict in which total victory had to be won before peace could be negotiated. He repeatedly urged that war should be limited in scope and ended as soon as possible, while Pitt maintained that the war was not being fought against troublesome doctrines but against a dangerous political, military and economic rival. Opposition numbers in the Commons posed no threat to the government's majority, and Fox and Grey knew that their best course was simply to maintain the Foxite connection as a viable and independent party so that the campaign for liberty could be continued when circumstances improved. They concentrated on consistent themes: that the war was unnecessary and government repression unjustified, and that ministers were cynically creating alarm in order to attack political opponents, suspend constitutional liberties, and push objectionable measures through parliament with indecent haste.

Foxites were the leading spokesmen against the prosecution and punishment of radicals, and against restrictions on public assembly and other popular rights. The cabinet, parliamentary majority and local authorities considered radical agitation a threat to public order and institutions, and especially dangerous in wartime. Courts dealt severely with such political offences as sedition, but there was also need for legislative action. Of special concern was the radical plan for a national reform convention. This seemed to be a direct challenge to parliament, and the government could hardly permit the congregation of a national body which claimed to represent the people more faithfully than the House of Commons. Unease grew because of the organisation of mass petitions against war and for parliamentary reform, while reports from paid informants persistently warned the authorities about radical agents who were touring the country to solicit support for the convention. Reports also referred to wild talk of a French invasion, which was expected to assist in the recovery of the people's just rights.

In May 1794 London radical leaders were arrested and their papers confiscated (some of these men were subsequently tried for treason). The 'committee of secrecy' informed the Commons that people had been arming themselves in preparation for the convention, and that there existed a plan to subvert the constitution. The government decided to suspend habeas corpus for one year. Radicals could now be held without trial. Fox protested that ministers were seeking an absolute power over every individual, and that the real threat to the constitution came from Pitt's administration, not the radicals. Pitt insisted that there was real danger of insurrection and that a temporary sacrifice of liberty was needed to safeguard the social and political order. The prime minister was backed in the Commons by Burke, Windham and Dundas, and conservatives who wanted a full range of preventive measures.

The mounting harvest crisis of the mid-1790s, and the refusal of committed radicals to retreat into inactivity, caused further unrest. In October 1795 stones were thrown at the king's coach as it carried him to the state opening of parliament. New measures were introduced to restore order. Having for some time been pressed by his supporters to act, Pitt had only been awaiting a suitable opportunity. He was disappointed that some political trials had not resulted in convictions, and that radical bodies seemed to be stepping up rather than suspending their agitation. Now the Seditious Meetings Act imposed restrictions on meetings of more than fifty people, and the Treasonable Practices Act redefined the offence of treason to encompass plans to harm the king, help invaders, or coerce parliament (spoken words were included in this offence). Foxites regarded these 'Two Acts' as proof that the government's real priority was to intimidate its critics, using national security as a pretext. Fox denounced the removal of rights without just cause, denied that the attack on the king's coach and recent reform meetings were closely connected, and challenged Pitt to verify the claim that reformers were engaging in sedition and treason. There was no need for repressive measures, said Fox, because existing laws were sufficient to deal with breaches of the peace. Fox agreed that the constitution needed to be defended, but against an aggressive executive, not against the British people.

Pitt defended the new measures. Though he respected the right of individuals to meet and discuss political questions, and their right of petition, he held that these rights were being abused. Reform meetings were a cover for revolutionary plotting, Pitt argued, and it was government's duty to prevent the abuse of rights while preserving those rights intact. Pitt and his supporters accused Fox of contesting parliament's competence and promoting disaffection. The opposition could not prevent the passage of the 'Two Acts' in 1795, nor the opening of subscriptions for local defence. Foxite MPs thought these funding arrangements illegal, since defence was parliament's responsibility, and people who chose not to contribute would be vulnerable to persecution. Again it seemed that the purpose was to combat anti-government opinion out of doors.

If the Foxites were right, the immediate level of danger to the state did not warrant the suspension of habeas corpus in 1794 and the 'Two Acts' of 1795. But if Pitt's principal concern was not merely to inconvenience his opponents, other motives, personal and political, assume greater significance. Pitt had to protect himself and his cabinet from possible political failures in the future, and guard against criticism from George III and the Portland Whigs. Domestic threats could be used to strengthen Pitt's position and silence complaints about lack of success in the war. Coercion also recommended itself when Pitt thought about what might happen if radical agitation continued unchecked. Added concerns were the possibility of a French invasion, and the need to encourage men of status and property to assist in defending the established order. For many reasons, therefore, government had to demonstrate energy and firmness, and the timing of measures was crucial. In 1794 Pitt wanted to cement his alliance with the Portland Whigs, who abhorred popular radicalism, and in 1795 public support for the war was fast declining.

Foxites continued to advocate moderate parliamentary reform after Grey's effort of 1793, though opposition MPs were by no means united on the question and it was never a priority for Fox and Grey. They wanted no association with plebeian radicals out of doors, moreover, and eschewed annual parliaments and manhood suffrage. Their version of reform involved only household suffrage and a limited redistribution of seats. In May 1797 Grey introduced another reform motion (it was too moderate for advanced radicals, and the distance between them and the Whig opposition grew wider than ever). Grey wanted to divide large counties, transfer seats to counties from corrupt boroughs, extend the county franchise to copyholders and some leaseholders, introduce a uniform householder suffrage in boroughs, and reduce electoral expenses and inconvenience by limiting the duration of the poll. He also favoured a reorganisation of electoral districts into single-member constituencies. In the Commons Fox declared that this reform plan would save the nation from misgovernment and ruin. It directly addressed the salient problems of the age: an unrepresentative legislature and an executive dependent on improper influence. Turning his attention to agitation out of doors, Fox suggested that the most effective way of discouraging extremists was to conciliate the much larger number of people who wanted moderate reform. Pitt was unimpressed, and he told the Commons that there was no great demand for reform, no need for it, and that this was not the time to consider the question. Grey's motion was heavily defeated.

This defeat prompted a Foxite secession from parliament. Fox himself stayed away from the Commons for nearly four years, though secession was incomplete, informal, and caused a great deal of argument among opposition politicians. The ambitious Grey came to regret the manoeuvre, and began to attend again late in 1798. Sheridan and Tierney, who both hoped to succeed Fox as opposition leader in the Commons, disagreed with the tactic and did not secede at all. Reformers out of doors complained about Fox's conduct and feared that liberal opinions would now be expressed in parliament even less often than before. Secession turned many people against Fox, because he seemed no longer to regard parliament as the appropriate place to state grievances. His critics accused him of bringing the Commons into disrepute. Secession was a sign of frustration (the apparent futility of opposition to Pitt had been indicated again by the 1796 general election, which confirmed the government's majority), but it was also rooted in honourable principle. It was a protest against government manipulation of the political process, and an attempt to deny Pitt the legitimacy afforded by parliamentary debate and division. The premises of Foxite politics were unaffected by secession and the controversy to which it gave rise: Pitt and George III were corrupt, their regime rested on coercion, and they were destroying liberty under cover of an unnecessary war. This was an important legacy for younger Whigs who came to the fore in the early nineteenth century, though in the short term secession harmed the Foxites and strengthened Pitt. In addition, when further repressive measures were introduced at the end of the 1790s there were fewer opposition MPs than usual to remonstrate against them. Habeas corpus was suspended again in 1798, for three years, the Newspaper Publication Act subjected publishers to stricter regulation, in 1799 the radical London Corresponding Society was suppressed and there were moves to combat oath-taking and other underground activity, and Combination Acts were passed in 1799 and 1800 to control workers' unions. These precautions were necessitated, said Pitt, by the continuing disturbances of the time and the dangerous influence of secret societies. The measures were designed to prevent rather than to punish, he insisted, and they accorded with the spirit of the constitution.

Through the 1790s and early 1800s there were periods of intense distress, and attendant outbreaks of violence, owing to economic dislocation, unemployment, high prices and poor harvests. Radical leaders pointed to what they said was the root cause of these troubles, misgovernment, and thereby attracted more support for their meetings and petitions. The home office, meanwhile, was constantly receiving reports about oath-taking, drilling and arming. Pitt resolved that there could be no sur-render on issues relating to the war, system of government, or maintenance of public order. Nevertheless, his ministry made some gestures to relieve suffering, improve poverty relief provisions and safeguard food supplies, deciding that limited state intervention of this kind was justifiable in times of crisis.

Pittite repression did not amount to a reign of terror. Frank O'Gorman argues that repressive legislation was necessary because informal and indirect methods of containing radicalism 'were no longer sufficient', and Clive Emsley insists that ministers diligently adhered to familiar constitutional practice and did not take on arbitrary powers. The priority was always to find a balance between respect for individual liberties and government's duty to maintain order.[3] John Ehrman rejects the Foxite claim about ulterior motives and asserts that Pitt only responded to dangers which no government could ignore.[4] It is difficult to accept the idea of a reign of terror. There were less than two hundred political prosecutions between 1793 and 1801, charges were often dropped, and trials could and did result in acquittal. The offence of treason was redefined in 1795, but most proceedings were on the lesser charge of sedition. Though emergency laws may have appeared harsh, they were only temporary and did not alter the constitution. Pitt's related goals were to deter radicals and encourage the loyalist majority to defend the established order. As this happened, further laws and trials became unnecessary. Yet reformers directly affected by repression would not have agreed that there was no reign of terror, and there were enough people held in prison without trial, or whose health, reputation and livelihood were harmed by arrest and trial, for a reign of terror to become embedded in the developing radical consciousness. Nevertheless, there were fewer prosecutions for political offences between 1796 and 1800 than between 1792 and 1795. Even while restrictions were being extended, the number of cases decreased. The content and duration of emergency laws were strictly defined, and ministers had to justify their use and renewal at the appropriate times. Certain liberties were untouched, notably the right of petition. Some forms of association were unaffected, and many types of premises were not included in restrictions on meetings.

Pitt's time and attention were not only taken up by parliamentary struggles, popular unrest and war strategy. Though some of the administrative and financial reforms of the 1780s could not carry on in wartime, efficient government and stable public finances were even more necessary during war than they had been before 1793, and some new measures related directly to problems created by the war. A new government department had to be created, for example, to deal with military affairs and the conduct of the war. Dundas assumed responsibility for these matters in 1794 on his appointment to the new post of secretary of state for war (he was already treasurer of the navy and president of the Indian board of control).

Economic and financial questions loomed large during the 1790s, and Pitt had increasingly to attend to these as it became clear that the war would not be as short as expected. He realised that success in war depended largely on economic strength and financial resources. Pitt's suspension in 1797 of specie payments by the Bank of England brought more flexibility into the money supply, stimulated business, and limited the loss of bullion (which was needed to pay for foreign grain and subsidies to Britain's continental allies). Pitt and his successors decided against a quick return to specie payments because they did not

73

want to restrain economic activity nor risk a loss of confidence in paper money. Pitt's plans for lowering the national debt could not work in wartime, though he tried to limit the debt's growth. Existing taxes were increased, especially those affecting property. The old land tax was reorganised, and there was a significant innovation, income tax, collection of which began in 1799. Opponents of income tax claimed that it was inquisitorial, unfairly heavy on the wealthy (who already supported a large tax burden), and that it would damage the economy and retard investment. It was also said to represent an unconstitutional enlargement of government power. But it soon came to be seen as a wartime necessity, and provided 28 per cent of all money raised for the war. The income tax began a new era in public finance, though this was probably not intentional. Indeed, it has been argued that Pitt's priority was not to raise money to fight a larger war, but to safeguard the financial reforms of the 1780s (especially the sinking fund).[5]

When Addington succeeded Pitt as prime minister in 1801 he committed his administration to peace and retrenchment. The Treaty of Amiens was concluded with France in March 1802. This made possible substantial cuts in public expenditure, especially on the army and navy. Income tax was ended, sinking fund arrangements reorganised, and Addington also reformed public accounting and the civil list. Peace brought a revival in trade, and all these developments combined to bring ministers a large majority at the 1802 general election. Initially ridiculed for its lack of quality, Addington's cabinet steadily improved its position, recruited talented allies, and took full advantage of royal confidence and lack of agreement among its parliamentary opponents. Pitt welcomed the peace treaty but complained about disarmament, as did Dundas, while Fox (prompted by Pitt's fall to return to active politics) supported both measures. Fox also advocated Catholic relief, as did Grenville, but Grenville disliked the peace of which Fox approved, and Pitt was no longer willing to associate himself with the Catholic cause. The Foxite party was in disarray at this time, because Tierney would no longer accept Fox's leadership (Tierney accepted junior office under Addington), and Grey disagreed with Fox's tactics. Grey saw more quickly than Fox that Napoleon did not want peace to last, and while Fox hoped to co-operate with Addington to preserve peace, Grey envisaged a new understanding with the Grenvillites. Fox eventually accepted Grey's analysis of the exigencies of the time.

Despite growing criticism of Addington late in 1802, Pitt refused to declare himself openly against the king's ministers. Peace with France broke down in May 1803, and Addington was blamed in some quarters for failing to prevent the resumption of war, and in others for Britain's lack of military preparedness. Urged by friends and followers to exert himself, Pitt preferred to wait. He realised that he could no longer count on Grenville, who had refused to abandon Catholic emancipation, and who believed that Britain's need for strong government at this juncture could only be met by a comprehensive coalition including all the most influential political leaders of the day. Grenville did not wish to promote or be part of a narrowly based Pittite administration, and his sense of alienation from Pitt became stronger when he reflected that Pitt's failure actively to oppose Addington probably indicated reluctance to join a new and wider political alliance.

The Addington government reintroduced income tax and simplified its collection (Addington proved to be a better administrator of the tax than Pitt had been), and tried to strengthen home defence and take advantage of a new wave of war patriotism. But political confusion increased. Foxites opposed the war, the Grenvillites demanded a more vigorous approach than the limited defensive strategy favoured by Addington, and Pitt manoeuvred to return to the premiership and conduct the war himself. Fox and Grey decided that the only way to keep Pitt out was to ally with Grenville. Grenville's anti-French stance was an obstacle, but Fox thought that he would accept an honourable peace. Co-operation also seemed possible because of definite points of agreement, particularly Catholic emancipation and the need to replace the discredited Addington administration. Early in 1804 George III suffered another period of illness, and all political leaders held back rather than risk further instability. In April, however, Addington's Commons majority fell sharply when the followers of Pitt, Grenville and Fox voted together on defence and the militia. Addington had also lost control of the Lords. He decided to resign. By now Pitt had added his weight to the pressure for a new ministry, and he made plain his wish to be its leader. Though he saw merit in ideas for a coalition government, Pitt upheld the (now recovered) king's free choice in the appointment of ministers to replace Addington's cabinet. This naturally meant the exclusion of Fox. Grenville, realising that the new government could not be the broad coalition he wanted, decided to remain with Fox in opposition. Foxites argued that Pitt's return as prime minister demonstrated yet again the dangerous extent of royal influence. Fox concluded that efforts to restrain the executive might have to await more favourable times (an excuse for his own periods of absence and inactivity): parliament was subservient, royal power seemed to be growing, and changes of government in 1801 and 1804 disguised an essential continuity, for the king was still in control, backed by the same advisers and acting upon the same political values as before.

Pitt's ministry of 1804 to 1806 combined his own friends with men who had served in Addington's cabinet. Its main strengths were royal approval, Pitt's personal prestige, talented ministers in key departments, and no division on Catholic emancipation. But there were also serious weaknesses. Pittites and Addingtonians argued about patronage and appointments, and failed to cohere effectively in office. Nor was Pitt the confident, sure-footed leader he had formerly been. Politics had changed since the 1790s, and he could no longer rely on the methods and ideas which had united his previous cabinet. The parliamentary opposition was also much stronger, while the ministerial team and support base upon which Pitt had formerly relied were fragmenting. Apart from Pitt, the only experienced figure in the cabinet was Dundas, Lord Melville, who resigned when accused of corruption in 1805.

Early in 1805 Pitt's cabinet desperately needed additional strength, an agreed war strategy and more back-bench support in the Commons. The willingness of Foxites and Grenvillites to act together disturbed Pitt, and he tried to gain new adherents, but George III was not prepared to make room in the cabinet for Moira (of the Carlton House interest, led by the Prince of Wales), and Tierney refused to join Pitt. The other option was an approach to Addington, some of whose followers were already allied (albeit uneasily) with Pitt. Addington retained royal favour, and Pitt agreed that he should be admitted to the cabinet. The prime minister insisted, however, that Addington must go to the House of Lords, to prevent him from undermining Pitt's authority in the Commons. Addington, now Viscount Sidmouth, joined Pitt's administration in January 1805 only to resign in June. He objected to Pitt's imperious manner and the lack of patronage for Addingtonians, offended Pitt by demanding that he should select Melville's successor in the cabinet, and believed that the prime minister was plotting against him. Meanwhile the loss of Melville was a serious blow to Pitt's energy and morale, and his opponents took advantage by reviving the Catholic question. Foxites and Grenvillites were defeated on this issue in May 1805, but ministers could not relax. Sidmouth's departure prompted Pitt to reopen negotiations with Grenville, Fox and George III, though nothing was settled respecting ministerial changes. The war continued to go badly, Pitt was unable to unite and direct his administration as he wished, and he found his leadership increasingly questioned. He died in January 1806. The cabinet could not survive without him (Eric Evans regards its collapse as almost inevitable in view of Pitt's failure to build up a parliamentary party and the lack of a dominant figure among his associates[6]), and the king had to look to his opponents. Grenville was invited to take the premiership, and George III could not insist on Fox's exclusion.

The Talents administration included Foxites, Grenvillites, former Portland Whigs (such as Windham, who had turned against Pitt after 1801), and Sidmouth. The last agreed to serve because of his attachment to the king and his belief that the nation needed as broadly based a ministry as possible, though he never trusted his cabinet colleagues. Foxites accepted Sidmouth as a means of neutralising George III and isolating the Pittites in opposition. Grenville was initially pleased to lead a ministry which encompassed a variety of opinions and groups, but he soon found the cabinet deeply divided on personal and public grounds. He added to the controversy by retaining a lucrative sinecure, and as auditor of the exchequer he was in a position to check and approve his own accounts as first lord of the treasury. Fox, for years an outspoken critic of corruption, accepted Grenville's decision to retain his sinecure in return for more say in government appointments. But this damaged Fox's reputation and affected his relationship with the progressive wing of Whig MPs led by the brewer Samuel Whitbread, who objected to Grenvillite greed and conservatism. Furthermore, Whitbread's group, along with reformers in the nation, were dismayed to find that Fox and Grey had no intention of making parliamentary reform a government policy. There was also consternation at Fox's willingness to work with Sidmouth, an ally of the court, and his readiness to postpone action on Catholic emancipation. In justification Fox claimed that royal influence would be broken only if he co-operated with George III's former advisers, including Sidmouth, and that shelving emancipation would make possible other successes. In particular Fox hoped to end the war and abolish the British slave trade, and of course he was well aware that the king and Sidmouth were both firm opponents of emancipation. Fox's reasoning may have been sound, but to outsiders he seemed once again to have compromised in order to take office, and as Fox established himself as the dominant force in the Talents cabinet, his attempt as foreign secretary to negotiate a peace with France led many to question his prudence and his understanding of European affairs.

Fox was intensely disappointed to find that Napoleon could not be persuaded to modify his political and territorial ambitions. Eventually Fox had to accept that continuation of the war was inevitable. His health deteriorated during the summer of 1806 and he died in December (worn out, claimed his nephew Lord Holland, by vexatious and carping opposition in the Commons). Grey succeeded Fox as foreign secretary and leader in the Commons, and established good relations with Grenville, but the ministry lacked a unifying cause. Sidmouth began to make difficulties after the 1806 general election, because his followers were not given a fair share of government boroughs. He objected to Grenville's idea that the most talented of the Pittites, George Canning, should be persuaded to join the cabinet and lead in the Commons when Grey inherited an earldom and went to the Lords (this elevation was imminent because Grey's father was well advanced in years). There were other quarrels. Some Foxites favoured parliamentary reform, but Sidmouth opposed it, and Grenvillites preferred to concentrate on the war effort and had no wish to stir up popular radicalism.

Nor did Grenville favour economical reform. He and his family did well out of sinecures and pensions, and considered patronage essential to sound government. The only major issues on which agreement between Grenvillites and Foxites could be guaranteed were the slave trade and Catholic emancipation, but on both they had to contend with resistance from Sidmouth and the court.

Fox did not live to see the passing of the government's bill to abolish the slave trade, but he had known it was coming. Grenville and Grey steered the measure through parliament, achieving the Talents' one genuine success in office. Economic, moral and strategic arguments for abolition had been presented for years by William Wilberforce and the 'Saints', a group of evangelical Christian MPs who began to promote a campaign for abolition in the 1780s. There was common ground between the 'Saints' and the followers of Grenville and Grey, as shown by A. D. Kriegel,[7] and together they overcame the resistance of gradualists like Sidmouth and Windham. Gradualists thought that unilateral withdrawal from the trade would simply deliver it to other nations, and that Britain should regulate rather than abolish its slave traffic. Significantly, abolition cut across the government–opposition divide in the Commons. Sidmouth and Windham spoke for those connected with the Talents ministry who disliked immediate abolition, and among opposition leaders there was disagreement between Canning and Perceval, who favoured the policy, and Viscount Castlereagh, who did not.

On the Catholic issue Grenvillite and Foxite ministers were forced to act sooner than they wanted because of pressure from Irish leaders, who would not agree to suspend their agitation for emancipation. This pressure seriously embarrassed the government, and Grenville and Grey decided to propose a mild form of relief (the admission of Catholics to higher ranks in the army) in order to forestall a petition for full emancipation. Sidmouth was persuaded to accept this plan, and managed to secure George III's grudging acquiescence, but then there arose an irreversible breach on the precise details of the government's proposal. Finally Grenville and Grey agreed to withdraw the relief measure, though they refused to comply with the king's demand for a guarantee that the issue would not be raised again. The Talents resigned on 24 March 1807, by which time it was clear that opposition leaders were ready to form an alternative ministry. Grenville and Grey welcomed the opportunity to resign, and their clash with the king was not the only reason for their departure. The Talents had lost control of the Commons, opinion out of doors was not favourable towards Catholic relief, home defence was in utter confusion, the cabinet had never recovered from the loss of Fox, and there was internal dissension (Grenville and Grey had alienated Sidmouth; Windham was outraged by Grenvillite accumulation of patronage). In addition, there was no breakthrough in the conflict with Napoleon, and continual disagreement on war strategy was as important as the king's resistance to Catholic relief in bringing the ministry down.

The experience of office had been burdensome, embarrassing and disheartening for Fox, Grenville and Grey, but at least the circumstances surrounding the Talents' fall brought some compensation. Foxites found their unity and identity strengthened by George III's actions in 1807 and their subsequent exclusion from power. Though Michael Roberts and A. D. Harvey accentuate the weaknesses of the Talents ministry, and suggest that veneration of it by later Whig politicians and propagandists was rather misplaced, R. W. Davis adds some balance and comments favourably on the Talents' proposal for Catholic relief: 'Often dismissed as a mere symbolic gesture, it was in fact no less important for being symbolic. It underlined the Whig commitment to principle, the principle of religious liberty, as opposed to Pittite expediency.... And whatever historians may think, the proposal was enough to get the Talents dismissed'.[8]

After the fall of the Talents, power passed to former allies and followers of Pitt, though it was some time before all components of the old Pittite alliance could be reunited. For a while the void left by Pitt remained all too obvious, for nobody seemed able to combine able and ambitious individuals into a successful team. Personal animosities persisted. Canning was behind much of this trouble. Highly impressive in debate, impatient for high office and dismissive of less gifted associates, he proved a difficult colleague and gained a reputation for intrigue and duplicity. Canning was foreign secretary in the Portland cabinet formed in March 1807, but he had to resign with the secretary

for war, Castlereagh, in September 1809, when the two quarrelled over military strategy (and subsequently fought a duel).
Portland, ill and ineffectual, did not provide the firm leadership
needed at this time, and was replaced as premier by Perceval.
Like Portland, Perceval was an opponent of Catholic emancipation. His administration began to take on a more confident
demeanour as its basis of support expanded and Castlereagh
and Sidmouth were recruited, and it survived alarms about
George III's failing health as well as pressure for the establishment of a new government of national unity including Grey
and Grenville. Perceval won the support of backbenchers in the
Commons and propertied classes in the nation, but was assass-
inated in May 1812 by a failed merchant who blamed the
government for his misfortunes. Lord Liverpool became prime
minister, though negotiations preceding his appointment were
complicated by George III's final and complete mental collapse
and the establishment of a regency under the Prince of Wales.
Restrictions on the constitutional power of the prince regent, as
defined in 1811, passed away in 1812, and he decided to confirm
Liverpool as premier. By this time Grey and Grenville realised
that the long association between the prince and the Whig
opposition was politically worthless.

The Liverpool government's priority was to conduct the
war vigorously, and from 1812 the tide began to turn against
Napoleon. On domestic matters the ministry was conservative. Most of those who had served under Perceval
remained in Liverpool's cabinet after June 1812, including
Eldon, Sidmouth and Castlereagh, and the ministry strengthened its position at the 1812 general election. The most
difficult political issue of the time, Catholic emancipation,
remained an open question in cabinet, a compromise which
enabled talented men of differing opinions to work together
under Liverpool. The arrangement made sense in wartime and
was continued beyond 1815. The prince regent knew that
Liverpool would fight France to the finish and obstruct concessions to the Catholics, matters on which he felt he could not
trust Grey and Grenville.

By this time the use of Whig and Tory party terminology was
widespread. The Foxite–Grenvillite alliance was increasingly
referred to as Whig. Toryism, which had lost its objectionable

political and dynastic meanings from the late seventeenth century, was being redefined as a government creed, and the Tory label distinguished Pitt's successors from supporters of Grey and Grenville. The party system was still undeveloped, however, and there was a limit to unity and coherence on both sides. Jonathan Clark has argued that political preference was determined mainly by religious affiliation, and that Catholic emancipation was a far more significant issue than parliamentary reform. James Sack emphasises the 'spiritual, Christian, Anglican' roots of conservative politics. The evolution of the early nineteenth-century Tory party also owed much to the 1794 union of Portland and Pitt, though Portland's following later disintegrated and he never described himself as a Tory. Most decisive for John Ehrman were Pitt's position on the royal prerogative and his association with Eldon, Castlereagh and Hawkesbury (Liverpool) in the administration of 1804 to 1806. They went on to dominate government into the postwar period.[9]

It is clear that party feeling developed on the Pittite side after Pitt's death as his former associates began to act more as a group in opposing the Talents. They returned to office, and at the 1807 election they defended the Church and the king's right to dismiss a ministry. These were vital rallying points, and political allegiances were clarified further by the second regency crisis, of 1810 to 1811, and the appointment of Liverpool's government in 1812. Agitation and disorder after the war gave rise to repressive legislation, which was called Tory policy by its critics, and by now the parliamentary opposition was consistently referred to as Whig. The old Pittite connection was finally reunited in 1821 when Grenvillites returned to the government side. Foxites were left as sole inheritors of the Whig name, while Toryism denoted a distinctive attachment to Church, crown, property, social hierarchy and conservative constitutionalism.

The basic unifying cause for Whigs remained Catholic emancipation, though it was an obstacle to advancement and unpopular at court, in parliament and among voters. Parliamentary reform had not been a Talents policy, and Grenvillites were reluctant to make it a party question. In order to maintain unity Grey accepted the Grenvillite ban, which annoyed pro-reform Foxites, and Grey was often accused by outdoor reformers of abandoning former commitments. Whig campaigns for economical reform were also inhibited by Grenvillites, who sought to maintain their incomes and privileges. Therefore radicals who revived the anti-corruption movement after 1807, inspired by revelations about official misconduct and elite immorality, made little distinction between government and opposition. The reluctance of Whig leaders to associate with extra-parliamentary radicals continued, and Grey was quick to condemn those who tried to bring the ruling classes and established institutions into contempt. Grey thought that radicals were helping the government by taking attention away from the misuse of royal powers and mismanagement of the war. He was also annoyed by the willingness of Whitbread and the progressive wing of opposition MPs to co-operate with radicals. Grenvillites were so offended that they tried to drive Whitbread from the Whig alliance.

The opposition's internal divisions increased. There was no agreed position on the conduct of the war, no effective leadership in the Commons, a disturbing incongruity between Whig libertarian rhetoric and the party's respect for privilege and hierarchy, and when bold initiatives were taken in parliament there was no guarantee of unity or success.[10] A bill to prevent the sale of parliamentary seats was pushed through in 1809, but only after ministers had amended it, and by relying on an oath that no money had changed hands this measure seemed likely to make corruption even more difficult to detect. In 1810 Whig MP Thomas Brand moved for a committee on the state of the representative system. He wanted to cut the maximum duration of parliaments from seven to three years, extend the vote to householders in boroughs and copyholders in counties, and redistribute seats from decayed boroughs to large unrepresented towns, with compensation to borough patrons. Similar to proposals made in the 1780s, and milder than Grey's scheme of 1797, Brand's plan was defeated in the Commons by a margin of two to one. Some Whigs continued to hope for parliamentary reform in later years, though it was not an opposition priority. There was also Whig involvement in agitation against the orders in council in 1812 (see below), but as before most opposition MPs eschewed close association with extra-parliamentary campaigns. Efforts to promote Catholic emancipation in parliament continued between 1812 and 1815. Grey accepted the need for securities for Church and state, including a royal veto on papal appointments to the Catholic Church in Ireland. Some of his colleagues objected, however, and Irish leaders also refused to accept these conditions. Attachment to the Catholic cause in these years brought the opposition a sense of purpose, but led to internal disagreements and a prolonged exclusion from office.

The continuing evolution of British radicalism

The French Revolution stimulated a massive increase in political discussion out of doors, and there was special interest in voting rights and theories of representation (along with parliament's independence, an important aspect of radicalism since the time of Wilkes). This growing political consciousness was not only the result of events in France. Domestic developments in preceding years had extended political participation and commitment. Meeting, petitioning, writing and argument increased at the end of the 1780s. People were moved by the regency crisis, by celebrations marking the centenary of the Glorious Revolution, and then by rapid political changes across the Channel. The French Revolution occurred at a time when large sections of British society were ready and able to engage in political activity.

Influential organisations arose to guide and articulate reform opinion. The Society for Constitutional Information (SCI), originally established in 1780, became active again. It consisted mainly of respectable radicals, educated and professional men who subscribed to some of Paine's ideas and had contacts with politicians in France. They mistrusted the parliamentary opposition and regarded its leaders as insincere reformers. The SCI favoured manhood suffrage and wider political education, pressed for electoral purity and an end to government corruption, and sought more influence for independent men of property. Meanwhile the London Corresponding Society (LCS), established in January 1792, brought together workers, shopkeepers, tailors, printers and artisans. Its secretary was Thomas Hardy, a shoemaker. The LCS communicated with and co-ordinated the activities of popular bodies in other large towns, encouraged political discussion, and favoured democratic reform. This entailed equal rights and government by consent, and LCS members were inspired by the vision of a generous, participatory constitution which they thought had existed before the decline into corruption and exclusivity.

The Society of the Friends of the People was formed in April 1792 by opposition MPs, young Whig aristocrats and wealthy gentlemen reformers. They wanted to make the Commons more representative, but theirs was a moderate and patrician approach to this problem. The Friends disliked innovation, condemned Paine, sent no messages of encouragement to French revolutionaries, and eschewed co-operation with other reform associations. The priorities of the Friends of the People differed from those of the SCI and LCS, and engendered continuing friction between opposition MPs and extra-parliamentary radicals. The two sides could not combine effectively in a movement for parliamentary reform. Foxite MPs expressed commitment to popular causes, but they were mostly from aristocratic families and sat for rotten boroughs. They wanted to guide and exploit public opinion, not submit to it. Leaders of the Friends of the People, in fact, attempted to use reform agitation for party purposes. They hoped to enlist outdoor support for the parliamentary opposition, to discredit Pitt and to deny influence to extreme radicals.

The quickening maturation of extra-parliamentary politics in the early 1790s prompted people of all classes to form associations, and in some towns respectable reformers offered advice and meeting rooms to plebeian groups. Radicalism had lost its former reliance on London, and was assuming forms quite unlike the gentlemanly county movement of Wyvill and his allies. Reform opinion was taking hold in the growing industrial and commercial centres of Birmingham, Manchester, Newcastle, Leeds, Nottingham and Sheffield. E. P. Thompson considers these developments 'the first stages in the political education of a class', as political consciousness spread from artisans and traders in traditional craft communities to the manufacturing districts of the Midlands and north.[11] In June 1792, the SCI dispatched hundreds of reform tracts to provincial radical clubs, and the number sent to each town probably indicates the relative strength and size of clubs at that time: 1,200 each to Sheffield, Norwich and Manchester, 600 to Birmingham, 500 to Cambridge, and 200 each to Derby, Belper, Liverpool and Glasgow.[12] Commitment and organisation were spreading, and delegates from over eighty reform groups met at a radical convention in Edinburgh in December 1792.

Parliamentary reform was not the only cause attracting mass support in this period. Protestant Dissenters had been agitating for repeal of the Test and Corporation Acts for several years, and the campaign against the slave trade was also being extended. In many towns the same individuals who had participated in repeal agitation, or attended meetings to protest against the slave trade, were also involved in the movement for parliamentary reform. This range of reform interests rested partly on a strong sense of grievance, whether prompted by lack of adequate representation in parliament, moral outrage against the slave traffic, or resentment about the imposition of civil disabilities on account of religious belief. Other complaints were added to these motivations: high prices, heavy taxation, the cost of government, wartime economic policies. Parliamentary reform was regarded as the necessary first step. Only a more representative legislature, it was thought, would respond to the people's honest protests.

The expansion of popular politics was facilitated by the continuing development of a political press. The annual sale of newspaper stamps rose from 14 million in 1780 to over 17 million in 1793. In June 1789 the number of newspapers circulating by post peaked at over 15,500 per day. Provincial titles devoted an increasing amount of space to political news and comment, and radical newspapers began to have readerships in the thousands rather than hundreds. Dror Wahrman has found that parliamentary reporting was a battleground. Editors and writers often put their own gloss on reports, fomenting conflicts of interpretation which intensified the discord between the state and its critics. This relationship between what went on in parliament, and how it was perceived and used out of doors, was one of the most volatile areas of contact between high and low politics, and Wahrman's work offers a further demonstration that press comment on public affairs was a vital resource for radicals.[13]

The French Revolution and attendant controversies furthered the political polarisation in many towns, especially in places where rival interests had long been competing for influence. Exclusive Anglican and conservative ruling factions were challenged by respectable reformers and Dissenters, whose wealth, intellectual life, social institutions and political ideas encouraged greater involvement in municipal affairs. Local conflicts began to involve mob violence. In July 1791 there were 'Church and King' disturbances in Birmingham, directed against reformers and Dissenters, who included the discoverer of oxygen, Joseph Priestley. June and December 1792 saw riots in Manchester. The targets were members of the radical Manchester Constitutional Society (established in October 1790), Dissenting chapels, and the offices of the pro-reform *Manchester Herald*. The local authorities did not intervene to stop the disorder.

As the French Revolution descended into violence and extremism, war broke out in Europe in April 1792, and many people who had welcomed the early reforms in France began to change their minds. Committed radicals, however, continued to call each other 'citizen', plant liberty trees, and grant honorary membership of their societies to French leaders. Wyvill and other moderates feared that the reform movement would forsake a sensible path for illegality and subversion, but commitment to violence never became widespread. Most radicals valued the French Revolution as a source of ideas and aspirations, not an experience they wished to recreate in every detail. They thought more in terms of recovering lost rights than demanding new ones, and the British constitution was seen as a guide and safeguard. John Belchem, James Epstein and John Stevenson have noted a genuine attachment to parliamentary government and the British heritage of constitutional rights.[14] Radicals wanted to extend these, not destroy them, and only a small minority ever contemplated armed insurrection. For the most part language and ideology continued to rest on a constitutionalist idiom. This concept has fascinated historians in recent times because of its links with the so-called 'linguistic turn', the intellectual processes behind the evolution of political theory and programme. Perhaps the most interesting point about theory and programme in the era of revolution is that reformers and anti-reformers made use of similar phrases, symbols and ideas in order to justify their own position and discredit that of their opponents.

Committed radicals were not very numerous, and their influence often depended on economic conditions. Recession in 1792 assisted recruitment, but there was a limit to radicalism's appeal even in hard times. Membership of the LCS did not exceed five thousand, and provincial societies were much smaller (though they may have had sympathisers who did not enrol as members). The LCS served as an important co-ordinating force, yet radicals across Britain were never united into a cohesive movement with an agreed programme, and there was persistent division between reformers of different social backgrounds. Respectable, propertied, professional and educated groups disliked the impatient spirit, admiration of Paine, demands for manhood suffrage and plans for national conventions associated with plebeian leaders, and there was deep disagreement in radical circles about the French Revolution and European war. In addition, government repression encouraged a loyalist backlash in many towns. There was great pressure to conform, and many reformers ceased their campaigning because they feared prosecution and ostracism.

Confidence in the Foxites as champions of reform decreased. After the opposition split of 1794 Fox's influence seemed to be in terminal decline, and though he was congratulated by prominent radicals, including Major John Cartwright (the Nottinghamshire squire who had been politically active since the 1770s), for speaking and voting against state repression, Fox and his followers could not change government policies. The opposition rarely committed itself to specific reforms, moreover, and chose not to establish close links with radical organisations across the country. And Fox alienated many influential people out of doors by maintaining that the French Revolution had taken a violent course only because of outside interference, that the French had justice on their side and better reasons for going to war than Britain, and that Pitt's ministry was unworthy of support while it acted so inexcusably at home and abroad.

Though many radicals suspended their reform agitation, others refused to desist and met with a severe response from magistrates, courts and government. Prominent reformers were imprisoned or transported for their political ideas and activity. There were many prosecutions for sedition. Even when prosecutions failed, the accused suffered in other ways owing to absence from and loss of employment, neighbourhood sanctions, legal costs, and the stigma of arrest and trial. Local and central authorities claimed that there existed a genuine threat to security and order, that they had to act swiftly, and that their goal was deterrence rather than punishment. The suspension of habeas corpus in 1794 gave a clear sign of intent.

At local level there was continuous persecution of reformers. In 1794 the leader of the Manchester Constitutional Society, wealthy cotton master Thomas Walker, was tried for conspiracy. Though he was acquitted, the trial was costly and Walker's health and business suffered. Other Manchester reformers were not willing to run the same risks. Sheffield reformers faced similar difficulties: Joseph Gales, editor of the *Sheffield Register*, fled abroad, and Henry Yorke spent two years in prison for conspiracy. London's radical leaders were tried for treason. Among the indicted were Thomas Hardy and John Thelwall of the LCS, and veteran reformer John Horne Tooke, who had been active since the time of Wilkes. They were acquitted at the end of 1794, to great celebration, but continuing persecution forced many metropolitan reformers into quiescence, and Hardy soon gave up active politics. Poor harvests and intense distress made mass support available for the reform campaign, though, and lack of success in the war prompted many peace meetings and petitions during 1795. The government was concerned that disaffection might spread to the armed forces, and it became clear that repression had not eliminated agitation completely. A committed core of reformers survived and continued campaigning in spite of official and unofficial restraints. In 1795 the Friends of the People issued declarations in favour of household suffrage and a reorganisation of electoral districts, but as material suffering and discontent mounted, the initiative passed to popular leaders and artisan radicalism. The LCS sponsored mass open-air meetings in London. Serious disturbances were followed by the 'Two Acts'. After 1795 radicals who wanted to carry on had to adhere to the new limitations. There could be no meetings of more than fifty people. In July 1797, when the LCS defied restrictions and organised a mass meeting, speakers were arrested and the assembly was dispersed by troops.

Towards the end of the 1790s frustration and resentment in some radical circles created more support for violent solutions. There were revolutionary cells on the fringes of British radicalism, and though they always lacked influence and numbers, they were able to plan and sometimes attempt armed risings. Among the conspirators were Irish leaders John Binns and James O'Coigly, both arrested in 1798, and a former colonial officer, Edward Despard, arrested in 1803. The schemes in which they were engaged drew together two revolutionary societies, the United Irishmen and United Englishmen, and LCS militants who had abandoned constitutional methods for insurrection. The number of extremists involved was small, and it is unclear how far they carried their organisation in these years, but they appear to have thought that simultaneous risings in Ireland, London and the north, with French aid, were not beyond them. Revolutionary plots were easily detected and crushed, however, and substantial French assistance was never forthcoming. There were conspiracies in the West Riding in 1802, but no serious outbreaks, and for the rest of the war the revolutionary underground remained weak and fragmented. The fact that some groups never gave up their idea of a revolutionary coup became evident in later years, though, especially in London. E. P. Thompson insists that the revolutionary underground cannot simply be dismissed as marginal and frail, and he prefers to regard wartime revolutionary activity as continuous, international and highly influential. Roger Wells maintains that it posed a genuine threat to the state.[15]

Food shortages and high prices during the late 1790s and early 1800s prompted more violence and unrest, and hardship was exploited by radicals as they organised meetings and petitions for peace and reform. There was persistent protest against government repression. The sense of injustice was an additional spur to action, and the state's interference with individual rights was taken as proof that reform was necessary. The idea of a reign of terror was reinforced by further coercive legislation between 1798 and 1800, particularly the suspension of habeas corpus, new restrictions on the press, and the suppression of the LCS. But popular radicalism had considerable staying power. In 1801 there were mass meetings to celebrate the expiry of the 'Two Acts' and restoration of habeas corpus. The government took these demonstrations as proof that danger still existed, renewed the acts and again suspended habeas corpus. Still there was no radical collapse. Popular political activity had developed too far to be easily contained, as may be seen in the work of E. P. Thompson on the spread of political consciousness, Gwyn Williams on artisan radicals, and Albert Goodwin on provincial reform societies in districts with strong Dissenting and reformist traditions.[16]

Reformers became more hopeful with the appointment of the Ministry of All the Talents after Pitt's death in 1806. Though it was predominantly Foxite in composition, this was not a progressive ministry. Nevertheless, the abolition of the slave trade in 1807 was regarded by reformers as an important step on the road to enlightenment and progress. Moral and economic grounds for abolition had been repeatedly outlined by parliamentary spokesmen for the cause, notably Wilberforce, but there was also effective organisation and mobilisation out of doors, owing partly to the energy and efforts of writer and lecturer Thomas Clarkson. During 1806 and 1807 there were numerous meetings and petitions on the slave trade, which became the most prominent political issue of the day. Abolition was a great victory for the reform spirit in parliament and nation.[17]

These years also saw an extension of the crusade against official corruption as information spread about improprieties in high places. The Melville affair of 1805 was followed by a scandal surrounding attempts by the Prince of Wales to subject the behaviour of his estranged wife Caroline of Brunswick to official investigation. Then came the disclosures of 1809 concerning another royal prince, the Duke of York, commander-in-chief of the army, whose former mistress, Mrs Mary Anne Clarke, had allegedly been selling military promotions. In this context radicals declared that patriotic duty required people to question elite authority, not to accept it regardless of revelations about corruption and depravity.

Some radicals demanded fundamental reforms while expressing support for the war. The war was no longer a conflict against liberty, they decided, but a crusade to defend liberty against Napoleon. Their language and goals changed, and there was an attempt to broaden radicalism's appeal in order to nullify the effects of official repression and conservative propaganda. Peter Spence also notes an ideological shift towards a form of romantic nationalism. Some spokesmen argued that government and society had been corrupted. Military failure abroad and scandals at home proved this, and indicated that Britain would soon be unable to ward off external threats. Constitutional reform was urgently necessary, not so much to restore to the people their just rights, but to reverse institutional and moral decline and thereby make the nation better able to resist foreign invasion. It is not clear how far this ideology spread. The change in radicalism may relate more to tactics than principles, and the picture is blurred by the flexible use of vocabulary and symbol. Words and signs wielded by critics of the governing elite were similar to those of the loyalists, though the two sides continued to define patriotism and duty in contrasting ways.[18]

Alongside criticism of aristocratic rule there was protest against specific wartime measures, notably the orders in council. These were designed to control and tax neutral trade, in response to Napoleon's attempt to destroy British commerce. The orders so angered the USA that, even after their removal, the Americans engaged in a war against Britain between 1812 and 1814. The removal of the orders in 1812 was greeted as a victory for extra-parliamentary agitation: the orders had been widely condemned for their deleterious effects on employment, profits, trade and industry. This protest about the economic consequences of war and government policy was combined with pressure for peace and parliamentary reform. Business communities in Manchester, Birmingham, Liverpool and other large towns, following up the activism of commercial groups during the earlier part of George III's reign, had demanded repeal of the orders, and were also complaining about the income tax. These developments further increased middle-class involvement in extra-parliamentary protest, and strengthened the political commitments of merchants, manufacturers, bankers and professionals. An associated phenomenon was the rise of the Friends of Peace, led by respectable urban notables, who were becoming more active in local politics and who could rely for financial, organisational and psychological support on a growing network of Nonconformist chapels. J. E. Cookson's study of the Friends of Peace elucidates their essential traits: group consciousness, provincialism, rational Christianity, religious grievances, criticism of the war and commercial policies, and an anti-oligarchical appeal to urban, industrial, non-Anglican middle classes. Dror Wahrman also notes the political importance of provincialism and civic pride in this era, and the affinity between radicalism and Dissent is underlined by John Seed and R. E. Richey. Jonathan Clark goes so far as to suggest that religious heterodoxy was the very source of radicalism, though J. E. Bradley contends that the origins of radicalism were primarily political, and 'only secondarily' theological.[19]

There was no weakening of disorder and protest during the final years of the war. Hunger, hardship and unemployment rose again, and luddism spread through the manufacturing areas of the Midlands and the north. Luddism was not simply a reaction to social and economic distress, and as a form of protest it was more thoughtful than the violence and machine-breaking of these years might suggest. Luddites were attempting to defend traditional community values and standards of living, and their activity was often highly disciplined. Political ideas and goals may have motivated some luddites. Though historians still disagree about the role of the popular political consciousness, it is clear that the labouring classes were directly affected by the economic consequences of war, and that radical leaders were able to direct their attention to heavy taxes, corrupt government, and the unmerited privileges of the ruling elite. Rising support for radical panaceas meant that older forms of protest were reassessed. What John Bohstedt has called the 'protocol of riot' was passing away. This had rested on customary relationships between the paternalistic establishment and a deferential people, but such contacts were missing in rapidly expanding industrial and commercial towns.[20] Another destabilising development was parliament's explicit adoption of a laissez-faire approach to social and economic questions. The state's responsibilities were being scaled down in this respect. Old laws regulating particular trades were allowed to lapse, making some workers even more vulnerable to machines and unskilled labour. They petitioned parliament for assistance, and luddism was also taken up as a viable alternative.

Luddites were motivated by a range of concerns: bad harvests, heavy taxes and misgovernment, alongside more immediate grievances about wage cuts, unemployment, mechanisation and rules of entry to specific trades. The use of violence was mostly deliberate, well organised and selective, and employers who introduced new machines were the main target. Sometimes the expression of political demands took priority. John Belchem, E. P. Thompson and John Dinwiddy insist that luddism must be viewed as an essentially political activity, while Malcolm Thomis and F. O. Darvall detect little political motivation or meaning.[21] This disagreement highlights the complex nature of protest in these years, and luddism cannot properly be separated from such events as the Manchester riot caused by the prince regent's refusal to replace his father's ministers in 1812, the celebration of Perceval's assassination in Nottingham and Leicester, and the speaking tours of veteran radical Major Cartwright. Attacks on mills and machines were occurring at the same time and in the same places as political agitation. Wartime protest was neither exclusively economic nor exclusively political.

Pressure for parliamentary reform increased towards the end of the war, primarily because of the difficult economic situation (when conditions improved after 1821 radical leaders would lose their mass following). Figureheads rose to inspire the movement: not only Cartwright, but the wealthy City radical Sir Francis Burdett, journalist William Cobbett, and Henry 'Orator' Hunt, who was of Wiltshire gentry stock. In higher intellectual circles, parliamentary reform was taken up by the group of writers, officials and politicians led by jurist and philosopher Jeremy Bentham, who had composed a tract on reform in 1809. This was not published until 1817, but Benthamite influence was already spreading before the end of the war, and parliamentary reform had become a matter for serious intellectual discussion. In some towns reformers once again became a force to be reckoned with in local political struggles, as in the early 1790s, and these struggles often merged with Church–Dissent rivalry, newspaper controversies and labour disputes. Reformers also had new organisations by 1815, notably the

Hampden Clubs promoted by Cartwright. His tours through the Midlands and the north in 1812 and 1813 were intended primarily to encourage meeting, petitioning and association. The original Hampden Club in London remained a highly respectable body whose membership fees kept out the lower ranks, in the hope that this would encourage Whig MPs to join. Elsewhere, in large provincial towns, the clubs were less exclusive.

Though extra-parliamentary radicalism survived the period of revolution and war, among its leaders there was constant disagreement on tactics. Cartwright was a pragmatist. He favoured co-operation with the progressive wing of Whig MPs and believed that the parliamentary opposition would eventually take up electoral reform as a party issue. But Cobbett and Hunt refused to trust the Whigs. They also preferred not to co-operate with commercial pressure groups. Cobbett and Hunt agreed on very little else, however, which added to the confusion. The two men strongly disliked each other, and while Hunt envisaged a mass movement uniting all the groups and resources of urban plebeian radicalism, Cobbett retained a nostalgic attachment to the yeomanry of old England. Cobbett merged radical politics with rural culture, and regarded country folk as the true 'common people' ground down by oppressive and expensive government.[22] Meanwhile Cartwright called for an alliance between Burdett, who had been returned as MP for 'radical' Westminster in 1807, and pro-reform Whig MPs, but the latter drew back because they wanted no embarrassing contact with Burdett's constituency supporters. Burdett himself disappointed many radicals. His success in Westminster was made possible by the exertions of Francis Place and the Westminster Committee, a body controlled by shopkeepers and tradesmen who had previously been active in the LCS. Though Burdett declared himself for annual parliaments, equal electoral districts and householder suffrage, he did not attempt to form a radical party in the Commons and showed no signs of a genuine commitment to popular politics. Burdett's ideas on reform owed more to the old Wyvill movement than to early nineteenth-century urban radicalism, and he still thought of reform primarily as a means of holding government to account and strengthening the influence of the country gentry.

By 1815 radicalism incorporated a range of political, social and economic grievances. Labourers and artisans were concerned about financial burdens imposed by the state, about the loss of status caused by mechanisation and an oversupply of labour, and they believed that their lack of representation in parliament deprived them of necessary security. They had not consented to war taxes, and had no say in the framing of laws by which they were governed. Lack of adequate representation also stirred merchants and manufacturers. They regarded income tax and the orders in council as proof that an aristocratic parliament cared nothing for the real needs of business communities. Parliamentary reform was considered a prerequisite for economic and social improvement. Though plebeian and respectable reformers used similar arguments, their aims and tactics diverged. After 1815 campaigners from different social backgrounds would find co-operation difficult because of mutual mistrust and a basic disagreement about the appropriate extent of reform.

Conservatism and loyalism

In the early 1790s, as alarm about radicalism and disorder increased, loyalists began to combine against the assertive reform societies. All social classes joined in this conservative reaction, not just those with wealth and property, and unlike their opponents loyalists did not have to contend with official interference or lack of funds. Conservative propaganda was remarkable for its quantity rather than quality, and the print crusade was activated even before France declared war on Britain in February 1793. War made the task of denouncing French revolutionary ideas, and those at home who allegedly embraced them, even easier. Extracts from Burke were issued in many forms, and conservative newspapers, pamphlets, tracts and periodicals outnumbered those of the radicals. Extra-parliamentary political controversy quickly went beyond what Burke and Paine had written. The discussion widened, and Gregory Claeys has shown that participants did not confine themselves to issues defined clearly in the *Reflections* or *Rights of Man*. Many related political, theological, social and economic matters were taken up. John Dinwiddy suggests that neither the case for reform nor the case against it were unanswerable, and that reception of these arguments was conditioned by prevalent circumstances, which enabled conservatives to misrepresent reformers as French-style revolutionaries and to assert that reform would lead to violent upheaval.[23]

Hostility was particularly strong towards plebeian radicalism, owing not only to what was demanded, but to who was demanding it. The agitation of common people, operating outside established structures of influence and patronage, and demonstrating a new political consciousness, alarmed and antagonised the propertied ranks. Here was a politics for the many rather than the few, but pressure from below drew forth repression from above, and radicalism went into partial retreat during the 1790s. Controversy continued, however, and the meaning of patriotism was hotly contested as conservative and radical argued about who were the better patriots: those who opposed reform and regarded established institutions as sacrosanct, or those who wanted to improve and preserve institutions by reforming them.

As well as a mass of propaganda, loyalists could rely on effective organisation. In November 1792 the lawyer John Reeves, an adviser to the home office, founded the Association for Preserving Liberty and Property against Republicans and Levellers. This project may have been undertaken with ministerial knowledge and approval. E. C. Black thinks so, though a more recent account maintains that Pitt did not know of it in advance, even if he and his colleagues were quick to turn it to their own purposes.[24] Based in London, the Reeves body established or made contact with similar groups in provincial towns. Soon these numbered over a thousand. They subjected known reformers to surveillance and intimidation, spread anti-radical literature, and worked with local authorities to prosecute writers and publishers of seditious material. In some towns a conservative reaction had been under way for many months. Reform mobilisation in Manchester, for example, had provoked the formation of a Church and King Club in March 1790, which was superseded by the local Association for Preserving Constitutional Order at the end of 1792. Manchester loyalists forged close links with the local authorities, and occasionally encouraged mob violence against reformers. The great extent and impressive organisation of conservative sentiment were indicated by the hundreds of loyal addresses submitted to king and parliament on the outbreak of the French war, by wide support for the prosecution of radicals and passing of information to local authorities, and by countless meetings and demonstrations displaying firm commitment to the established order in state and society. Loyalists warmly welcomed repressive legislation designed to combat subversive activities. The number of petitioners who supported the 'Two Acts' of 1795 outnumbered those against by two to one.

Historians disagree about the impact of repressive laws and popular loyalism on the reform movement. Donald Ginter suggests that some loyalist associations were captured by reformers, but evidence for this is patchy, and Robert Dozier considers it much more likely that large sections of the reform movement were diverted away from anti-establishment activity and turned towards loyalism.[25] Official repression and the so-called reign of terror were less important in subduing radicalism than the force of public opinion, and Pitt was not the oppressive demon his critics considered him to be. Furthermore, much of the violent disorder arose because of social and economic problems, and the government did try to address these. Pitt responded to hunger and distress. Ian Christie points out that welfare provisions were not ungenerous. They promoted order and contributed to the fundamental political stability which ensured that Britain would not have revolution. Institutions survived wartime crises, writes David Eastwood, because they were able to prove their worth and stimulate active voluntary effort in their defence.[26]

Government repression and popular loyalism forced radicals to adopt patriotic language and struggle with conservatism on its own terms. They could never match the loyalists' public display and fervid propaganda. State occasions, royal birthdays and victories over the French evoked a mass response, which was directed against reformers and given staunchly conservative meanings. This popular nationalist participation also involved a significant change in political and social thought. According to Robert Hole, there was a departure from the older religious basis for arguments about sanction and restraint. Religion was still important in defining and enforcing duty, but new arguments about duty were formulated primarily in reaction to the problems of the 1790s. Radicals often focused on goals, and demanded reform in order to achieve these, but conservatives focused on social control, which required a proper appreciation of duty.[27]

Through the 1790s and into the early 1800s, British politics were increasingly shaped by the force of popular loyalism. Pitt admitted that government repression would have been ineffective without mass approval. Despite all the demonstrations for peace and reform, there was still wide support for the ministry and the war. The conflict against France was hailed as a patriotic struggle. British interests and institutions were obviously at stake, and the French did not appear to be willing to negotiate. Conservatives also believed that the parliamentary opposition could not be trusted. A continuous flood of conservative propaganda disseminated loyalist rhetoric, which was uttered from the pulpit too as Anglicans, Wesleyan Methodists, the Church of Scotland, and some Dissenting congregations upheld the values of hierarchy and obedience. Novels and cartoons reinforced the loyalist concept of duty, and over 2 million copies of the *Cheap Repository Tracts* were distributed between 1795 and 1798. A new conservative periodical, the *Anti-Jacobin*, was established in 1797. George III became a powerful patriotic symbol. Linda Colley views the monarch as a nucleus for emotional and political attachment, though James Sack suggests that Pitt rather than the king was the main focus for wartime loyalism.[28]

The volunteer movement also provoked a mass response, and its uniforms, banners and parades were open displays of patriotism (though selfish motives were at work as well, relating to the local status of those who participated). Pitt's administration approved the establishment of armed units in 1794 and appealed directly to loyalists for funds. Volunteers intimidated reformers and inspired national pride, and these functions were far more significant than the contribution made by volunteer units to home defence.

In some ways the volunteer movement exacerbated the problem of how to control popular loyalism. There was much discussion about arming the volunteers, and ministers had grave misgivings about recruitment from the lower classes.

Some volunteers proved to be independent rather than deferential in spirit. They refused to act against food rioters in 1795, 1797, 1800 and 1801, and demanded the right to select their own officers. The volunteer system was reformed in 1801 to improve discipline, and there was more reliance on a permanent local militia. This improved the nation's defences while continuing the marginalisation of radicals. Half a million men were involved in home defence by 1804, when there was a serious invasion scare.[29]

Public celebration of victories over the French, loyalist meetings, addresses to the government, and waves of excitement marking the renewal of war in 1803 after a brief peace, and the king's resistance to Catholic emancipation in 1801 and 1807, demonstrated the continuing vitality and success of loyalism. Even in towns where radicalism was strong, reform leaders and publicists were constantly subjected to surveillance and pressure. Radicalism evinced a remarkable capacity for survival, but it is also clear that popular loyalism remained strong and well organised, and, as Jonathan Clark has argued mainly with reference to the upper levels of British society, that traditional conservative and hierarchical principles maintained a firm intellectual dominance.[30]

The most important reform of the early nineteenth century was the abolition of the British slave trade in 1807, but even this was open to differing interpretations. Regarded by some as a victory for the reform spirit, by others it was given a distinctly conservative emphasis. As a fundamental reform in wartime, loyalists brandished it to show that Britain's constitution, laws and government were not incompatible with true liberty. This had a similar impact to the acquittal of Hardy and his radical associates in 1794. Acquittal had assisted the loyalist cause because it proved that the British state was not what radicals declared it to be; radical arguments would have been strengthened only if Hardy and the others were convicted on questionable evidence. The abolition of the slave trade established the superiority of British freedom and manners, and this measure of justice for the African race increased national self-confidence. Engaged in a war against military despotism and territorial aggrandisement, it would not have been fitting for the British government and people to put off abolition of the slave trade. Linda Colley regards abolition as 'a means to uphold the reputation of the existing order against both radicals at home and the French enemy'. It enhanced Britain's international leadership, and demonstrated the worth of British influence and institutions. The ruling elite saw an opportunity to take a popular course without surrendering any power, and by responding to pressure on the slave trade drew attention away from parliament's refusal to give way on other matters, particularly electoral reform. Abolition showed that there was no need to question the established order. It 'made large numbers of Britons feel important, benign and above all, patrons and possessors of liberty' and 'reassured them that their country was worthy of their attachment and of other nations' envy'.[31]

Conclusion

Revolution and war abroad brought momentous change in British politics as new ideas and problems merged with older conflicts. Price, Burke and Paine, and the controversialists they inspired, battled for men's minds and added urgency and bitterness to the political struggles of these years. In high politics the Whigs divided over issues of revolution, war and peace, and the disintegration of Pitt's conservative alliance after 1801 was followed by a series of brief ministries and further political instability. On war strategy, Catholic relief, parliamentary and economical reform, royal influence and other prominent questions no consensus was possible. Extra-parliamentary political activity and interest increased. Though radical organisations were often weak and vulnerable, and did not secure the reforms they sought, they were highly significant. Radicalism matured as a cause and consequence of growing enthusiasm for reform, a more effective expression of grievances, the wider involvement both of numbers and sorts of people, reasoned argument as well as emotional responses, and a sense of self-worth and collective interest. Most reformers were constitutionalists and disliked violence, though there were extremists who saw in violence the only way to force the ruling elite to make concessions. Indeed, respectable and plebeian radicals alike found no easy answer to the question of how to reform parliament when parliament refused to respond to outdoor pressure. Popular loyalism was also a striking feature of the era of revolution and war, and the growth of popular political participation was promoted even more successfully by conservatives than it was by radicals.

Notes

1 B. W. Hill, 'Fox and Burke: the Whig party and the question of principles 1784–89', *EHR*, 89, 1974, pp. 1–24.

2 G. M. Ditchfield, 'The parliamentary struggle over the repeal of the Test and Corporation Acts', *EHR*, 89, 1974, pp. 551–77.

3 F. O'Gorman, 'Pitt and the "Tory" reaction', in H. T. Dickinson (ed.), *Britain and the French Revolution 1789–1815*, Basingstoke, 1989, p. 33; C. Emsley, 'An aspect of Pitt's "terror": prosecutions for sedition during the 1790s', *SH*, 6, 1981, pp. 155–84, and 'Repression, "terror" and the rule of law in England during the decade of the French Revolution', *EHR*, 100, 1985, pp. 801–25.

4 J. Ehrman, *The Younger Pitt. The Reluctant Transition*, London, 1983, pp. 398–400.

5 R. Cooper, 'William Pitt, taxation, and the needs of war', *JBS*, 22, 1982, pp. 94–103.

6 E. J. Evans, *The Forging of the Modern State 1783–1870*, 2nd edn, London, 1996, p. 66.

7 A. D. Kriegel, 'A convergence of ethics: Saints and Whigs in British antislavery', *JBS*, 26, 1987, pp. 423–50.

8 M. Roberts, 'The fall of the Talents, March 1807', *EHR*, 50, 1935, pp. 61–77; A. D. Harvey, 'The Ministry of All the Talents: the Whigs in office February 1806 to March 1807', *HJ*, 15, 1972, pp. 619–48; R. W. Davis, 'Whigs in the age of Fox and Grey', *PH*, 12, 1993, p. 204.

9 J. C. D. Clark, *English Society 1688–1832: Ideology, Social Structure and Political Practice during the Ancien Regime*, Cambridge, 1985, pp. 89, 235–42, 247, 267–78, 290, 317–22, 358–71, 382–92; J. J. Sack, *From Jacobite to Conservative. Reaction and Orthodoxy in Britain 1760–1832*, Cambridge, 1993, p. 2; D. Wilkinson, 'The Pitt–Portland coalition of 1794 and the origins of the "Tory" party', *History*, 83, 1998, pp. 249–64; J. Ehrman, *The Younger Pitt. The Consuming Struggle*, London, 1996, pp. 675–6.

10 M. Roberts, *The Whig Party 1807–12*, 2nd edn, London, 1965, and 'The leadership of the Whig party in the House of Commons from 1807 to 1815', *EHR*, 50, 1935, pp. 620–38; D. Rapp, 'The left-wing Whigs: Whitbread, the Mountain and reform 1809–15', *JBS*, 21, 1982, pp. 35–66; A. D. Kriegel, 'Liberty and Whiggery in early nineteenth-

century England', *JMH*, 52, 1980, pp. 253–78; E. A. Smith, *Lord Grey 1761–1845*, 2nd edn, Stroud, 1996, chs 4, 5.

11 E. P. Thompson, *The Making of the English Working Class*, rev. edn, London, 1980, ch. 5. On developments in Manchester, Sheffield and Nottingham see M. J. Turner, *Reform and Respectability. The Making of a Middle-Class Liberalism in Early Nineteenth-Century Manchester*, Manchester, 1995, pp. 38–55; J. Stevenson, *Artisans and Democrats. Sheffield in the French Revolution 1789–97*, Sheffield, 1989; J. Beckett, 'Responses to war: Nottingham in the French Revolutionary and Napoleonic wars, 1793–1815', *Midland History*, 22, 1997, pp. 71–84.

12 C. B. Cone, *The English Jacobins. Reformers in Late Eighteenth-Century England*, New York, 1968, pp. 125–6.

13 D. Wahrman, 'Virtual representation: parliamentary reporting and languages of class in the 1790s', *P&P*, 136, 1992, pp. 83–113.

14 J. Belchem, *Popular Radicalism in Nineteenth Century Britain*, Basingstoke, 1996, p. 1; J. Epstein, *Radical Expression: Political Language, Ritual and Symbol in England 1790–1850*, New York, 1994, pp. 3–28; J. Stevenson, 'Popular radicalism and popular protest', in Dickinson, *Britain and the French Revolution*, pp. 72–3.

15 Thompson, *Working Class*, pp. 515–42; R. Wells, 'English society and revolutionary politics in the 1790s: the case for insurrection', in M. Philp (ed.), *The French Revolution and British Popular Politics*, Cambridge, 1991, pp. 188–226.

16 Thompson, *Working Class*, chs 5, 14; G. A. Williams, *Artisans and Sans-Culottes. Popular Movements in France and England during the French Revolution*, London, 1968; A. Goodwin, *The Friends of Liberty. The English Democratic Movement in the Age of the French Revolution*, London, 1979, chs 2, 5, 10, 12.

17 D. Turley, *The Culture of English Antislavery 1780–1860*, London, 1991; R. Blackburn, *The Overthrow of Colonial Slavery 1776–1848*, London, 1988, chs 2, 4, 8; R. J. Hind, 'William Wilberforce and the perceptions of the British people', *HR*, 60, 1987, pp. 321–35; S. Drescher, 'Whose abolition? Popular pressure and the ending of the British slave trade', *P&P*, 143, 1994, pp. 136–66.

18 Belchem, *Popular Radicalism*, pp. 27–8; P. E. Spence, *The Birth of Romantic Radicalism: War, Popular Politics and English Radical Reformism 1800–15*, Aldershot, 1996; P. Harling, 'The Duke of York affair and the complexities of wartime patriotism', *HJ*, 34, 1996, pp. 936–84.

19 J. E. Cookson, *The Friends of Peace. Anti-war Liberalism in England 1793–1815*, Cambridge, 1982; D. Wahrman, 'National society, communal culture: an argument about the recent historiography of eighteenth-century Britain', *SH*, 17, 1992, pp. 43–72; J. Seed,

'Gentlemen Dissenters. The social and political meanings of rational Dissent in the 1770s and 1780s', *HJ*, 28, 1985, pp. 299–325; R. E. Richey, 'The origins of English radicalism: the changing rationale for Dissent', *Eighteenth Century Studies*, 7, 1973–4, pp. 179–92; Clark, *English Society*, ch. 5; J. E. Bradley, *Religion, Revolution and English Radicalism*, Cambridge, 1990, pp. 134, 138.

20 J. Bohstedt, *Riots and Community Politics in England and Wales 1790–1810*, London, 1983.

21 Belchem, *Popular Radicalism*, p. 34; Thompson, *Working Class*, pp. 569–659; J. R. Dinwiddy, 'Luddism and politics in the northern counties', *SH*, 4, 1979, pp. 33–63; M. I. Thomis, *The Luddites: Machine Breaking in Regency England*, Newton Abbot, 1970, pp. 78, 95; F. O. Darvall, *Popular Disturbances and Public Order in Regency England*, 2nd edn, Oxford, 1969, p. 317; J. Stevenson, *Popular Disturbances in England 1700–1832*, 2nd edn, London, 1992, pp. 193–201.

22 J. Belchem, *'Orator' Hunt. Henry Hunt and English Working-Class Radicalism*, Oxford, 1985; I. Dyck, *William Cobbett and Rural Political Culture*, Cambridge, 1992.

23 G. Claeys, 'The French Revolution debate and British political thought', *History of Political Thought*, 11, 1990, pp. 59–80; J. R. Dinwiddy, 'Interpretations of Anti-Jacobinism', in Philp, *French Revolution and British Popular Politics*, pp. 38–49.

24 E. C. Black, *The Association. British Extra-Parliamentary Political Organisation 1769–93*, Cambridge, Mass., 1963, ch. 7 (esp. p. 237); M. Duffy, 'William Pitt and the origins of the loyalist association movement of 1792', *HJ*, 39, 1996, pp. 943–62.

25 D. E. Ginter, 'The loyalist association movement of 1792–93 and British public opinion', *HJ*, 9, 1966, pp. 179–90; R. R. Dozier, *For King, Constitution and Country. The English Loyalists and the French Revolution*, Lexington, 1983, pp. 192–3.

26 I. R. Christie, *Stress and Stability in Late Eighteenth-Century Britain. Reflections on the British Avoidance of Revolution*, Oxford, 1984, chs 3, 4; D. Eastwood, 'Patriotism and the English state in the 1790s', in Philp, *French Revolution and British Popular Politics*, pp. 146–68.

27 R. Hole, *Pulpits, Politics and Public Order in England 1760–1832*, Cambridge, 1989, chs 7–11.

28 L. Colley, *Britons. Forging the Nation*, London, 1992, ch. 5, and 'The apotheosis of George III: loyalty, royalty and the British nation 1760–1820', *P&P*, 102, 1984, pp. 94–129; Sack, *From Jacobite to Conservative*, pp. 113, 131, 134.

29 J. R. Western, 'The volunteer movement as an anti-revolutionary force', *EHR*, 71, 1956, pp. 603–14; J. E. Cookson, 'The English volunteer movement of the French wars 1793–1815: some contexts', *HJ*,

32, 1989, pp. 867–91; L. Colley, 'Whose nation? Class and class consciousness in Britain 1750–1830', *P&P*, 113, 1986, pp. 97–117.

30 Clark, *English Society*, *passim*.

31 Colley, *Britons*, pp. 358–60; J. Walvin, 'Freedom and slavery and the shaping of Victorian Britain', *Slavery and Abolition*, 15, 1994, pp. 246–59.

3

Parliament and people

Introduction

After 1815 there was further tension and unrest, owing to the economic consequences of the French wars, criticism of financial and economic policies, and continuing resentment about the high cost of government and corruption in high places. It was by no means clear that the ruling elite had the political will and practical ability to deal with these problems. Special interest groups, notably financiers and landowners, obstructed certain reforms, and the Liverpool government's authority in parliament was frequently brought into question. An upsurge in popular radicalism added to the political instability of the time, though the reform movement was divided on goals and tactics, and there was little co-operation between plebeian activists and more moderate, middle-class reformers. Economic distress, which stimulated much of the extra-parliamentary agitation, eventually subsided, and in the 1820s there was a reassessment of radical ideas and methods. Liverpool's ministry had countered agitation with repression, and this effort to maintain law and order drew attention away from the government's financial and political shortcomings. Meanwhile the Whig opposition split on the issue of repression, and Whig success in exploiting unease about the government's financial and economic management could not be continued once the ministers adopted a bolder approach to these matters. Social and economic conditions improved in the early 1820s. Liverpool's administration became more confident and secure, and ministers implemented a series of constructive policies. Unresolved questions continued to defy easy solution, however, and political turmoil increased again after 1827.

Postwar economic and political problems

Economic dislocation during the war left a difficult legacy, and many regions continued to suffer from rising poverty, hunger, slack trade and unemployment. Merchants, manufacturers, farmers and workers struggled to adjust to peacetime conditions. The situation was exacerbated by cuts in public spending, cancellation of war orders, and the return of demobilised servicemen. Attention turned increasingly to the impact of war on profits, wages, output, capital and fund-holding, and popular resentment grew as the war and government policies were blamed for prevalent hardship.

During the war there appears to have been an income shift towards landowners and away from labourers and capital-owners, and of the last two groups labour was relatively better off because wages rose more than profits. It was generally assumed that income was also transferred to fund-holders. Resentment against those who had done well during the war prompted a revival of interest in economical reform. The idea spread that the nation was suffering because of the extravagance, greed and corruption of the ruling elite, which had used the expansion of government during wartime further to enrich itself at the community's expense.[1] Pitt's financial measures, hailed by his successors and admirers as proof of his genius, and widely reckoned to be the main reason for Britain's ability to fight and win the war against France, began to be questioned. Many subsequent commentators have joined in this criticism. They claim that Pitt should have introduced income tax earlier to slow down the growth of the national debt, that he was wrong to maintain the sinking fund in wartime, that he should have secured better terms for loans in order to relieve taxpayers, and that his war taxes were highly detrimental because they imposed unequal burdens and failed to promote lasting economic progress.[2]

The immediate postwar grievances with which Liverpool's government had to contend related specifically to the value and availability of cash, the 1815 corn law, and the massively swollen national debt. On the first point there were loud complaints, especially from businessmen large and small, about the shortage of cash and depreciation of notes issued since 1797. The corn law, passed before Napoleon's final defeat, prohibited the importation of foreign wheat until the home price reached 80s a quarter (lower prices were prescribed for rye, barley, oats and other grains). Ministers were concerned primarily to assist British agriculture through the difficult transition from war to peace. But the new measure was widely condemned as a selfish piece of legislation which served the interests of landowners, who controlled parliament, by keeping up farm rents and food prices. This harmed the labouring classes by raising the cost of food, and business by restricting demand for British manufactures. Workers at home had less money to spend on these goods, and foreigners would not take them because they could not pay in grain. Meanwhile the national debt was so great that contemporaries genuinely feared national bankruptcy. Interest charges on the debt now took up more than half of government's total expenditure. Taxation had risen and, it was claimed, would gradually impoverish the middle and lower classes in order to satisfy the ruling elite and its parasitic allies, notably financial interests and government creditors.

Liverpool's government had to address these matters quickly, but ministers suffered a massive handicap. It was difficult for them to manage the House of Commons. The waning away of executive patronage and the process of economical reform since the 1780s meant that traditional means of control were no longer available. Some contemporaries complained that patronage and influence had been diminished too quickly, and that stable and efficient government was impossible without them. Despite these protests the limitation of executive influence could not be reversed, and the independence of the Commons from government control was emphatically demonstrated in March 1816, when Liverpool's ministry proposed to continue income tax in peacetime at a reduced rate. The majority of MPs voted to remove it. This was a serious defeat, and hindered government efforts to restore public finances after the long and costly war.

Income tax had become an essential source of revenue and was vital to the ministers' budget plans. It did not seem possible to make good the loss of revenue from income tax without imposing new burdens or adding to the national debt, a problem exacerbated by growing demands for cheaper government. Ministers were taken aback by pressure for retrenchment and the ever more insistent calls for the suppression of waste and corruption. In the postwar years economical reform was energetically taken up by a progressive section of Whigs, led after 1815 by Whitbread's successor, Henry Brougham, whose reform credentials and extra-parliamentary popularity had been confirmed by his agitation against the orders in council and income tax. Cheap government was also a cause championed by such radical MPs as Joseph Hume, and supported in the publications of William Cobbett. Under these mounting pressures the government's financial planning collapsed. New economies were continually demanded, out of doors as well as in parliament (over four hundred petitions were submitted against continuation of the income tax), at a time when the government's spending commitments could not be rapidly reduced. For several years Liverpool's ministry was desperately short of money.

To get measures through the Commons when patronage was in decline, and when government was plagued by complicated needs and expectations, ministers had to rely heavily on argument and persuasion. Castlereagh was leader in the Commons, but oratory was not his strength. He was more effective at privately negotiating with and cajoling backbenchers. Debating assistance was given by Canning, who joined Liverpool's cabinet in 1816, and by Robert Peel, a talented young politician who had been attached to the government since 1810 in junior offices and would be promoted to the cabinet in 1822. Though Liverpool's administration was considerably stronger than its immediate predecessors, it was never totally dominant in parliament. Nevertheless, at no time during Liverpool's premiership did a majority of MPs wish to drive him out and let in the Whigs. Liverpool sometimes relied on this, and by making it known that defeat in a particular division would mean the cabinet's resignation, he managed to force Tory backbenchers into line.

In place of patronage, party discipline would have been an alternative method of control. But party was still in its infancy. With patronage fading and party a rudimentary framework in parliamentary politics, and with the volume of government business rapidly expanding, Liverpool's administration did not have an easy time in the postwar period. Yet there was continuity in goals, assumptions, leadership and personnel, which was a source of strength alongside the weaknesses. This paradox has been noted by Norman Gash: a conservative policy developed more quickly than a conservative party, and the Liverpool administration lasted for fifteen years without perfecting its parliamentary organisation.[3]

General elections could be useful to governments, for they normally confirmed an administration in power. Liverpool's ministry called one in 1818, a year before it was due, in order to take advantage of a brief economic recovery and the decline of popular unrest (which had been particularly alarming in the first half of 1817). This election brought some gains for the opposition, however, and indicated strong indignation against government's failure to stabilise the public finances and alleviate the postwar economic depression. Liverpool complained that the new House of Commons might be as unreliable as its predecessor, and contemporaries noted an independent spirit among new MPs, many of whom refused to commit themselves to the government. Ministers had to earn parliamentary approval, and could not expect to have it unless they proved their competence in managing the nation's affairs.

Radical mobilisation and the mass platform

Economic depression and popular unrest created more support for organised radicalism. Radicals called for a range of political, social and economic changes, including public retrenchment, lower taxes, repeal of the 1815 corn law, and protection for wages and employment. As before, parliamentary reform was the priority because it would make possible improvements in so many other areas, and would force the legislature to respond to the people's needs more diligently. To radicals, the electoral system was too anomalous and seemed increasingly out of date. They pointed to the control of county seats by great landed families, the bizarre mixture of borough franchises, the disproportionately heavy share of constituencies in southern England, the large number of decayed boroughs and lack of direct representation for large towns. Plebeian radicals tended to focus on the vote, while the transfer of seats to commercial and industrial towns was the main aim of respectable middle-class reformers, who wanted more men of their own kind, successful in business and the professions, to be elected to parliament. They believed that reform would facilitate a more vigorous promotion of local interests.

By now popular activists had many points of contact with elite politicians. Some historians have argued that the petitioning, dinners, public assemblies, lobbying and correspondence of these years demonstrate a high level of popular political commitment and awareness, and that the unreformed parliament was more influenced by pressure from without than is often assumed.[4] The increase in political knowledge owed much to the continuing growth of the press. Anti-establishment journalists, authors, lampoonists, satirists and illustrators rose to have unprecedented influence. They included T. J. Wooler, George Cruikshank and William Hone. In 1816 Cobbett, the leading radical writer of the age, began to publish editorials from his *Political Register* as cheap, single, unstamped sheets. This 'Twopenny Trash' gained a mass readership (see Document 6). Weekly instalments sometimes sold over sixty thousand copies. Inevitably there was a conservative reaction. Over 130 prosecutions for seditious and blasphemous libel occurred between 1817 and 1821. Reformers again faced persecution and surveillance by loyalists, and the Constitutional Association was established to co-ordinate efforts against radical writers, printers and booksellers. Local political struggles continued as reformers confronted conservatives (normally the latter controlled local government). Anti-reform clubs and associations were established or revived to assist local and central authorities. Cobbett fled to the USA in 1817 when he was required to pay stamp duty on his 'Twopenny Trash', and the prominent radical and freethinker Richard Carlile was accused and convicted of blasphemy after republishing some of Paine's works. Carlile spent most of the period between 1819 and 1825 in prison for his press activities.

Economic distress and radical mobilisation were closely linked. As had long been their practice, radical leaders argued that the ultimate cause of material hardship was misgovernment, which could be corrected only by parliamentary reform. The reform movement benefited from a new wave of organisation. Provincial Hampden Clubs were open to all who could pay a penny a week. They were democratic in spirit, and the goal of manhood suffrage had strong support throughout the northern industrial regions. There were also Union Societies, which campaigned for the vote while seeking to educate workers and elevate their character. Radical agitation spread as a result of mass meetings and petitioning. Cartwright helped to inspire a truly nationwide campaign, and two thousand reform petitions were sent to parliament in 1817 and 1818 combined. This was a zealous, inclusive movement, likened by Elie Halevy to Protestant evangelicalism on account of its plebeian organisation, small subscriptions, open-air meetings and itinerant missionaries. Agitation was strongest in districts which had a radical past, and many campaigners were already experienced in the arts of organisation and mobilisation. Craig Calhoun argues that the basic resources of collective action were community and tradition. Though broader concerns were becoming more important, these were not the original promoters of popular political activity.[5]

Cartwright, Cobbett, Hunt and their followers were developing a non-revolutionary radical constitutionalism. They wanted no violence, knowing that to engage in illegal conduct would be to provoke official repression and lose public sympathy. Most radicals concentrated on subjecting the unreformed system to sustained pressure through press, petition and mass meeting. As in previous years, however, it was not clear what campaigners could do if parliament refused to reform itself. Reform petitions were not taken very seriously by the ruling elite. Cartwright advocated an older method, conventions, and declared that large unrepresented towns should select 'legislative attorneys' to present the people's wishes to government. Though he did not intend this as a threatening manoeuvre, ministers, MPs, and most men of property and influence still regarded the reform convention as an alternative parliament and an unconstitutional rival to the properly convened legislature.

Radical agitation gave rise to the usual reports from spies and informers about arming, drilling and other preparations for insurrection. Some extremists did attach themselves to the postwar reform movement. In 1815 and 1816 they tried to turn mass pressure to their own purposes. One of the more head-strong groups, the Spenceans (followers of Thomas Spence, who had died in 1814), pursued egalitarian and republican goals and advocated nationalisation of the land. The Spenceans needed celebrity speakers to draw the crowds. They made contact with the ambitious Hunt, whose longing for fame and applause meant that he needed the crowds. But Hunt was no revolutionary. He was evolving the 'mass platform', a means of extending political participation to bring large numbers behind the demand for parliamentary reform, and this depended on disciplined action and legitimacy.[6] Hunt initially co-operated with the Spenceans because they agreed to keep proceedings peaceful. A mass meeting at Spa Fields, London, on 15 November 1816 was addressed by Hunt and passed off without incident, though it was notable for provocative display of the 'cap of liberty', used in the 1790s by French revolutionaries. As James Epstein explains, appropriation of this controversial symbol by postwar British radicals inevitably added to the mounting tension.[7] A second Spa Fields meeting, on 2 December 1816, was planned by extremists to coincide with an armed rising. It was easily crushed, but rumours about uprisings in the provinces persisted. January 1817 saw a Hampden Club convention in London, which attracted delegates from all over the country. Unrest continued as resentment about falling wages, unemployment and rising food prices increased, and economic grievances merged even more closely with the demand for parliamentary reform. On 28 January 1817 the window of the prince regent's coach was smashed by a mob as he travelled to parliament. This caused great outrage and alarm. Liverpool's government responded with measures to suspend habeas corpus, restrict the right of public assembly, preserve the loyalty and discipline of soldiers, and protect the person of the prince regent.

Repression did not end the agitation. If anything, reformers became all the more determined and insistent. Mass mobilis-ation had developed too far, and economic distress was too serious, for popular radicalism to be peremptorily crushed in 1817. John Belchem stresses its defiant, celebratory character,[8] and the growth of libertarian aspirations was clearly demonstrated by provincial delegates to the Hampden Club meeting in London, for they forced it to take up manhood suffrage even though Cartwright had committed himself to household suffrage in order to appease Burdett. The assertiveness of these delegates was a symptom of widespread radical commitment in the nation. But there remained both a fundamental disagreement about aims and personal rivalries among the reform movement's figureheads. Hunt, Cobbett and Cartwright all quarrelled with each other during the London conference, and after the decision for manhood suffrage, a victory for Hunt and the northern clubs, Burdett turned away from the popular campaign.

The campaign began to lurch out of control. There was more desperation, because of hunger and suffering, and some ill-advised conduct owing to the influence of injudicious local leaders. In the spring of 1817 came the March of the Blanketeers, a plan for reform petitioners to march from Manchester to London (carrying blankets for shelter against the cold). Local authorities refused to believe that the march would be peaceful, and the plan implicitly threatened physical force because marchers expected to gain adherents along the way, making the Blanketeers a huge and irresistible body when they reached London. Manchester magistrates and loyalists decided that this march could not be allowed to proceed. Radical organisers were arrested and the marchers dispersed. In June there was an attempted insurrection in Derbyshire, the Pentridge Rising, which involved about three hundred stockingers, ironworkers and labourers. The rising was weak in terms of preparation, arming and discipline. Many men were forced to take part against their will, and it soon became clear that the whole project had been inspired by government agents, notably 'Oliver the Spy' (a convicted debtor named W. J. Richards). Nevertheless, three Pentridge men were executed and thirty were transported. There was general protest about these punishments and the use of spies to entrap poor workers, but ministers, the parliamentary majority, and respectable opinion out of doors held that property and order were in grave danger, and loyalists considered a severe response entirely justifiable.

After Pentridge, popular agitation temporarily declined. A good harvest in 1817 and some signs of economic recovery eased the tension, though many radical leaders and publicists did not suspend their activities. They had not been cowed into submission by official repression. Indeed, ministers were disappointed when treason proceedings against the Spa Fields ringleaders failed in the summer of 1817, and by the acquittal of Wooler and Hone, who were both tried for libel. In London and the provinces some political prosecutions had to be dropped because of flimsy evidence, and many radicals realised that imposing conformity would be more difficult for government in peacetime than it had been during the war. Habeas corpus was restored in 1818, and restrictions on public assembly lapsed. Radical leaders prepared for a revival of agitation. Hunt continued to advocate the mass platform, with its wide appeal and stimulating public display. He presented himself as a champion of the common folk, repudiating both Burdettite moderation and the timeworn tactics of Cartwright. Burdett's constituency, Westminster, had the largest borough electorate in the country, and Hunt was an unsuccessful parliamentary candidate there in 1818. Though it was still controlled by the Westminster Committee, the influence of old LCS men had declined as the constituency prospered, and the Committee was now dominated by moderates who wanted to co-operate with the Whigs. Hunt eschewed this policy completely, and condemned Burdett as a traitor to the reform cause. Hunt and his followers also broke with Cartwright. The idea of a movement led by independent gentlemen, pressing for household suffrage on the grounds that representation should correspond with payment of direct tax, seemed outdated. Cartwright and Burdett had envisaged the Hampden Clubs as a continuation of Wyvill's association movement of the 1780s, but the rise of Hunt prevented this and permanently divided the popular campaign.

Meanwhile respectable radicalism flourished in the postwar years. Wealthy, educated and propertied groups were active, often interesting themselves primarily in local issues (such as municipal government, or local trade and manufacturing). Sectional concerns could also be related to wider questions, like the corn laws, as in Manchester where textile masters were worried about the impact of corn regulations on wages and profits in industry.[9] The notion that business interests were not being treated fairly by parliament strengthened the case for parliamentary reform. Middle-class liberals assumed that the whole community would benefit from repeal of the corn laws and a substantial change in the electoral system, though they were equivocal about the upsurge of popular radicalism. Reform was necessary, they agreed, but not manhood suffrage and annual parliaments. Uneasy about what they saw as the threatening language and irresponsible tactics of plebeian agitators, many respectable reformers mistrusted independent popular political activity and complained that the workers always tended to follow the wrong leaders. Plebeian assertiveness was to be regretted, moreover, because it would frighten off men of property and influence who might otherwise agree to join in a responsible, well conducted reform campaign. After the March of Blanketeers in 1817, respectable reformers expressed sympathy for the suffering workers and condemned the coercive methods employed by Manchester authorities. But they were above all concerned that such projects would discredit the reform cause (see Document 7). If wealthy and respectable men did not come forward to press for reform, it was feared, the initiative would increasingly be taken by unreliable demagogues who would lead the labouring classes into all manner of inappropriate courses. Middle-class reformers strongly disliked Hunt, whom they dismissed as a vain publicity-seeker.

The relative social and political peace of 1818 did not last. Trade slackened again and 1819 was another difficult year. Political and economic goals became more explicitly combined. Hunt had appeared on the same platform as the London shipwrights' leader John Gast, for example, and parliamentary reform was associated with the workers' right to a decent standard of living. In 1819 there was an unprecedented popular mobilisation for reform. Hunt went to Manchester in January and adopted a more menacing tone than previously, suggesting that the people should abandon reform petitions and present a direct 'Remonstrance' to the prince regent demanding manhood suffrage and annual parliaments. Most large towns by now had active radical associations and regular reform meetings. Delegates and orators circulated from place to place, and the number attending meetings swelled because of the deepening economic slump. There were plans for the formation of a national reform union. The government was alarmed by reports of drilling in formation, often directed by former soldiers, but reformers claimed that they practised drilling only in order to parade in a disciplined fashion on the way to their meeting places.

There were mass open-air assemblies in most large towns through June and July 1819. Liverpool's ministry, parliament, local authorities, and many middle-class reformers were worried about the proliferation and character of these demonstrations, and government informants maintained that insurrectionary plotting lay behind them. Conservatives banded together again. In Manchester they formed a Committee to Strengthen the Civil Power. The persecution of radical newspapers was stepped up, and special constables were recruited in disturbed areas. Panic and enmity increased. The Birmingham meeting of 12 July which was called to elect a 'legislative attorney' to represent the town at a planned national convention revived fears about an alternative parliament. The home secretary, Sidmouth, declared all such proceedings illegal. But the agitation went on, building up a seemingly unstoppable momentum. At the end of July a royal proclamation was issued against seditious libels, drilling and unlawful assembly. The home office was in regular communication with magistrates all over the country. Rising tension soon resulted in confrontation and bloodshed, at the 'Peterloo Massacre' in Manchester on 16 August, when local magistrates sent in armed yeomanry and then regular troops to disperse an assembly of 60,000 people as it was being addressed by Hunt. Eleven people died and more than 400 were wounded.

At the time, Peterloo promised to be a turning point, although historians have long disagreed about its significance, its causes and where to apportion blame.[10] Peterloo sparked off a general protest and there were impassioned calls for redress. Even commentators who had formerly condemned the reform movement declared that those in authority were more culpable than those who had simply wanted to meet together and express grievances. Radicals raised their campaign against misgovernment to the level of a righteous crusade. Large and indignant meetings took place all over the country. Burdett restored his contacts with Cartwright and Hunt, and he publicly condemned the use of force in Manchester. More petitions demanding reform were submitted to parliament and the crown. Free on bail after the Manchester meeting, Hunt was greeted by a huge crowd when he returned to London in September. Cobbett arrived from America in November, bringing with him the physical remains of Thomas Paine for ceremonial burial (Paine had died in 1809). Radical propaganda was published in huge quantities, and reformers now rallied an impressive moral force against the establishment. But they did not secure parliamentary reform in 1819 and 1820, and they did not even gain redress for Peterloo. There was no official inquiry into the events of 16 August 1819, and inquests, trials and other efforts to attach responsibility to government, magistrates and yeomanry were entirely unsuccessful. Though extremists hoped for an armed rising to avenge the Peterloo martyrs, they gained no backing from the mainstream reform movement. Hunt urged his followers strictly to adhere to constitutional protest, and though many radicals believed that the use of force was a legitimate response to oppression, it was not clear that Peterloo had justified this drastic course. Hunt probably overestimated the opportunities created by the massacre. John Belchem points out that concern about Peterloo proved less powerful in the nation than hostility to the independent mass reform campaign promoted by Hunt.[11]

Liverpool's ministry recovered its composure and regained the initiative soon after Peterloo. New repressive measures, the 'Six Acts', were implemented, and these effectively weakened the popular movement. Prominent reformers were removed by the trials which followed the popular mobilisation of 1819. Hunt was sentenced to two and a half years in prison for unlawful assembly and inciting contempt towards government and constitution. Some Manchester and Lancashire radical leaders were also imprisoned. Burdett was fined and sentenced to three months in prison for his public remarks about Peterloo. Cartwright, Wooler and others were punished for their participation in meetings leading up to 16 August, and there were further press prosecutions.

Though the mobilisation was seriously weakened, vigorous protest activity continued. Fewer numbers were involved, but they were still able effectively to articulate their grievances.

Parliamentary reform, redress for Peterloo and repeal of the Six Acts were their principal aims. There were also strikes and riots in this period, which had more to do with high prices, falling wages and unemployment than with Peterloo. Anger and desperation prompted some advanced radicals to resort to violence. For the revolutionary underground this was a deliberate strategy. The Cato Street Conspiracy, concocted by a group of Spenceans led by Arthur Thistlewood, was a plot to murder cabinet ministers at dinner. It was easily uncovered. Arrests were made in February 1820, followed by five executions and five transportations for life. Obviously there was still a commitment to armed rising in some quarters, but the revolutionary spirit was always limited in terms of influence and numbers. There is no evidence that Thistlewood's faction had close contacts with any provincial groups, though such links were assumed by the authorities to exist. There were serious disturbances in 1820 to increase these suspicions, notably rioting and a general strike in Glasgow, and an armed rising in Huddersfield. Ministers also received reports of armed gatherings near Barnsley, and a plan to attack the barracks in Sheffield. More trials followed. It was generally believed that the Cato Street Conspiracy was not an isolated incident. Liverpool's government and local authorities acted swiftly, however, and the danger receded. Then the economic situation began to improve again. Civil disorder had justified the ministers' repressive stance, which had substantial support, but the popular appeal of radical leaders subsequently faded.

There was one last burst of radical activity in the immediate postwar period, before the economic prosperity and relative political peace of the mid-1820s deprived anti-establishment speakers and organisers of their mass following. For much of 1820 and 1821 attention was focused on the Queen Caroline controversy. The unpopular prince regent had long since separated from his wife Caroline, and had repeatedly pressed for official inquiries into her scandalous conduct. His own sexual morals were no better than hers, but he hated her intensely and had engaged in years of accusation and vendetta. She had moved abroad in return for an annual grant. When the prince succeeded as George IV in 1820 he called for his wife's name to be removed from the Anglican liturgy, and instructed ministers to arrange a divorce. But Caroline announced that she would be returning to England to claim her rights as queen, and her pose as a wronged woman and a symbol of resistance to oppression gathered enormous sympathy from the common people.

Radical politicians and journalists, including Cobbett and London alderman Matthew Wood, sided with the queen, and there was great excitement as she was received in London by huge crowds in June 1820. Writers and caricaturists intensified their attacks on king, ministers and the whole rotten system of government. Popular commotion increased. It had deep community roots. Discussion ranged over sexual relationships, marriage, family, gender roles, public morals and private virtue. Despite the queen's questionable character, the fact that this agitation focused on a woman had sentimental resonance. The controversy was carried on in a language of chivalry, alongside more salacious and seedy material, and many of the queen's supporters in London and the provinces were women. There was widespread indignation at the parliamentary proceedings against her. Revelations about Caroline's private life added to the scandal and attracted all the more interest out of doors. T. W. Laqueur suggests that the scandal-mongering took attention away from serious political issues, while Anna Clark argues that scandal and melodrama did not trivialise the Queen Caroline affair, but made it more (rather than less) politically significant. A deluge of publications encouraged mass participation in the controversy on both sides, as supporters of the queen vied with defenders of king and government.[12]

The queen's supporters depicted her as a brave woman standing up to a wicked king and corrupt ministers who had violated the people's liberty, and there was great celebration when the government's bill of pains and penalties was withdrawn. Public figures who had spoken out against the queen were subjected to insults and mob attack. But the excitement quickly faded. There was disappointment early in 1821 because the parliamentary opposition could not pass motions against the government's treatment of the queen, and her acceptance of a grant and a house ended her pose as the people's ally against tyranny and injustice. When Caroline arrived at George IV's coronation in June 1821 and demanded to be crowned, she was refused admittance. She died in August, by which time her cause had lost its power and appeal. Her funeral procession was marked by serious disturbances, but these were of no lasting importance. Popular protest had been weakened after Peterloo by the Six Acts and the imprisonment of radical leaders. Liverpool's administration survived the Queen Caroline affair, prosperity began to grow and prices to fall, and though the decline of mass political participation was masked by the commotion surrounding the queen's return, it is significant that only a thousand people gathered in Manchester in August 1820 to mark the anniversary of Peterloo.

Economic recovery and the expansion of trade coincided with a period of more confident and competent government. The mass platform collapsed, and radical leaders were no longer able to foment popular agitation and channel this pressure against the establishment. But many of them remained active. Popular politics changed during the 1820s as more attention was given to educational work and economic theories, and efforts were made to expand the radical press and strengthen trade unions. One result was the elaboration of a popular, anti-capitalist political economy which treated labour as the sole creator of wealth. This has been analysed by Noel Thompson, and its premise was that workers were deprived of the whole produce of their labour. Their main problem was not mis-government or the corrupt parliament, therefore, but an unequal distribution of economic power, though this inequality was usually explained in political terms because it had political causes. The establishment of co-operative societies became a favoured response to the problem of economic inequality. These societies promoted a free exchange of products and services and were designed to eliminate competition (along the lines suggested by their originator, the manufacturer and social reformer Robert Owen). As John Belchem has demonstrated, popular radicalism became highly eclectic in these years. There was still a strong commitment to parliamentary reform, but new ideas and organisations were arising, and these were not exclusively tied to political goals. Reform clubs, radical news-papers and the unstamped press, strikes and machine-breaking, trade unionism and co-operation indicate the range of plebeian concerns during the 1820s. Agitation on wage rates and

121

employment conditions continued alongside demands for the vote.[13]

Popular radicalism was still divided. Carlile and the admirers of Paine, for example, advanced arguments rooted in natural rights, republicanism, rationalism and free thought, and abandoned popular assemblies and reform societies. In marked contrast, Hunt and his followers relied on indigenous popular constitutionalism, community responses, inclusive organisation, public display and charismatic leadership, trusting that the mass platform could be recreated when the time was right.

Meanwhile most respectable reformers were relieved that the mass mobilisation had come to an end. They hoped now to carry forward their own campaigns, through sensible argument, calm debate and wide publicity, while studiously avoiding illegality and violence. They were convinced that the government would eventually have to take notice of reform demands proceeding from propertied, wealthy, educated businessmen and professionals. Some of these groups continued to focus on the corn regulations, which they said limited the supply of food for labourers and interfered with the trade and profits of manufacturers and merchants (hence restricting the number of workers they could afford to employ). Corn law repeal was a rallying cause. There was anger among middle-class reformers in Manchester in 1826 when Liverpool's government temporarily removed restrictions on the entry of foreign grain because of a poor harvest and brief economic recession. Protesters argued that the reasons for a temporary suspension of the corn laws were equally applicable to their full repeal.

Respectable radicals grew in confidence and influence during the 1820s, and among their broad range of activities was involvement in 'improving' educational, social and cultural ventures, notably mechanics' institutes, medical dispensaries, literary clubs, charities, University College in London, and the Society for the Diffusion of Useful Knowledge. Some of these institutional supports added force to demands for freer trade and greater civil and religious liberty. There was an ever closer association between liberal newspapers and local reform leaders: groups formed around Edward Baines of the *Leeds Mercury*, for example, and Archibald Prentice of the *Manchester Gazette* (see Document 8). Moderate pro-reform organisations thrived. Some Manchester liberals joined the Cheshire Whig Club, which was dominated by Whig nobles and MPs but also included respectable reformers from across the north-west. Shared ideas, institutions, interests and goals gave middle-class reformers a sense of identity and purpose. Many of them were bound together by Protestant Dissent, a predilection for liberal political economy, and the belief that growing towns should return their own representatives to parliament. Proud and assertive, these spokesmen stepped up their attacks on exclusivity, inefficiency and privilege, for so long the salient features of aristocratic government.

The 1820s became a time of growing influence for the Benthamites, who maintained that permanent social and economic progress would be impossible without structural reforms. They and their allies subjected institutions to the test of reason, and affirmed that government should promote the greatest happiness of the greatest number. Bentham himself was now an old man (seventy-five in 1823), but he had unequivocally embraced parliamentary reform during the war, and this commitment was shared by his friends and followers, including James Mill, who worked in the India Office, Joseph Parkes, a solicitor who would later rise to prominence in Birmingham politics, and Francis Place, the veteran organiser of artisan radicalism in London. Benthamites were behind the foundation of the *Westminster Review* in 1824. This periodical rapidly established itself as the country's leading exponent of rational radicalism. Bentham had formerly assumed that once informed about useful and beneficial policies, legislators would naturally seek to implement them. But he and his allies had since decided that elite selfishness and corruption made this impossible. The only way to win concessions, therefore, was through intimidation. This could be achieved by an organised reform movement, backed by mass agitation, with goals clearly articulated by enlightened and respectable leaders. These leaders would not actually resort to violence, but they would be prepared to threaten it implicitly, with menacing language and conduct. The aim was to alarm the ruling classes and force them to abandon their resistance to reform.[14] It was difficult to generate such a movement in a time of peace and prosperity, however, and respectable reformers generally had no wish to co-operate closely with plebeian radicals. They found the latter too rash and irresponsible, and accused them of harming the reform cause, alienating moderates, and creating support for government repression. Another stumbling block was continual disagreement among middle-class reformers on the question of whether they should try to work with the Whigs.

The Liverpool administration after the war

Between 1801 and 1812 there was political flux, and the separation of the Pittite alliance created more scope for the exercise of royal influence at decisive moments. But from 1812 a measure of ministerial stability returned. Liverpool's cabinet hardly changed in personnel before the end of the war. Apart from the prime minister, its dominant figures were Castlereagh, Sidmouth and Eldon. The most significant changes in the postwar period were the appointment to cabinet office of Canning in 1816, F. J. Robinson in 1818 and the Duke of Wellington in 1819. Liverpool's administration initially had a reasonably secure parliamentary majority, gained prestige for its successful conclusion of the war, and enjoyed royal favour. The prince regent was not the political force his father had been before 1810, which strengthened the prime minister (especially if backed by a united cabinet) in his dealings with the crown. Liverpool could be firm when necessary. He benefited from the absence of a clear rival for the premiership, and from the division between the prince and the Whigs before the end of the war. Liverpool and his colleagues usually had fewer problems in dealing with the crown than in trying to manage the Commons. In troubled times or on particularly sensitive issues, the government found that a parliamentary majority could not be taken for granted.

Nevertheless, this proved to be a stable and long-lasting ministry. There was gradually a clearer demarcation between government and opposition, both in attitudes and affiliations, though it is not clear that this brought a remarkable increase in party cohesion. In fact, Norman Gash, J. E. Cookson and Peter Fraser suggest that party was getting weaker in these years, not stronger. On the other hand, Arthur Aspinall and R. G. Thorne discern a clear sense of party after 1815, Frank O'Gorman writes of a two-party system under Liverpool, and Jonathan Clark regards party as permanent and continuous, albeit 'periodically recast' in times of unusual political excitement.[15] Cohesion may have been increasing, but irregular attendance and incomplete party discipline still characterised parliamentary politics at this time, otherwise the government would not have found it so difficult to secure a majority on particular questions. Shared concerns did draw MPs together, though, and voters too, and it is not surprising to find that parties closed ranks in response to particular experiences, needs and problems. Tories sought to defend established institutions during the years of postwar distress, for example, while Whigs coalesced in the routines of opposition and shared a continuing commitment to Catholic emancipation, civil liberties and restriction of the royal prerogative.

Postwar economic problems created widespread unrest, and repression was the response of government, parliament and local authorities, whose attitudes were still shaped by revolution and war. Public men, it was thought, were obliged to protect property and suppress disorder, and the root causes of popular agitation were not properly their concern. The early nineteenth century saw the rise of the laissez-faire state. Though Liverpool and his colleagues were concerned about the people's welfare, they maintained that government could do little directly to help, and they backed public works schemes and inquiries into the system of poor relief mainly because they thought it would be politically dangerous to do nothing. On the whole Liverpool's ministry wanted to scale down rather than add to government's responsibilities. Ministers and their supporters, however, could not fail to respond to mass meetings, seditious speeches and literature, and the expansion of radical associations linked by itinerant political missionaries.

Food riots, strikes, luddism, arson and other disorders after the war prompted the stationing of troops in disturbed districts, and there were a number of special commissions and executions during 1816. These were followed by the so-called 'Gagging Acts' of 1817, including suspension of habeas corpus and new restrictions on public assembly, brought on by the attack on the prince regent's coach and subsequent parliamentary reports which stated that radical agitation was revolutionary in intent. The evidence was highly questionable, and ministers exaggerated the danger for their own purposes. Some remembered the 1790s and felt they could take no chances. The Pentridge Rising was followed by a special commission in Derby, which meted out further harsh punishments, and though there was controversy over the employment of spies and informants, home secretary Sidmouth insisted that it was government's duty to act swiftly against threats to property and order. Prosecutions for sedition and blasphemy also increased at this time (some of these failed in 1817, much to Sidmouth's disappointment).

Through 1819 there was growing alarm at the rapid increase in extra-parliamentary agitation. Radical leaders seemed to want a final reckoning. Mass mobilisation built up to a climax in the summer, which came at Peterloo. Sidmouth congratulated the Manchester authorities for their conduct on 16 August, as did the prince regent, and these insensitive gestures added to the turmoil as intense moral condemnation arose against those who had employed troops against an apparently peaceful and unarmed crowd. In private, ministers complained that the Manchester magistrates had acted unwisely (ministers thought they should have waited until the Peterloo meeting had finished: then it would have been easier to arrest the organisers and speakers if there was evidence of unlawful assembly). But the cabinet had firmly to support the magistrates in public, in order to reassure local authorities in other disturbed regions of the government's backing. To the ministry and its supporters, Peterloo confirmed the need for further coercive legislation. The Six Acts prohibited drilling and military-style exercises, authorised the confiscation of arms and seizure of seditious and blasphemous literature, imposed new restrictions on the press and the right of assembly, and facilitated the bringing of cases to trial. These emergency measures secured comfortable majorities in parliament, where they had the backing of both the government's regular supporters and the Grenvillites. The Cato Street Conspiracy then created a general wave of sympathy for ministers, as intended murder victims, and unrest in Scotland, south Lancashire and west Yorkshire was taken to justify government repression. This brought independent MPs into line, and the ministry's ability to attract more support out of doors had some effect at the 1820 general election. Soon economic conditions improved and discontent began to die down.

There had probably never been a genuine revolutionary threat in these years and, despite what their critics claimed, ministers had not set out to impose a harsh coercive regime. Postwar emergency measures were far milder than Pitt's had been, and less effective in wiping out popular agitation than in convincing backbenchers in the Commons and propertied classes in the country of the government's sense of responsibility. Maintaining public order was not the ministry's only concern, and not always the main one. Tierney remarked in 1817 that the government was in trouble because of the state of the revenue, not some threat of revolution.

The postwar radical upsurge divided and frustrated the Whigs. Most of them agreed that disorder and disloyalty had to be suppressed, but many objected to the manner in which this was attempted. Foxites denied that popular agitation was the problem Tories claimed it to be. Grenvillites left the opposition in 1817, favouring repression, while Grey condemned both the government for its repressive measures and the radicals for dangerously raising the expectations of a distressed people. Some Foxites suggested that parliamentary reform had become more urgently necessary than ever, and that it would calm the nation and protect rather than destroy established institutions. Yet it was not clear what kind of reform would bring these benefits, and few MPs, of whatever party or connection, were willing to countenance the advanced schemes of plebeian radicals. Conservatives in parliament and out of doors insisted that parliamentary reform was unnecessary. The variety of voting qualifications was an advantage, they maintained, for the flexible system admitted all interests and classes, including workers (particularly in scot and lot and pot-walloper boroughs). Representation could not be judged according to numbers, but properly rested on property and rank, and representation had always been virtual rather than direct. No person or place was unrepresented, thought defenders of the existing arrangements, because MPs put the national interest above the local and sectional concerns of their own constituencies. The vote was a trust, not a right, and could not be extended to those who might use it irresponsibly. Memories of previous periods of unrest prompted conservatives to repeat old arguments that reform would lead to chaos and possibly social and political revolution.

Loyalists and conservatives out of doors offered continued assistance to the government, increasing the pressure on reformers, facilitating the prosecution of radical publishers and writers, and forming associations to assist in preserving public order. There was general support for the Liverpool government in difficult times, as it tried to defend respected institutions. Though there were some opposition gains at the 1818 general election, ministers could still depend on a Commons majority, and the 1820 general election necessitated by the death of George III (by statute an election was required within six months of the sovereign's death) did not alter the relative strengths of government and opposition. Furthermore, government could normally rely on the support of landed gentry, Church, universities and municipal corporations. Postwar Toryism rested on this union of interest among holders of property and privilege. Tories were content with the existing order. They opposed disturbing and unnecessary change, and trusted Liverpool's administration to respond to new situations by employing conservative ideas and methods. They wanted social peace, economic prosperity and political stability after the long war. Repression in 1817 and 1819 won the approval and co-operation of organised extra-parliamentary conservatism, particularly Pitt Clubs, yeomanry units and loyal associations in aid of the civil power. This voluntary loyalist activity was not as vigorous as it had been in wartime, but was nevertheless a useful asset to Liverpool's government. It was influential even in large towns where radicalism was strong. As in past times, ministers found that they could rely on the inveterate suspicion with which the propertied classes contemplated plebeian assertiveness.

Of more lasting concern to the government than popular agitation were financial and economic problems. There may have been a lack of confidence and expertise within the government on these matters. Few politicians could deal proficiently with abstract economic questions, and not until the mid-1820s did the cabinet's command of commercial and financial details become more convincing (and even then there was much disagreement among ministers). The most controversial matters after 1815 related to the unstable currency, agricultural protection and the government's urgent need for revenue.

Financial instability had seriously disturbed business, trade and credit, and there had been rising inflation since the suspension of specie payments in 1797. Though the flexible currency facilitated wartime industrial expansion, by 1815 inflation had detrimentally affected lower-class living standards. Many merchants and manufacturers were demanding an end to the paper system and a return to 'sound money', because they considered the latter more convenient for commerce. The parliamentary opposition was also pressing for the resumption of specie payments. Liverpool and his colleagues did not want to make any hasty moves, however, and they had to respect the Bank of England's advice against premature resumption (ministers needed to co-operate with the Bank: its loans were essential because of the loss of income tax). The government postponed resumption in 1816 and 1818, but increasing pressure necessitated the appointment of a Commons finance committee in 1819. The committee was chaired by Peel, and it recommended resumption in four stages between 1820 and 1823. In practice, note issues were reduced too quickly. This created further controversy, and there were many radicals, businessmen and provincial bankers who opposed resumption on the grounds that it would worsen the postwar depression. Ministers were accused of being too concerned to protect the interests of fundholders, the creditors of the nation who would now benefit from interest payments in money of increased value. Agricultural distress reinforced this argument. The problems of landowners and farmers were traced by some commentators to deflationary pressures resulting from resumption of specie payments. Thomas Attwood, the Birmingham banker and ironmaster, emerged as a leading opponent of the government's financial policy, but it was generally believed that the financial reforms would work well, and that they were necessary. This was certainly the view of the Bank of England, most political economists, opposition MPs and the business interests which depended on foreign markets. The nation needed a stable currency, they argued, and gold was its best possible basis.

One of the tests of the government's financial competence was the extent to which it carried retrenchment. There were ceaseless demands for more savings. Liverpool and his colleagues made a genuine effort to end waste and control expenditure, while complaining about the government's lack of funds. The loss of income tax meant increases in indirect taxation, which pressed more severely on the poor than on the wealthy, and more loans, which in turn added to the national debt. Savings were made, but critics asserted that ministers were not going far enough. Liverpool protested that it would be dangerous to carry retrenchment too far, since government had to have the resources to perform its proper functions. There were heavy reductions in the civil and military establishments, the civil list and official salaries, but pressure for retrenchment did not quickly recede.

British agriculture did not adjust well to the change from war to peace. The prospect of declining farm prices and rents created alarm, and currency reforms hardly dispelled this growing anxiety. Debt became a serious problem. Many farmers and landlords had prospered while agriculture boomed during the war, and they had taken out loans when prices were high and demand was rising. Now they had to pay heavy interest at a time of falling prices and new competitive forces. They welcomed the 1815 corn law and expected ever more government assistance, but the government was reluctant to interfere because it had no wish to take on further responsibilities. Ministers called upon farmers and landowners to adapt to new conditions and rely less on protective regulations. But Liverpool's administration needed the political support of landlords and knew that agriculture was still a big employer. The cabinet was also disturbed by anti-protectionist criticism of the 1815 corn law, and disappointed to find that the law was not working as intended. It brought no stability in price or supply, and farm incomes were falling. This satisfied neither producer nor consumer. The act was too rigid: it veered between total prohibition on imports when the price of corn was below 80s a quarter, and unrestricted entry when the price rose above that figure. The landed interests demanded something more than the 1815 corn law. Ministers agreed to revise their policy, but for national rather than sectional reasons. They sought to safeguard food supplies when the population was known to be rapidly expanding. Liverpool and his colleagues therefore tried again to oblige agriculture to adjust to peacetime conditions, in order to help consumers as well as producers. According to the ministers' rhetoric, they had to attend to the needs of the whole community, not just one part of it. They had a duty to balance all the great interests of the nation. The corn law of 1822 implemented a sliding scale of duties. It was intended to be more flexible than the 1815 act, but it brought no solution because the sliding scale was not to operate until the 80s entry price was reached, and this never happened while the 1822 measure was in force. As pressure from the opponents of agricultural protection increased, landowners and farmers still complained that government could do more to help, and the corn question continued to be controversial and divisive through the 1820s.

Meanwhile ministers were engaged in a constant struggle to balance the budget. In the postwar years they raided the sinking fund (a departure from Pitt's policy), increased indirect taxation and borrowed to redeem existing debt. The government was vulnerable on financial questions. This offered hope to the parliamentary opposition, whose leaders repeatedly argued that ministers were signally failing to stabilise the nation's finances and had nothing to offer but hazardous stopgaps. Almost two-thirds of public expenditure now went to service the national debt, and it was not possible to balance the budget by manipulating the remaining third. The government needed more revenue and a bolder approach to financial problems. Hence Liverpool made sound finance his priority, knowing that this would win support in the Commons and in the nation, and that the disappointing election results of 1818 made regaining the control which had been lost in 1816 on income tax even more urgent. Clearly, financial improvements would deprive the opposition of its best chance to undermine the ministry's position. In 1819 the government resumed specie payments and announced plans to reorganise the sinking fund, foster debt redemption, curb inflation and introduce new taxes. This programme (rather than Peterloo) made 1819 a vital year in the history of Liverpool's administration, for here was the beginning of financial recovery. But it was still imperative to increase revenue, particularly from customs and excise. Therefore the 1820s saw a sustained effort to promote commercial and industrial expansion.

The parliamentary opposition

The Foxite–Grenvillite alliance had never been very secure. Between the end of the war and the Grenvillite defection of 1817 there was persistent internal argument, though Grey did his best to keep the opposition united. He and Tierney thought it best to refrain from trying to do too much, believing that if the opposition was active, it would be even more difficult to keep it together. The progressive wing wanted more meaningful commitment to reforms and constantly complained about Grenvillite conservatism, while the Grenvillites put pressure on Grey to keep pro-reform Whigs in line. Quarrels broke out over specific issues, notably the 1815 corn law. Grenville considered it an improper use of political power by landowners, and he disliked intervention by the state in economic affairs. But Grey endorsed protection for the landed interests and welcomed the corn law as a means of ensuring a regular supply of corn and promoting price stability. Grey also realised that the measure was very unpopular out of doors, however, and though the Whigs claimed to be the party of the people, most of them voted with the ministry on corn. Many Whig MPs were themselves landowners, and their aristocratic leaders possessed some of the largest estates in the country. As Tierney noted, Whig support for the 1815 corn law allowed radicals to argue even more forcefully than before that government and opposition were as selfish and untrustworthy as each other. Another problem was the continuing lack of effective leadership in the Commons. Tierney was accepted as leader there from 1817, but he resigned in 1821 because of the party's internal divisions. The Whigs had no recognised leader in the Commons until Viscount Althorp assumed this responsibility in 1830.

By this time the opposition consisted mainly of old Foxites and their heirs and associates. Most of the Grenvillites seceded in 1817. They joined Liverpool's conservative alliance four years later. The split was occasioned by a disagreement about the ministry's response to postwar radical agitation. Foxites were still presenting themselves as guardians of liberty, and ministers as servants of the corrupt court, but Grenville insisted that all governments had a duty to maintain order. His union with Grey came to an end when he voted for suspension of habeas corpus.

Grenvillites did not join Liverpool immediately, but when the opportunity arose the prime minister was quick to purchase their support. In 1821 Liverpool finally reunited the old Pittite connection which had crumbled after 1801. Grenvillites controlled twenty seats in the Commons. These were now added to the government's majority, there was a dukedom for Grenville's nephew the Marquess of Buckingham, and Buckingham's cousin Charles Wynn was taken into the cabinet.

The loss of the Grenvillites was a blow to Grey, but opposition numbers in parliament eventually rose again and Grey's son-in-law, J. G. Lambton, hoped that a remodelled Whig opposition would now be able to identify itself openly with progressive causes. Grey believed that unity was more important than commitment to specific measures, however, and he had no wish to push anti-reform peers like Fitzwilliam (who had been reunited with Fox after 1801) over to the government side. To those who questioned his consistency, Grey declared that he would simply destroy his party if he tried to commit it to parliamentary reform. Why hinder Whig usefulness on other questions, he asked, just for the sake of firmer commitment to parliamentary reform? Grey's strategy was to keep opposition credible by focusing on three main goals: public retrenchment, a non-interventionist foreign policy and Catholic emancipation. Though Grey personally favoured moderate parliamentary reform, this was not a party policy and if any Whig MP wished to propose it he had to do so in his individual capacity.

Retrenchment remained an invaluable cause for the Whigs. It promoted unity (unlike parliamentary reform), and was an issue on which they could exploit the ministry's lack of strong speakers in the Commons. Cheaper government was a theme taken up with great alacrity by both Tierney and Brougham. They attacked the court as well as the ministry, demanding reductions in the civil list and objecting to all special grants to the crown, including those made to encourage George III's surviving sons to marry and produce legitimate heirs after the death of the prince regent's only child, Princess Charlotte, in 1817. The 1816 session was highly successful for the opposition because attention was focused on taxation and expenditure, and financial management became very difficult for ministers once they lost the Commons vote on income tax. But in 1817 radical agitation pushed financial questions into the background. In response to government repression some Whigs strongly condemned the ministers for their arbitrary interference with the people's rights, uttering arguments that were solidly in the Foxite tradition. Lord John Russell, one of the rising young Whigs in the Commons, claimed that the constitution was most endangered not by radicals but by those who denied the need for reform. Radical MP Burdett joined in the protest against the measures of 1817, and he accused ministers of creating alarm in order to destroy the reform movement. But the opposition never mustered more than a hundred votes against the government's repressive bills (and of course Grenvillites voted with ministers). Whigs then tried to turn parliamentary and public attention back to finance, a more promising issue for them. Some wanted to reinvigorate the party by declaring for moderate parliamentary reform. Though Fitzwilliam lent his considerable support to the protest about 'Oliver the Spy' after the Pentridge Rising, he and his friends still opposed an open party commitment to parliamentary reform. Grey and Tierney agreed that the party should concentrate on defending liberty and forcing cuts in public expenditure.

In 1818 economic conditions improved and popular radicalism appeared to lose ground, but even in these calmer times Grey would not commit the Whigs to parliamentary reform. He had noticed how easy it was for ministers to take advantage of unrest in 1817 after being shaken by Commons defeats on finance in 1816. This made Grey all the more determined to avoid constitutional questions and revive the attack on the government's financial policies. Financial muddle and the ministry's apparent unwillingness to do anything about postwar economic depression helped to produce some gains for the Whigs at the 1818 general election, but ministers soon responded with determined efforts to promote sound finance in 1819, demonstrating the government's competence and narrowing Whig options in the process.

As Brougham, Tierney, Holland and other prominent Whigs demanded that opposition should be more energetic, Grey maintained that there could be no firm commitment to parliamentary reform and no close association with the radicals. Meanwhile Russell was gathering support from Whig MPs for a piecemeal disfranchisement of corrupt boroughs. Holland was sure that all sections of the opposition would back this, but Grey was doubtful. In prevalent conditions it seemed impossible to design a reform that would unite the party, and win respectable support out of doors, without assisting the radicals. Peterloo and extra-parliamentary protest presented new opportunities, and Whig leaders believed that they could guide or at least take advantage of this pressure. Grey was not ready to press for parliamentary reform, but he attempted to use Peterloo to discredit both the Liverpool government and plebeian radicalism. He denounced the massacre and demanded a public inquiry, while stressing that the conduct of Hunt and his cohorts gave the government an excuse to restrict liberty. It is significant, however, that most Whigs were stirred not by the massacre itself, but by the government's decision to strip Fitzwilliam of his lord lieutenancy of the West Riding when he publicly condemned the Manchester authorities: this humiliation of a senior Whig peer seemed to matter more than redress for reformers. The parliamentary opposition made little progress in the aftermath of Peterloo. Ministers passed new emergency laws with comfortable majorities, and Whigs refused to co-operate with radicals out of doors. Grey's middle course was followed by most Whigs in the Commons. They criticised government repression, pressed for an inquiry into Peterloo, and reproached the radicals for improper tactics and goals. Grey was annoyed, though, because some of his allies welcomed the Six Acts as necessary precautions in the conditions of the time.

The opposition was not united, therefore, and Grey was irritated by continuing arguments. Some Whigs regarded the sentences meted out to Hunt and other radical leaders in 1820 as excessive, while others deemed harsh punishments appropriate. Grey was shocked by some of the language used in the House of Lords, which reminded him of the early years of the French Revolution. Whigs were disconcerted, moreover, by decisive ministerial majorities in parliament after Peterloo. Lambton decided that the Whigs would have no future as a viable party, and no support out of doors, unless they committed themselves to parliamentary reform. Grey temporised. Perhaps the party could take up the issue when circumstances improved, he told Lambton. Grey blamed the radicals for this difficult situation, for they had discredited reform so badly that a clear commitment from the parliamentary opposition might be counterproductive. Grey stated that Whigs were still free to propose reform as individuals, though, and Lambton and Russell took full advantage of this dispensation.

In December 1819 they both addressed the Commons on parliamentary reform. Lambton gave notice of a plan to abolish rotten boroughs, shorten the duration of parliaments, and enfranchise copyholders and rate-paying householders. Lambton was offended by Holland's private criticism of the scheme, but Grey also thought it too drastic. Meanwhile Russell had formulated a less controversial strategy, designed to eradicate abuses and preserve the constitution from decay while leaving its essential features unimpaired. Russell had in mind the gradual alteration of the representative system, and he told the Commons that the cardinal requirement was a transfer of seats. When a borough was convicted of bribery and corruption, Russell argued, it should lose its seats. These could be transferred to a large town or county. In the past, elective rights had been awarded and removed in accordance with the changing population, wealth and importance of particular places. This was nothing new, Russell said, and to begin the present operation he proposed to award the seats of a corrupt Cornish borough, Grampound, to a populous town. Once this process of identifying and disfranchising corrupt boroughs began, Russell thought, the electoral system would gradually reform itself. But Castlereagh, the leader of the House, strongly objected to Russell's plan. While it was appropriate to punish corrupt voters, Castlereagh explained, a general reform scheme could not work because every case had to be treated according to its circumstances. Castlereagh argued that Russell should have confined himself to one case, not outlined a general and continuous process of reform. Russell therefore withdrew his plan and announced that he would in due course introduce a bill specifically to disfranchise Grampound and transfer its seats to a large town.

Russell was true to his word, and during the disfranchisement bill's committee stages in February 1821 he pressed forcefully for Grampound's seats to be awarded to Leeds. The county and boroughs of Cornwall already returned forty-four MPs, he stated, and it would not be appropriate for the seats to go to Grampound's neighbouring hundreds (a customary remedy for corruption) when the thriving industrial town of Leeds lacked direct representation. But Russell's proposal aroused heated argument, and many MPs did not wish to establish a precedent for the future. Eventually it was decided that the Grampound seats should be transferred to the county of Yorkshire. Russell's defeat again prompted some Whigs to urge their party leaders unequivocally to take up parliamentary reform, but Grey repeated that this should remain a matter of individual judgement rather than party policy. Lambton prepared a bill to shorten the duration of parliaments to three years, revise constituency boundaries in England and Wales, and enfranchise all copyholders, leaseholders, resident householders and payers of direct tax. In April 1821 he moved for a committee to consider the representative system, intending to submit his bill for discussion, but the proposal was easily defeated.

By this time the opposition was deeply engaged in the Queen Caroline controversy. This came as an important opportunity for the Whigs, but it also created difficulties. Though they welcomed the chance to attack court and ministry, some Whig leaders disapproved of Caroline's character and the nature of her extra-parliamentary support, and were reluctant to identify themselves closely with a campaign they found sordid and disreputable. Nevertheless, they did try to take advantage of what was a perilous situation for the ministers. Relations between cabinet and king deteriorated. There was an upsurge in agitation out of doors, and the introduction of the bill of pains and penalties led to rancorous debates in the Lords as peers considered evidence relating to the queen's adultery. There were strong objections to certain parts of the bill. Some peers considered its wording too degrading to monarchy. Others wanted to pass it without a divorce clause. Grey, Lord Lansdowne and senior Whigs denounced the 'Queen's trial', but sought to retain objectionable parts of the bill in the hope that more peers would turn against the government. In November the Lords passed the bill by a slim majority. Ministers knew they could not carry it through the Commons, so they abandoned it. Whigs celebrated, and some of them expected a change of ministers. There was much speculation, but in the event the king was not prepared to revive his old connection with the Whigs nor turn for advice to men who had condemned the bill of pains and penalties. Furthermore, had George IV dismissed Liverpool, Grey would probably not have been able to form a lasting administration. Grey knew that his party was not united, and he was reluctant to take office while the Queen Caroline affair was the leading issue of the day. Lambton, Fitzwilliam, Holland and other Whigs had insisted all along that the 'Queen's trial' should not be made a party question, and that the Whigs should not be seen to have made use of the affair for party purposes. A close association with the queen or her radical supporters, they thought, would be degrading. There was also the problem posed by Brougham, who was committed to the queen. He would insist on being leader of the House of Commons in any new Whig ministry, but Grey did not trust him. In addition, the Whigs were still numerically weak in parliament. Grey doubted that a Whig cabinet would be able to control the Commons, and he was painfully aware that this cabinet would have to deal with the queen. The coronation and wording of the liturgy still had to be arranged, and the king would oppose any move to settle these matters in Caroline's favour. For a number of reasons, therefore, Grey did not want to take office at this juncture, even if he were given the opportunity.

Liverpool's administration was not unaffected by agitation out of doors, royal displeasure, and pressure from the parliamentary opposition, but it survived. The prime minister's main concern at this time was Canning's resignation. In earlier years Canning had been on close terms with the queen, and in 1820 he decided not to support the parliamentary proceedings against her. Canning also resented the fact that he had not yet been promoted to a senior post in the cabinet (he was still president of the board of control). He left the cabinet in December 1820. Liverpool and other ministers were worried that this would make them more vulnerable: though a difficult colleague, Canning was one of the best speakers in the Commons. This was far more important to the cabinet than the threat posed by the queen and her supporters. The crisis passed, however, and Caroline's popularity faded. Whigs were unable to pass motions censuring the government's treatment of the queen and the removal of her name from the liturgy. The opposition's lack of success in this respect soon prompted Whig allies of the queen to fall silent. The party leadership was still held back by concern for its honour and reputation, and it chose not to place itself at the head of any popular movement in the country. Grey was relieved when Caroline died in August 1821, Russell distanced himself from outdoor reformers, and on economic and financial questions there was less boldness and energy on the opposition side than in previous years. Whigs were unable build up more support in parliament or nation in the period following the 'Queen's trial'.

There was continual argument about parliamentary reform. Some Whigs (Fitzwilliam and his friends) were unwilling to sanction reform, and though it appeared that most of the party might be persuaded to back a moderate plan, it was not clear that this would win sufficient public approval. The decline of radicalism in the more prosperous conditions of the 1820s meant that there no longer seemed to be so much interest in the question out of doors, while the prevalent opinion in parliament was that Liverpool's ministry was providing good government. In April 1826 Russell tried to bring parliamentary reform before the Commons for debate, but his efforts now seemed irrelevant because the ministry's more constructive policies during the 1820s proved that necessary improvements could be gained from the unreformed legislature. Hardly any reference was made in parliament to the state of the representative system during the mid-1820s, and the Commons received no reform petitions at all between 1824 and 1829.

Meanwhile Grey continued to believe that party unity was more important than a definite commitment to particular policies. Parliamentary reform was not the issue to unite the party, he thought, and in any case the type of reform required to attract popular support for the Whigs, and genuinely to improve political life, would involve much more than the moderate schemes advanced in recent times. Grey spoke of transferring at least a hundred seats, reducing the duration of parliaments to five years, and extending the county franchise to copyholders, but he despaired of persuading Fitzwilliam and other party grandees to approve such a plan.

Whigs preferred to act upon the one question on which they could all agree, Catholic emancipation. In May 1819 a motion was defeated in the Commons by only two votes. Peel, rapidly establishing a reputation as the Protestant champion in the lower house, was uneasy about the narrowness of this margin and doubted that emancipation could be put off for much longer. Liverpool also realised that trouble lay ahead. In 1821 an emancipation bill passed the Commons and was rejected by the Lords, and the prime minister recommended that George IV should not commit himself on the question, in case he robbed the government of room to manoeuvre in the future (Liverpool expected the matter to be raised again before a new House of Commons was returned at the next general election). Emancipation remained an open question in cabinet. Liverpool could not risk losing talented ministers who favoured emancipation, since they were responsible for some of the government's most important policies of the early 1820s. Meanwhile Grey held that the Whig association with the Catholic cause was essential to the party's identity and unity. Emancipation remained one of the Whigs' main goals, along with restraining the corrupt executive and defeating its designs against liberty. The return of the liberal, pro-Catholic Canning to Liverpool's ministry in 1822 led some Whigs to think that more progressive policies would ensue, and that Canning's rise would bring Catholic emancipation closer. Holland, Brougham and Russell thought so, but Grey had long believed that the Whigs could depend on Canning for nothing.

Other opposition goals during the 1820s included retrenchment and cheaper government, the abolition of sinecures, and lower taxation. Whigs also interested themselves in the controversy over the corn laws, appealing to Tory squires on the government's back benches, and asserting that the ministry was not doing enough for agriculture. Individual Whigs also championed popular education, penal reform and the cause of liberty abroad. But Liverpool's government was more secure and successful in the 1820s. Moderate reforms, expanding trade and rising prosperity made the task of opposition increasingly difficult. Grey became more depressed and pessimistic. He hardly attended the parliamentary sessions of 1823, 1824 and 1825, and party discipline suffered. The issue on which Whigs were most active and united was the Catholic question, but this was not enough to establish Grey's party as an influential opposition. In February 1826 Grey resigned the Whig leadership to Lansdowne.

'Liberal' Toryism and unresolved problems

Liverpool's administration withstood the pressures of the postwar years. Indeed, periods of adversity bound ministers together and strengthened their sense of collective identity. Even the breach with George IV over his attempted divorce was not fatal, and despite the king's resistance Liverpool repeatedly tried to bring Canning back into the cabinet, and eventually succeeded (George IV had been deeply offended by Canning's refusal to support the bill of pains and penalties). Liverpool's cabinet gradually secured itself in power. It was noted for the ability of individual ministers and for competent administration, and it benefited considerably from the weaknesses of the Whig opposition, economic recovery in the early 1820s, the crown's declining political influence, and George IV's lack of an alternative set of advisers who could command a parliamentary majority.

There were some important ministerial changes. Peel became home secretary in January 1822. Later that year depression and overwork got the better of Castlereagh, and he committed suicide. Canning was brought back to succeed him as foreign secretary and leader in the Commons. Liverpool overcame the objections of senior Tories as well as the king to bring back a man who had made many enemies because of his arrogance and ambition. Canning was considered too liberal by some, and his support for Catholic emancipation was held against him, but the prime minister insisted that the cabinet could not go on unless Canning returned. Others resented Canning's rise and complained of his influence over Liverpool (Canning's relations with more conservative cabinet colleagues, notably Wellington, would frequently be close to breaking point). In January 1823 Robinson became chancellor of the exchequer, and in October William Huskisson joined the cabinet as president of the board of trade. Peel, Canning, Robinson and Huskisson added substantially to the cabinet's talent and influence. Liverpool continued to guide general policy. A highly respected figure, pragmatic and conciliatory, Liverpool kept the ministry united and oversaw the personnel changes of 1822 and 1823 with great tact. The new ministers created for the government a reputation for progressivism and efficiency. Now that postwar difficulties were receding, a more flexible approach to political, social and economic problems was possible. The new mood and the new men brought about a period of 'liberal' Toryism.

There was no sharp break with the past, however, and the ministers who rose to dominate government during the 1820s were not really new. They had been shaping policy for years in junior posts. Ministerial changes brought no ideological shift; 'liberal' Toryism was more a matter of different methods. It is also clear that the immediate cause of cabinet changes was political necessity. Defeats in the Commons during 1821 forced Liverpool to try to strengthen the government's front bench there, in order to improve the ministry's reputation after the 'Queen's trial', to prevent the king from replacing ministers, and to attract more support in the lower house. This is not to deny the significance of the new appointments. Toryism as a governing creed lost some of its former conservative, managerial rigidity after 1821, and there was a more obvious commitment to economic progress, social improvement and administrative expertise. This accorded with the talents and views of dominant ministers, but also with the needs and opportunities of the time. Policies could now be framed and implemented in a period of prosperity and social peace.

'Liberal' Toryism is a useful concept, and rests on a combination of men, measures and prevalent conditions. It offers a framework for comparing the government of the 1820s with that of 1812 to 1821, though it cannot be taken to indicate a conscious, intentional or sudden change from one set of policies to another. Though Liverpool's cabinet became a reforming ministry, there was no question of structural change. Reforms were confined to administrative, financial, commercial and social spheres, and ministers were determined that the established order in Church and state should be shielded from innovation just as strenuously as before.

Older accounts of the Liverpool administration, such as those of W. R. Brock and Derek Beales, stress the differences between 'reactionary' and 'liberal' phases of Toryism, but more recent interpretations assume an underlying continuity. Boyd Hilton assesses the ministerial changes of the early 1820s in the light of Liverpool's capacity for artful political manoeuvre, and J. E. Cookson suggests that the appointments are significant mainly because of what they reveal about the environment within which government had to operate. Norman Gash argues that many policies would have been the same even had Peel, Canning, Robinson and Huskisson not joined the cabinet at this time. Ministerial changes did not bring a totally new direction, writes Gash, because Liverpool's cabinet was reorganised to implement measures already under consideration.[16]

A commitment to sound finance and the determination to raise more revenue from customs and excise predate the appointments of 1822 and 1823, though commercial and financial improvements did become more obvious as responsibility for them passed to Robinson and Huskisson along with Liverpool. These three ministers shared a strong attachment to liberal economic ideas and sought to accelerate the movement towards freer trade. The government was also influenced by advice from prominent political economists, pressure from business communities in ports and large trading towns, reports from parliamentary committees, and the economic policies of foreign states. Robinson, Huskisson and Liverpool assumed that government could most successfully assist industry and commerce by removing obstacles to economic activity and following a course of non-intervention. Many duties were reduced or removed, the navigation laws were relaxed, and taxes were cut. Growing trade brought in more revenue and enabled the ministry to experiment with the budget and sinking fund arrangements. There were banking reforms and further efforts to stabilise the currency, seen as essential for sustained economic improvement. But the approach remained more pragmatic than ideological. Boyd Hilton and John Derry have shown that liberal economic theory was used to justify rather than originate measures, and that ministers employed only those idioms and ideas that best suited their immediate objectives.[17] Commercial and financial reforms were cautious rather than thorough, partly because of heated protest from shipping, commercial and manufacturing interests which had prospered behind protective tariffs and were likely to suffer from freer trade. An economic crisis in 1825 and 1826 temporarily interrupted the growth in prosperity and confidence, making the government even more wary. In addition, ministers had no wish to create difficulties in parliament by pushing reforms too far too quickly. They were still committed to maintaining a balance of interests in the nation, with the state as arbiter.

Ministers were acutely aware of the need for a settlement of the corn question. The controversies to which this had given rise forced them constantly to assure landowners and farmers that government would respect their wishes. But it was extremely difficult to frame an agricultural policy which would appease the landed interests without harming other classes in the community. Ministers thought that the rapid expansion of trade was bound to assist agriculture, and that general prosperity would be a safeguard against agricultural depression. Farmers and landowners wanted another corn law, however, since the 1822 measure had done nothing to protect the home grower or promote price stability. Some landed men also wanted a depreciation of the currency, to recreate the favourable inflationary conditions of wartime. Ministers resisted. They said they could not favour one section of the community at the expense of everyone else, and urged the landed interests to modernise farming techniques, use land more efficiently, and reorganise production in accordance with the requirements of available markets. Economic and financial difficulties in 1825 and 1826 brought forth a wave of condemnation against the government's liberalisation policies. Strikes and riots occurred in many regions. Demands grew for freer trade to be abandoned, and Huskisson was singled out for particular abuse. His critics claimed that he should not have reduced so many tariffs, while free traders insisted that problems had arisen only because Huskisson had not gone far enough. The enlargement of economic freedom was not reversed, and a liberal approach was seen in other areas too: in Peel's reform of the criminal code, Canning's support for liberal and constitutional states abroad, and the government's decision to accept repeal of the Combination Acts in 1824. All these policies attracted varying degrees of criticism.

The ministry stood firm. Distress was temporary and would soon pass, Liverpool argued, and government would do more harm than good by interfering in economic and social affairs.

Landowners demanded action, but in the spring of 1826 ministers announced that nothing could be done to settle the corn question in view of the proximity of a general election: the new parliament would have to deal with it. Then the government secured a temporary relaxation of corn regulations because a poor harvest raised alarm about food shortages. Agriculturalists feared that this would be a step towards full repeal, and organised further protests, while those radicals who advocated corn law repeal were annoyed that ministers had provided for only a temporary suspension.

Even more controversial than the corn question, and also in need of a decisive manoeuvre, was the issue of Catholic emancipation. Peel became increasingly uncomfortable as his fellow ministers in the Commons spoke and voted for emancipation, and he had to work under a leader in the Commons, Canning, who was one of the Catholics' strongest advocates. Liverpool insisted that emancipation must remain an open question in cabinet, for this was the only way to ensure sound government. Ministers could be for or against emancipation as individuals, but the administration's position was strictly neutral, a compromise enabling men of talent to co-operate in office even if they disagreed with each other on the most divisive issue of the age (an issue, moreover, which they all knew had contributed to the fall of ministries in 1801 and 1807).

The situation changed during the 1820s. The Commons passed emancipation bills in 1821, 1822 and 1825, all of which were defeated in the Lords. It seemed that the two branches of the legislature were heading for serious conflict, and Liverpool, Peel, the rest of the cabinet and a majority of outside commentators saw that eventually, as on so many other questions, the decision of the Commons would prevail. The matter was complicated by the rise of Canning and by serious unrest in Ireland. Canning favoured emancipation, and as he emerged as one of the most influential ministers during the mid-1820s it was widely expected that he would exert himself to carry an emancipation bill. But this embarrassed him. Canning had to respect Liverpool's wish that emancipation should remain an open question in cabinet, and he knew that king, Tory party and public opinion were against concessions. He searched for a way to aid the Catholic cause and prove that he had not abandoned former convictions without endangering his political future and position in the cabinet. Disturbances in Ireland did not permit procrastination, however. Agitation was fomented by the Catholic Association, led by Dublin lawyer Daniel O'Connell and supported by Catholic priests and gentry and the mass of the Irish peasantry. The Association was suppressed by parliament in 1825, but O'Connell subsequently revived it in a new form.

Following the Lords' rejection of Burdett's emancipation bill of 1825, Peel told Liverpool that he intended to resign from the cabinet. His views on the Catholic question were not those of the majority in the Commons, and he regretted having to speak against all four of his ministerial colleagues in the lower house (Canning, Huskisson, Robinson and Wynn). The prime minister was also considering resignation at this juncture, and the cabinet was then thrown into turmoil by Canning's recommendation that Catholic emancipation should no longer be an open question. Canning's enemies in the cabinet insisted that he should resign if he was no longer prepared to accept the government's neutral stance, but Liverpool maintained that the ministry could not carry on without him. Liverpool persuaded Canning to relent, and the crisis ended when Peel agreed to remain in place. Peel did not wish to be blamed for bringing the ministry down, and he had been assured by colleagues that resignation would not be best way to serve the Protestant cause.

For the Whigs, Catholic emancipation was a unifying purpose, but there was still no agreed position on parliamentary reform. In Liverpool's administration the situation was reversed. Ministers looked upon the settled constitution as an essential framework for effective administration, social progress and economic improvement, and they maintained that it should be passed on intact to later generations. Tories generally thought that there was no overwhelming demand for parliamentary reform, no need for it, and no obvious advantages to be gained by it. Liverpool never thought of taking the initiative on this issue, and his cabinet was rather more united in opposition to parliamentary reform than it was on Catholic emancipation. Economic progress and the government's commercial and financial policies made arguments for parliamentary reform less persuasive. Lansdowne recognised this, commenting that even committed radicals lost interest in reform when the nation prospered. Liverpool, Canning, Peel and their colleagues were trying to tackle the problems which gave rise to pressure for structural change, in order to remove that pressure. This strategy was successful. Administrative, financial and commercial improvements began to silence the demand for parliamentary reform. Ministers were able to preserve aristocratic government by claiming to rule for the benefit of the whole nation, not just special interests, and by demonstrating competence and flexibility. Liverpool's administration won the approval of moderate mainstream opinion in the country, and moved to occupy the centre ground of politics in the 1820s.

But pressure on the corn and Catholic issues from inside and outside parliament could not be subdued, and at times the ministers' relations with their own backbenchers were seriously strained. The cabinet may have hoped that the general election of June 1826 would clarify the situation and present government with some pleasing options. It had already been decided that the corn regulations should be revised. Huskisson stated his preference for a small fixed duty rather than a sliding scale, but agriculturalists protested that they needed more protection, not less. They realised, however, that commercial reforms had left agriculture vulnerable as the last great interest still benefiting from protective barriers. Landowners also knew that Liverpool's ministry had made much of its duty to put national above sectional concerns. The prime minister was sorry that the 1822 corn law had been a failure, and the cabinet decided to make another effort in the new parliament after the 1826 election. Liverpool favoured an amended sliding scale of duties. Canning, Huskisson, Robinson and most of the cabinet agreed on this, and they were reassured by reports from the continent that European grain surpluses were not as large as had previously been predicted. Hence the British market would not be flooded with cheap foreign grain if the corn regulations were amended. At the election, in some urban constituencies, critics of the corn laws did well, but Catholic emancipation proved to be the dominant issue in many areas. There were victories for emancipation candidates in Ireland, while the 'No Popery' cry had considerable effect in England. On balance the Protestant gain at the 1826 general election may have been thirty seats, though G. I. T. Machin suggests a figure of sixteen.[18]

Various calculations were made, but it was hard to predict the temper of the new House of Commons. Preparations were made for major debates on corn and Catholics, scheduled to begin in March 1827. Before this, however, the government began to disintegrate. Liverpool suffered a serious stroke on 17 February 1827, and it quickly became obvious that he would not recover sufficiently to remain in public life. For years he had managed to balance forces within the cabinet, and had persuaded its members to work together despite their personal animosities and differing ideas on prominent public issues. Liverpool never lost the respect of his cabinet colleagues and political supporters, and his sensible course during the 1820s had rested on a principle with which many contemporaries agreed: government should not attempt to do too much, though it should act when appropriate to achieve conservative goals. Particularly difficult decisions had been postponed, however, and this may have been a mark not of Liverpool's tactical genius but of his lack of vision and boldness. Outstanding questions had not been resolved by the time he was forced to give up the premiership, an unfortunate legacy to his successors. Yet Liverpool had shrewdly decided (like Pitt before him) that in order to conserve, one had to be flexible, and early nineteenth-century Toryism splintered when it lost his leadership.

Conclusion

The Liverpool government came through the troubles of the difficult postwar years, finding it easy to rally support for property, order and conservative constitutionalism in times of popular agitation. Managing the Commons and restoring the national finances were more serious problems for the cabinet than the postwar radical campaign. In 1816 ministers suffered setbacks in parliament, especially on financial questions, and became increasingly vulnerable to criticism. It was several years before public finance was brought under control. Meanwhile, in 1817, ministers recovered the political initiative because of a radical upsurge and fears of disorder. In 1818 there was some improvement in trade, and popular agitation declined, but ministers experienced more difficulty in parliament on financial and economic questions (Liverpool often said that the government's real problem was in parliament, not in the nation). Unprecedented radical agitation in 1819 again restored the ministers' fortunes, and in this year they also adopted a bolder approach to finance. Peterloo was a shock, but the ministry's emergency legislation was welcomed by propertied ranks out of doors and even by some followers and allies of Grey in parliament. Liverpool's administration survived the Queen Caroline affair, and in the 1820s it appeared more confident and secure. Imaginative policies were pursued in line with new political and economic conditions. Changes in cabinet personnel brought greater influence for Canning, Peel and Huskisson, and the years of 'liberal' Toryism saw important reforms in nonconstitutional spheres. The government proved itself willing and able to respond to new circumstances. Here was a consummation of Pitt's creed of trustworthy and competent government. But there were unresolved problems for Liverpool's successors, especially corn, Catholics, and (to a lesser extent) parliamentary reform. In the spring of 1827 the Whigs, who for years had been struggling to maintain unity and morale, wondered if Liverpool's stroke would make possible their political recovery.

E. P. Thompson's phrase 'the heroic age of popular radicalism'[19] indicates the courage and commitment of those involved in postwar reform agitation. Radicalism developed into a mass movement after 1815 and posed a genuine threat to the established order, with its confident display, defiant and emotive slogans, and inclusive mobilisation. James Vernon's examination of this democratic and libertarian form of popular politics highlights the struggle between competing interpretations of the constitution. Of special importance were 'the political uses of outdoor spaces' and the 'language of the meeting-place'.[20] Reform associations arose to popularise ideas, goals and methods, and it is significant that many of them were named after John Hampden, the seventeenth-century opponent of Charles I's arbitrary rule. The continued growth of political consciousness after 1815 was a cause and effect of the expansion of the press and perfection of extra-parliamentary organisation. Though agitation declined after 1821, it provided a fund of experiences and examples to be drawn upon in later years. As in the 1790s, the ruling elite had been made aware of pressure from below. This was a development that could never be reversed, and though the insurrectionary fringe was not very influential, there was a dangerous ambiguity in the Huntite mass platform: strictly legal conduct did not preclude an implied threat of violence if demands were not satisfied. But protest was not just the affair of plebeian agitators. Powerful middle-class groups, especially merchants and manufacturers, condemned the government's economic policies and demanded more representation in parliament for their interests and localities. Respectable reformers welcomed the period of calm and plenty in the 1820s because this made possible the types of discussion and campaigning they most favoured: measured, constructive, non-violent. It was not clear what would happen if respectable radicalism came to full fruition, and if political and economic problems prompted a revival in mass mobilisation.

Notes

1 G. Hueckel, 'War and the British economy 1793–1815: a general equilibrium analysis', *Explorations in Economic History*, 10, 1973, pp. 365–96; P. Harling, *The Waning of 'Old Corruption'. The Politics of Economical Reform in Britain 1779–1846*, Oxford, 1996, ch. 4.

2 P. O'Brien, 'Political biography and Pitt the Younger as chancellor of the exchequer', *History*, 83, 1998, pp. 225–33.

3 N. Gash, 'Lord Liverpool and the foundation of Conservative policy', in Lord Butler (ed.), *The Conservatives. A History from their Origins to 1965*, London, 1977, p. 38.

4 J. A. Phillips, 'Popular politics in unreformed England', *JMH*, 52, 1980, pp. 599–625; P. Fraser, 'Public petitioning and parliament before 1832', *History*, 46, 1961, pp. 195–211; P. Brett, 'Political dinners in early nineteenth-century Britain: platform, meeting place and battleground', *History*, 81, 1996, pp. 527–52.

5 E. Halevy, *The Liberal Awakening 1815–30*, rev. edn, London, 1961, pp. 13–14; C. Calhoun, *The Question of Class Struggle. Social Foundations of Popular Radicalism during the Industrial Revolution*, Oxford, 1982.

6 J. Belchem, 'Henry Hunt and the evolution of the mass platform', *EHR*, 93, 1978, pp. 739–73.

7 J. Epstein, 'Understanding the cap of liberty: symbolic practice

and social conflict in early nineteenth-century England', *P&P*, 122, 1989, pp. 75–118.

8 J. Belchem, *Popular Radicalism in Nineteenth Century Britain*, Basingstoke, 1996, pp. 41–2.

9 M. J. Turner, *Reform and Respectability. The Making of a Middle-Class Liberalism in Early Nineteenth-Century Manchester*, Manchester, 1995, pp. 233–53.

10 See for example D. Read, *Peterloo. The Massacre and its Background*, 2nd edn, London, 1973; E. P. Thompson, *The Making of the English Working Class*, rev. edn, London, 1980, pp. 734–60; R. Walmsley, *Peterloo: The Case Reopened*, Manchester, 1969; *Manchester Region History Review*, 3, 1989, Peterloo Massacre special issue.

11 Belchem, 'Hunt and the mass platform', pp. 771–2.

12 C. Calhoun, *The Question of Class Struggle. Social Foundations of Popular Radicalism during the Industrial Revolution*, Oxford, 1982, pp. 105–15; Belchem, *Popular Radicalism*, pp. 49–50; J. Stevenson, *Popular Disturbances in England 1700–1832*, 2nd edn, London, 1992, pp. 245–51; T. W. Laqueur, 'The Queen Caroline affair: politics as art in the reign of George IV', *JMH*, 54, 1982, pp. 417–66; A. Clark, 'Queen Caroline and the sexual politics of popular culture in London 1820', *Representations*, 31, 1990, pp. 47–68; J. Fulcher, 'The loyalist response to the Queen Caroline agitations', *JBS*, 34, 1995, pp. 481–502.

13 N. Thompson, *The People's Science. The Popular Political Economy of Exploitation and Crisis 1816–34*, Cambridge, 1984; Belchem, *Popular Radicalism*, pp. 51–9.

14 J. Hamburger, *James Mill and the Art of Revolution*, New Haven, 1963; J. R. Dinwiddy, *Bentham*, Oxford, 1989, ch. 5, and 'Bentham's transition to political radicalism 1809–10', *JHI*, 36, 1975, pp. 683–700.

15 N. Gash, *Aristocracy and People. Britain 1815–65*, London, 1979, pp. 71–2; J. E. Cookson, *Lord Liverpool's Administration: The Crucial Years 1815–22*, Edinburgh, 1975, pp. 39–41; P. Fraser, 'Party voting in the House of Commons 1812–27', *EHR*, 98, 1983, pp. 763–84; A. Aspinall, 'English party organisation in the early nineteenth century', *EHR*, 41, 1926, pp. 389–411; R. G. Thorne, *The House of Commons 1790–1820*, London, 1986, vol. I, pp. 345–55; B. W. Hill, 'Executive monarchy and the challenge of the parties 1689–1832: two concepts of government and two historiographical interpretations', *HJ*, 13, 1970, pp. 379–401; F. O'Gorman, *The Emergence of the British Two-Party System, 1760–1832*, London, 1982, pp. 63–4, and 'Party politics in the early nineteenth century, 1812–32', *EHR*, 102, 1987, pp. 63–88; J. C. D. Clark, 'A general theory of party, opposition and government, 1688–1832', *HJ*, 23, 1980, pp. 295–325.

16 W. R. Brock, *Lord Liverpool and Liberal Toryism 1820 to 1827,* Cambridge, 1939, pp. 172–3, 182–3, 191–2; D. Beales, *From Castlereagh to Gladstone,* London, 1969, pp. 22–4, 78–9; A. J. B. Hilton, 'Lord Liverpool: the art of politics and the practice of government', *TRHS,* 5th series, 38, 1988, pp. 147–70; Cookson, *Lord Liverpool's Administration,* pp. 395–401; Gash, 'Liverpool and Conservative policy', pp. 48–9.

17 A. J. B. Hilton, *Corn, Cash and Commerce. The Economic Policies of the Tory Governments 1815–30,* Oxford, 1977; J. Derry, *Politics in the Age of Fox, Pitt and Liverpool,* Basingstoke, 1990, pp. 189–91.

18 G. I. T. Machin, *The Catholic Question in English Politics 1820–30,* Oxford, 1964, pp. 85–6.

19 Thompson, *Working Class,* p. 603.

20 J. Vernon, *Politics and the People. A Study in English Political Culture c. 1815–67,* Cambridge, 1993, ch. 6.

4

Instability and reform

Introduction

Liverpool's retirement from public life was followed by a period of political confusion. Tory and Whig connections fell apart during 1827, as two brief ministries under Canning and Viscount Goderich increased rather than allayed the bitterness and instability. Political realignment continued, but no lasting administration could be formed. Wellington became prime minister in 1828, only to resign in 1830, and he was unable to reunite the Tory party. Pressure had been building up for several years on key issues, particularly the corn laws, Catholic emancipation and parliamentary reform, and the manner in which Wellington's government addressed these problems encouraged both Whig revival and popular agitation. Extra-parliamentary political activity became more vital and influential than ever before at the end of the 1820s. Plebeian and respectable forms of radicalism were developing quickly, and reform campaigners had been evolving new organisations and methods of propaganda to direct opinion against the established order. Pressure from below had more impact because of instability at the top, and as parliamentary reform became the dominant issue of the time, the Whigs were finally able to form an administration, after more than twenty years in opposition. Grey's government resolved to settle the reform question. Ministers faced innumerable problems, however, in framing and passing a reform bill. Extra-parliamentary pressure was unremitting, owing to the volatile combination of economic distress and political turmoil, and conservative elements resisted until they had little choice but to give way in the early summer of 1832.

Canning, Goderich and political flux

After Liverpool's stroke there were protracted negotiations involving king, ministers and Tory backbenchers. Canning insisted on the premiership, and he was backed by the progressive section of Liverpool's cabinet (apart from Peel), by some influential backbenchers and by George IV. The king thought that the Tory government would fall without Canning, and had no wish to call on the Whigs. His relations with Canning had improved since the 'Queen's trial'. Canning flattered him, made him feel important, and had gratified the king soon after returning to the cabinet in 1822 by taking as his private secretary the son of George IV's mistress, Lady Conyngham. But Canning was opposed and disliked by a large number of Tory MPs, who objected to his liberal views, and Wellington and other peers in Liverpool's cabinet decided that they could not serve under him. They had long found him to be an ungentlemanly schemer, and did not trust him on corn, Catholics, or foreign policy.

The king was urged to make Wellington premier, but when George IV suggested that the cabinet should select its own leader, Wellington insisted that appointment of the prime minister was the king's constitutional responsibility. Canning was confirmed as Liverpool's successor in April 1827. Seven ministers who had served under Liverpool resigned, including Peel, Wellington and Eldon. Peel explained that the Catholic question was the only one on which he disagreed with Canning, and that resignation was a matter of honour and duty. But this did not mean that Peel was willing to lead a new ultra-conservative party, the course recommended by his friends and admirers. Peel's tendency to keep his own counsel and his refusal to commit himself disappointed many on the Tory side.

Canning improved his standing at court by convincing George IV that there had been a concerted plot to restrict the king's choice of prime minister. The king railed against the disloyalty of the departed Tory leaders and came to regard them as personal enemies. Political discussion began to focus again on the nature of the royal prerogative, and George IV believed that his wishes had made a difference in determining the succession to Liverpool. Indeed, when dominant politicians could not agree among themselves it was inevitable that the opportunities for royal intervention would increase.

Though Canning at last had what he always wanted, the premiership, he could not form an administration by depending solely on his adherents within the crumbling Tory party. He had to turn to favourably disposed Whigs. Tierney, Holland, Lansdowne and Brougham preferred Canning to other possible candidates for the premiership, and they decided to offer him support as a means of breaking up Liverpool's Tory alliance, enhancing Whig influence, and preventing the appointment of a firmly anti-Catholic administration. Three Whigs joined Canning's cabinet – Lansdowne, Tierney and the Earl of Carlisle – but they had to agree that emancipation would remain an open question, as requested by the king. There may have been some confusion on this point, however, and historians have argued about the precise status of the Catholic question after the spring of 1827.[1]

Intrigue and rancour increased. With the addition of the Whigs, Canning's cabinet numbered fifteen. Only six had served under Liverpool. Tories who stayed with Canning were assailed by those who had departed (in all over forty office-holders in various government departments resigned rather than serve under Canning). The Whigs were also deeply divided. Grey was astounded by the willingness of some of his closest friends to co-operate with Canning, whom he had regarded as a low-born, unprincipled charlatan since the days of Pitt. Grey became more active at this time, arguing with Holland, Fitzwilliam, Brougham and others who favoured coalition, and claiming that he had not in fact entrusted the leadership of the Whig connection to Lansdowne. Grey condemned those who joined Canning's administration for defiling their Whig identity and for failing to obtain guarantees on the Catholic question or any other vital issue. Many Whigs followed Grey's line and refused to back Canning's ministry. While those who joined Canning did so mainly because they expected him to settle the Catholic question, E. A. Wasson has shown that other Whigs were moved by different motives and goals. They did not trust Canning, differed with him on parliamentary reform, and wanted to promote more discipline on the Whig side. Rather than accept a new coalition, they set out to unite and strengthen the Whig party.[2]

Canning tried to forge an alliance of liberal Tories and conservative Whigs. Michael Bentley notes that former concerns about intra-party balance were superseded by notions of inter-party fusion. Paradoxically, the disorganisation of the late 1820s arose at the end of a decade in which party identities had been growing stronger. Derek Beales finds that the 'independent' MP was becoming less common than the partisan, and David Large suggests that party affiliations had grown more obvious in the Lords. Arthur Aspinall regards the late 1820s as a chaotic interlude in the process of party evolution: rather than a two-party divide, the years between 1827 and 1830 witnessed a 'group system' (as had prevailed between 1801 and 1812), and development of a clear two-party framework was punctuated by periods of disarray.[3]

By the time of Canning's appointment as premier the anticipated debates on corn and Catholic emancipation had already started. Canning introduced corn proposals (mainly the work of Liverpool and Huskisson) on 1 March 1827, and Burdett's motion for Catholic emancipation was made on 5 March. The corn bill would have replaced the inoperative sliding scale of 1822 with a less restrictive scale of duties, to operate around the pivot price of 60s a quarter. As the price fell the duty would rise. When the British harvest was adequate, therefore, foreign corn would be kept out, but importation would be easier when home supplies were deficient. The Commons passed the corn bill, but Canning abandoned it in June (to much consternation among reformers and business interests out of doors) when Wellington carried a wrecking amendment in the Lords. Animosity between Canningites and obdurate Tories deepened, as did the friction between Grey's followers and those Whigs who supported the Canning government. During the corn debate in the Lords Grey forcefully condemned the new coalition, as a result of which there was a temporary breach with Holland. Meanwhile the Catholic debate in the Commons was notable for Peel's speech on the second day. As usual he argued against concession. Burdett's motion was narrowly defeated. This was the first time since 1819 that the Commons had decided against emancipation, and a similar motion had been passed as recently as

1825. Anti-Catholic MPs were comforted by this evidence that the 1826 general election had strengthened their position, but rumours abounded that Canning would personally take up the Catholic issue during the next session.

The prime minister's Whig allies urged him to make this decisive move. In fact they seemed always to be making trouble in cabinet, particularly when accused by critics in the Commons and Lords of abandoning principles in order to take office. Canning turned increasingly to foreign affairs. A crisis had developed in the eastern Mediterranean, where Greek rebels were struggling against their Turkish overlords. But to the strains of leadership and heavy burden of official business was added serious illness, and Canning died on 8 August. His ministry had not yet had sufficient time to consolidate its position in parliament, and Canning's unexpected death further increased the confusion in high politics.

Viscount Goderich, secretary for war and the colonies, was acceptable to both the Canningite and Whig sections of the administration, and he briefly took over as prime minister. As Frederick Robinson, he had held cabinet office under Liverpool, but though a highly experienced politician, Goderich was not a strong character. He lacked Canning's influence. He could not stand up to the king, who appointed him precisely for this reason, nor to cabinet colleagues, who constantly quarrelled about policy and promotions. In this situation Goderich's health and resolve broke down. There was a damaging controversy concerning British intervention in the Greek rebellion, and ministers could not agree on a chairman of the Commons finance committee. Goderich resigned in January 1828, unable to keep Canning's ministry together. Membership of the Goderich cabinet had been disagreeable and embarrassing for all concerned. Opinion was divided as to whether Canning's death and Goderich's failure would lead to further political change or a return to the practices and alignments of Liverpool's day.

The Wellington government

As the Canningite–Whig coalition lost its way, George IV turned back to recalcitrant Tories and sought to restore relations with Wellington and Peel. They agreed to form an administration.

There was an obvious need for more settled and stable government, which they thought they could supply, and they were also influenced by their strong sense of duty and reputation as public figures. Another motive was their desire to reunite Liverpool's old conservative alliance and thereby restore a political configuration with which they were familiar. Wellington became prime minister. Peel became leader in the Commons, and resumed his former office of home secretary.

With Canning dead, Peel was generally acknowledged to be the most skilful debater in the lower house. He was also respected for his proficiency as an administrator. Peel's concerns set the tone for Wellington's ministry, particularly in its early stages. He insisted that it should operate on the same basis as Liverpool's administration, and that Canningites must be included. This would facilitate Tory reunion and ensure that the Wellington cabinet would not lack ministerial experience or talented speakers. The inclusion of Canningites annoyed more conservative-minded Tories, but Peel maintained that the government should not be exclusive and that he could not face the Commons as leader unless he had wider support than that offered by anti-Canning politicians on the Tory side. The Canningites Huskisson, the Earl of Dudley, Viscount Palmerston and Charles Grant agreed to stay on under Wellington, and the Whigs Lansdowne, Carlisle and Tierney were replaced. But Wellington never trusted the Canningites, and he resented the manner in which they tended always to act together. The new prime minister was tactless. He disliked the discussion and compromise which were now essential to cabinet government, grew annoyed when others disagreed with him, and did not have the patience to bargain with colleagues and deal calmly with applications for favours and patronage. Wellington was unable to provide the sense of continuity and means of conciliation which had been so important to Liverpool's premiership.

George IV had made only a few requests about men and measures (notably that Grey should be excluded and that Catholic emancipation should not become a government policy), but this relative freedom did not relieve the ministry from internal dissension and outside pressure. The corn and Catholic questions required urgent attention, and the issue of parliamentary reform was about to be revived. The events of 1827 created lasting suspicion and enmity. Huskisson became increasingly uncomfortable as Wellington publicly denied that he had agreed to persevere with certain Canningite policies. Whigs (and Canning's widow) accused Huskisson of inconsistency, and Goderich made some wounding claims about the problems of the previous government. Wellington showed no sign of accepting the Canningite strategy of persuading parliament and nation that government was able to respond to new needs. He cared little for popularity out of doors, denied that established institutions needed reform, and had always found Canning's progressive reputation and use of the press thoroughly disgusting.

Grey was ready to give the new ministry a fair trial. Rumours that Wellington would make friendly overtures to Grey prompted a great deal of speculation, and may have prolonged Whig disunity, but no such contact was made. Nevertheless, Grey assumed that Wellington would provide strong government, told friends that he disagreed with the duke only on Catholic emancipation, and suggested that opposition should be restrained in case it enabled ministers to rally support and so prevent Whig revival. Whigs and reformers were pleasantly surprised when the Wellington ministry withdrew its initial resistance to repeal of the Test and Corporation Acts. An annual indemnity exempted Protestant Dissenters from the penalties prescribed in these acts, but Dissenting sects had focused increasingly on the principle of religious tests. Their agitation and propaganda spread quickly during 1827 and 1828, and assistance was offered by Russell, Holland and other prominent Whigs. Opinion in the Commons and out of doors was turning against outdated civil disabilities imposed on the basis of religious faith, and against old statutes which had been intended to make public office the preserve of Anglican communicants.

For Russell, religious toleration was an illustrious old Foxite cause and a valuable unifying issue for Whigs, and he introduced a motion to repeal the Test and Corporation Acts in February 1828. The ministry yielded when it became clear that the Commons would pass Russell's motion. Peel was frustrated by his inability to control the lower house, but reassured by Church leaders who thought that the acts in question tended to demean the Anglican communion by requiring all office-holders to receive it. Peel did not surrender completely. He ensured that office-holders would be obliged to make a declaration that they would not use their positions to endanger the Church. Russell complained, as did Dissenting leaders out of doors, but they had to accept the declaration as the price of repeal.

Repeal of the Test and Corporation Acts was an important event for the Whigs. Many of their supporters were Dissenters, and many Dissenters were voters. Repeal was a success for determined opposition. It promoted Whig recovery after all the anger and division caused by coalition government in 1827. Repeal also suggested that Wellington's ministry could not manage the Commons. Indeed, ultra Tories were angered by the government's readiness to accept repeal, and they began to question the ministers' authority. Furthermore, many contemporaries believed that repeal would strengthen the case for Catholic emancipation, though few people can have expected that emancipation would follow quickly. As G. I. T. Machin suggests, parliament would probably not have repealed the Test and Corporation Acts had subsequent developments been foreseen. Yet repeal and emancipation had often been considered together, and in 1827 supporters of the Canning ministry had argued that repeal should not be taken up because it would make progress towards Catholic emancipation, the greater prize, more difficult.[4]

Wellington's ministry was torn asunder by disputes concerning corn duties and the disfranchisement of two corrupt boroughs, East Retford in Nottinghamshire and Penryn in Cornwall. Huskisson and the Canningite ministers wished to reintroduce the failed corn bill of 1827, but Wellington maintained that government had to respect the interests of landowners and farmers. After much argument the prime minister was the only one in the cabinet who refused to accept Huskisson's plan. There were several threats of resignation before a compromise was agreed, and in due course the new corn law of 1828 implemented a less liberal sliding scale of duties than that proposed in 1827. Peel warned that the reputation and dignity of government would suffer if ministerial disputes continued. Wellington had been amazed to find himself overruled in his own cabinet, however, and was sorry the

Canningites had not resigned. Then Huskisson gave him the opportunity he needed to reconstruct the ministry. The Canningites wanted the East Retford and Penryn seats to be transferred to large unrepresented towns, while other ministers favoured a merging of these corrupt boroughs with their neighbouring hundreds. Finally the cabinet decided that this latter course should be pursued with respect to East Retford, and that Penryn's seats should be transferred to a populous town, probably Manchester, which had secured the public endorsement of Russell. The House of Lords voted against the enfranchisement of Manchester, however, and Huskisson assumed that this invalidated the cabinet's agreement. In the Commons on 19 May 1828, goaded by opposition MPs and mindful of his public commitment to the enfranchisement of a large town, Huskisson voted against the transfer of East Retford's seats to its neighbouring hundred and departed from what Peel still regarded as a settled government policy.

Huskisson apologised to Wellington and as a gesture of courtesy offered to resign. The prime minister immediately accepted this resignation, and refused to let a surprised and embarrassed Huskisson change his mind. The other Canningite ministers left the government in protest. Wellington was pleased to be rid of them. Peel had refused to intervene on their behalf, annoyed by Huskisson's conduct and tired of the constant effort to keep the peace between the Canningites and Wellington. But Peel also realised that the departure of four capable ministers would weaken the cabinet, narrow its base of support, and create trouble for him as leader in the Commons. Whigs were encouraged by these developments. They noted the connection between Huskisson's resignation and the question of parliamentary reform. They saw how difficult it was for Wellington to find replacements for the departed ministers, and hoped that the ministry's problems would provide an opportunity to press more vigorously for Catholic emancipation. This opportunity came almost at once. Wellington appointed William Vesey Fitzgerald as president of the board of trade in place of Charles Grant, which necessitated a by-election in Clare (Fitzgerald's Irish constituency) because MPs who accepted government office had to obtain their constituents' approval. In July 1828 Fitzgerald was defeated in Clare by Daniel O'Connell, who had inspired mass agitation in Ireland since the suppression of the Catholic Association in 1825, and who saw in the Clare election a means of forcing the Wellington government to attend to Irish grievances. As a Catholic, O'Connell could not take his seat in the Commons. This in itself added to the controversy on emancipation, but Wellington and Peel also saw that the Clare situation could be recreated all over Ireland at the next general election. A significant part of the representative system would be paralysed.

Matters were complicated by serious unrest in Ireland (much of which was beyond O'Connell's control). In view of rural outrages, the destruction of property, and attacks on landlords and rent collectors, Peel thought that coercive legislation would be necessary, but he knew that this would not be sanctioned by the Commons. Ministerial deliberation was also affected by the Commons division of 8 May 1828. Burdett's emancipation proposal had passed by a majority of six, the first time such a motion had passed since the 1826 general election. Wellington's public remarks about the Catholic question subsequently became notably moderate. Indeed, for many years he had accepted that emancipation would eventually become unavoidable, and that political leaders were bound to ponder over the precise details in readiness for the moment when concessions had to be made.[5] Peel now concluded that the time had come to grant Catholic emancipation. However objectionable it remained to him in principle, emancipation had been rendered urgently necessary by prevalent circumstances, particularly the situation in Ireland and the mood of the Commons. But Peel was reluctant publicly to promote a settlement, which he deemed essential, because he would be accused of treachery to the Protestant cause. Though convinced of the logical soundness of his own pragmatic reasoning, Peel doubted that government supporters in parliament and the nation could be persuaded to see things his way. He told Wellington he wanted to resign, and changed his mind only because the prime minister insisted that without Peel, the government would collapse.

As rumours spread about the cabinet's decision to take up the Catholic question, government supporters became uneasy and anti-Catholic agitation out of doors quickly increased. The liberal press and reform societies countered with pressure for emancipation, and unrest continued in Ireland. Wellington and Peel decided that it was their duty to propose a settlement. This entailed difficult negotiations with senior Anglican clergy, who soon declared themselves against concession, and with George IV. The king adhered to the position of his father and insisted that he could never consent to emancipation. Eventually Wellington and Peel forced him to agree that ministers ought to discuss the question. But his fits of depression and violent mood changes made the king impossible to control, and after sanctioning the government's draft emancipation bill early in 1829 he subsequently rejected it. George IV sought the guidance of anyone who could relieve him of pressure, notably his ultra-conservative brother, the Duke of Cumberland. The king repeatedly threatened to replace Wellington's ministry, only to relent when in the presence of those who advised differently. In March 1829 he apparently accepted the ministers' resignations. Then he agreed to reinstate them and accept their emancipation bill on the grounds that no alternative cabinet could be formed.

Parliamentary debates on emancipation were extremely bitter, and campaigning increased in the country as supporters and opponents of the government's measure tried to influence the outcome. Peel was subjected to intense personal abuse, and criticism of Wellington by the Earl of Winchilsea resulted in a duel. The emancipation bill was passed by large majorities in both houses of parliament. It secured Whig and Canningite support, while the remnants of Liverpool's old Tory alliance were now in turmoil. Peel had maintained that there was less danger in removing Catholic disabilities than in trying to retain them, but many Tories in parliament and out of doors were outraged that a Tory government had so violated the established order in Church and state. It was no great comfort to them that the ministry had balanced emancipation with two safeguards, the abolition of O'Connell's revived Catholic Association, and disfranchisement of Ireland's 40s freeholders. These measures were intended to promote social peace and effective government in Ireland, and to restore landlord influence in Irish constituencies. Whigs, Canningites and O'Connell accepted them in return for emancipation, an arrangement condemned by many reformers out of doors.

The government's standing in the nation and at court declined considerably, and in parliament former supporters became inveterate foes. Ultra Tories now devoted all their energies to punishing Wellington and Peel. Meanwhile emancipation did not make possible a rapprochement with the Canningites, for they mistrusted Wellington and preferred to remain in opposition. Some of them made contact with Whig leaders, in case Wellington resigned and made way for a coalition government of the type formed by Canning in 1827. But the Canningites were no longer a united force,[6] and the Whigs had still not entirely recovered from the split of 1827. Some Whigs who had supported Canning's administration were slow to re-establish cordial links with the followers of Grey. Allegiances were so unclear that in February 1830 Holland declared party to be a thing of the past. Confusion continued. Whigs and Canningites frequently voted with Wellington's government in order to defeat the ultra Tories, and some of the latter took up parliamentary reform on the grounds that emancipation would not have been passed by a more representative legislature.

Parliamentary reform succeeded emancipation as the dominant issue of the day, and various proposals were made in the Commons during the session of 1830. Reform agitation increased again out of doors, largely because of economic distress, and the instability in high politics encouraged reformers to believe that resistance to a lowering of the franchise and redistribution of seats could not continue for much longer. Treatment of the reform question in the Commons during 1830 depended more on enmities within parliament, however, than on pressure from without. Ultra Tory the Marquess of Blandford was heavily defeated when he proposed an extensive plan of reform in February. This involved the disfranchisement of corrupt boroughs, redistribution of seats to counties and large towns, disqualification of non-resident voters, extension of the scot and lot franchise to all boroughs, exclusion of placemen from the Commons, and payment of MPs. Russell's proposal to enfranchise Manchester, Leeds and Birmingham was also defeated in February, after Peel made a highly effective speech against it, and in May O'Connell's motion for manhood suffrage, the ballot and triennial parliaments received only thirteen votes. Russell then introduced a scheme to reduce the number of MPs returned by small boroughs and increase the representation of growing towns and large counties. Huskisson saw Russell's plan in advance, and said that though he could not vote for it himself, something similar would almost certainly be passed in due course. In the event, some Canningites sided with Russell, as did many Whig MPs, the small number of radical members, and a group of ultra Tories, but the proposal was defeated by over a hundred votes on 28 May 1830.

The revived reform movement in the country was not yet strong enough to trouble the Commons, and only fourteen reform petitions were received during the session of 1830. The Whigs did not wish to inconvenience Wellington's ministry too greatly, moreover, for fear of assisting the ultras and the court (still rumoured to be plotting against the cabinet). Yet Whig interest in parliamentary reform was growing. The need to eliminate abuses seemed incontestable, and changing political circumstances offered a chance to end the Whigs' long period out of office and draw respectable opinion behind their version of reform. Canningites were less enthusiastic. Parliamentary reform had never been one of Canning's goals, and his followers were now concerned most of all to decide whether constructive government (and their own political future) would best be secured by an understanding with the Whigs or reunion with Wellington and Peel. For ultra Tories, parliamentary reform was necessary because of the government's surrender on Catholic emancipation: it would finally free the Commons from ministerial dictation and ensure that such a betrayal of the national interests could never happen again.

Peel's position on parliamentary reform had been made clear during the debates of 1830. He opposed needless tampering with the constitution, and condemned the idea that representation should rest on numbers rather than interests. Though it was appropriate to root out electoral corruption, Peel thought, parliament should not be tied to any specific procedure for the redistribution of seats, and in any case the constructive measures of recent years proved that parliamentary reform was not required for useful improvements in other fields. Indeed, Wellington's government had assisted trade and cut taxes, and was practising retrenchment, and as home secretary Peel had implemented further penal reforms and improved metropolitan policing. During and after the 1830 session it was predicted that Wellington and Peel, though opponents of parliamentary reform, would introduce a moderate reform bill in order to satisfy respectable opinion, quell plebeian agitation, and strengthen the ministry's position in the Commons, where it had no reliable majority. Yet Wellington was unmoved by extra-parliamentary pressure, and he did not believe that various opposition groups in the Commons would ever combine to bring his administration down.

Wellington miscalculated badly. He underestimated the new vigour and unity demonstrated by Whigs in 1830. Viscount Althorp became their recognised leader in the Commons, and Grey began to favour a more active opposition to Wellington (though he warned his allies that the Whigs were not yet ready to replace the duke's cabinet). Canningites sided increasingly with the Whigs, and it was clear that the government would soon come under increasing pressure in the Commons, especially on parliamentary reform and public finance. The settlement of the Catholic question gave Wellington too high an opinion of his influence and his ministry's strength. He grew irritated as Peel warned about the situation in the Commons and urged that the prime minister should bargain for additional support. The 1830 general election, necessitated by George IV's death in June, failed to make the government's position any more secure, which disappointed its supporters and encouraged its opponents. Parliamentary reform had emerged as the main issue in many constituencies, along with the government's failure to respond quickly enough to economic problems and urban and rural unrest.

Pressed by Peel to reinforce the government's front bench in the Commons, Wellington agreed that negotiations could begin before the assembly of the new parliament. He and Peel decided to approach Canningites as individuals rather than a group, not wishing to recreate the situation of 1828. Approaches to ultra Tories and to Whigs were ruled out. Those ultras who had apparently given up opposition could not be trusted, Peel thought, and Wellington believed that Whigs would expect too many guarantees on men and measures in return for their goodwill. The leading Canningite, Huskisson, who had reportedly been considering a return to the cabinet, was killed in a railway accident in September 1830. Overtures were made to Palmerston, but he wanted cabinet posts for his friends and by now preferred the Whigs to the government. Wellington was glad that negotiations failed. He had done as his cabinet colleagues wanted, was content for the ministry to carry on unchanged, and consistently argued that it was stronger than Peel thought. Wellington contemptuously dismissed press attacks and criticism from the Whigs.

Grey believed that Wellington's administration was close to ruin, and made it known that if he was invited to form a government he would make parliamentary reform a condition of taking office. Grey was assured by Holland, on good authority, that most Canningites were ready to support him as premier, and it seemed that the only way Wellington could revive the ministry's fortunes was to introduce a reform bill: this would probably divide the Whigs, Grey would be obliged to support it because of previous commitments (as had happened with Catholic emancipation), and radical agitation in the country would be undermined. Wellington had no intention of taking up reform, however, and he was annoyed by suggestions that he would even consider it. His insincere approach to the Canningites was followed by a clear indication that he wished to rely squarely on an anti-reform Toryism. He could win back ultra support, he thought, and deal a decisive blow to the reform movement. On 2 November 1830 Wellington spoke so strongly against reform in the Lords that his audience was stunned (see Document 9). The reform press immediately raised a clamour against the government, and extra-parliamentary agitation increased. Cabinet ministers and government supporters in the Commons could not believe that the prime minister had been so insensitive. The government now had no room to manoeuvre.

Wellington had seriously misjudged parliament's mood and public opinion, and his speech harmed rather than improved the ministry's prospects for survival. Jonathan Clark maintains that Wellington made a reasonable and justifiable attempt to gain ultra support and rally Tories against a threat to the constitution. But many historians, including Asa Briggs, Eric Evans, Elie Halevy, John Cannon and Norman Gash, suggest that Wellington's speech cannot be regarded as anything but an extraordinary error.[7] The prime minister did not win over the ultras. He exasperated those Tories who still backed his government, encouraged reformers in parliament and out of doors to step up their campaigning, and forced the uncommitted to take sides. The speech polarised opinion. Yet Wellington was confident that the crisis would pass and that, as with Catholic emancipation, there could be no settlement without his participation. Since he would not yield, reform could not proceed. His opponents did not accept this analysis. In the Commons Brougham gave notice of a reform proposal, to be introduced on 16 November 1830. Peel, who doubted the government's ability to overcome Brougham, sought a way to relinquish office without dishonour (and leave the reform question to be settled by someone else). Before Brougham's motion came to be debated, ministers were defeated in the Commons on a civil list vote. Having decided that this vote would be a matter of confidence, the cabinet resigned.

Wellington's government could not survive the crisis brought on by the prime minister's anti-reform speech of 2 November. Since 1828 it had offended too many of its own supporters, particularly by carrying Catholic emancipation. It was very unpopular out of doors. Wellington attached little importance to shifts in public opinion, and never sought to improve relations with the press. As James Sack points out, influential Tory newspapers had turned against the government before its fall at the end of 1830.[8] Many of them had initially welcomed Wellington's appointment as premier. They subsequently condemned emancipation, and now pointed out that the ministry was leaving agriculture, manufacturing and shipping in a considerably worse condition than it found them. New energy and unity on the Whig side had increased the government's problems, and relations between the cabinet's leading figures, Wellington and Peel, deteriorated. Peel had wanted to resign for many months. The government was too weak to stand, he thought, and yet Wellington refused to strengthen it. Its inability to conduct affairs firmly and efficiently was damaging Peel's reputation, and Wellington's speech against reform was the final straw. Parliament and people would not let the matter be sidelined. Previously Peel had expressed a willingness to support moderate parliamentary reform. This was now impossible, for the kind of measure needed to satisfy the parliamentary opposition and outdoor agitators would not be in the Tories' interests. Branded a traitor on Catholic emancipation, moreover, Peel was not prepared to risk the same thing on reform. For political and personal reasons he longed to go into opposition.

Radical revival

The instability in high politics after 1827, the fracturing of Toryism and appointment of a Whig-dominated coalition ministry led by Grey in November 1830 occurred in the context of growing excitement out of doors. High and low politics were merging. Extra-parliamentary agitation rose considerably at the time of the corn and Catholic debates in 1827, as reformers pressed for free trade in corn and greater religious toleration. Calls for repeal of the Test and Corporation Acts in 1827 and 1828 further increased political participation, as did the 1828 corn law (which many commentators found too moderate) and the prospect of a redistribution of parliamentary seats from East Retford and Penryn.[9] Repeal of the Test and Corporation Acts and the relaxation of corn regulations heightened the progressive mood, and these breakthroughs were greeted by reformers as important defeats for conservatism. In the later months of 1828 and into 1829 there followed mobilisation for and against Catholic emancipation as it became clear that Wellington's government was preparing to propose a settlement. Press, meeting and petition were marshalled. The *Westminster Review* of January 1829 denounced the Protestant ascendancy as a system of oppression, argued that Catholics no longer posed any political danger, and asserted that every group within the nation should have an influence appropriate to its size and importance. Reformers welcomed Catholic emancipation and celebrated the most significant victory for the progressive spirit in living memory, though some were angry about the disfranchisement of Ireland's 40s freeholders. About 200,000 voters were affected, and reformers objected to the idea that some rights could be gained only if others were surrendered.

Poor harvests and the return of economic depression in the late 1820s brought severe hardship. There were strikes and disturbances in large northern towns. Agitation for parliamentary reform revived, with organisation and direction given by new radical bodies. The National Union of the Working Classes (NUWC), based in London, was formed by radical members of the Metropolitan Trades Union. They gave political goals priority over labour issues, established close links with the unstamped press, and divided into small classes (like the LCS during the 1790s) for discussion of public affairs. In the NUWC there was some approval for the principles of Paine and Owen. The London Radical Reform Association (RRA) was more respectable in composition and moderate in character, and the Birmingham Political Union (BPU) established itself as the leading reform association in the provinces. Its membership was unusually eclectic, for social and economic conditions in Birmingham facilitated cross-class co-operation. The BPU's leader, Thomas Attwood, believed that parliamentary reform would make possible currency reform, but he did not expect all BPU members to subscribe to his own inflationary preferences. The BPU resolutions of January 1830 declared that Birmingham's distress had never been worse, that distress was attributable to misgovernment, and that the remedy was parliamentary reform.

Reformers drew confidence from recent events. Amendment of the Irish county franchise suggested that other parts of the electoral system could also be changed, and Catholic emancipation was nothing less than a fundamental constitutional reform. Further structural reforms might follow, for emancipation had been a crushing disappointment for anti-reformers and had divided the anti-reform forces in parliament. In addition, the Catholic Association had shown what mass agitation could achieve, and O'Connell was now joining in the demand for parliamentary reform (in league with the Benthamites).[10] But it was some time before large numbers of workers turned from labour disputes towards a more focused agitation for reform. Radical leaders, particularly Cobbett and Hunt, argued among themselves, and the Whig opposition was still not prepared to associate closely with the extra-parliamentary movement. Whig spokesmen openly condemned both the plebeian radicals and the Benthamites.

Local and regional differences also inhibited the advance of the reform movement. Many reformers were inspired by specific local concerns, which were not necessarily shared by campaigners elsewhere. The financial ideas of Attwood in Birmingham had little appeal in Manchester, for instance, where textile masters favoured the gold standard and deflationary controls. Manchester industrialists had welcomed the resumption of specie payments in 1819 because they considered 'sound money' good for business and credit, and knew that deflation would make their products more competitive abroad (Lancashire textile firms exhibited a marked orientation towards the export trade). Asa Briggs has emphasised that the collaboration between lower and middle classes in Birmingham was more difficult to achieve in other large towns. Birmingham was less socially fragmented. Its economy was based on small workshops and regular personal contact between employers and workers. In Leeds and Manchester, systems of production promoted conflict rather than friendly contact between masters and men. In addition, while Birmingham's reform leaders were most interested in currency questions, in Manchester some reformers associated parliamentary reform with corn law repeal, and in Leeds factory regulation was a priority. Therefore Birmingham's united effort was not possible in other towns where social, political and economic conditions were quite different.[11]

In many towns several competing political unions appeared, with members drawn from distinct social backgrounds. In Leeds there were eventually three separate unions. The Manchester Political Union, established in November 1830, was dominated by shopkeepers and small businessmen. Denied any influence in its proceedings, local workers soon formed an alternative body, the Political Union of the Working Classes (PUWC). Then in September 1831 the wealthy middle-class reformers of Manchester established their own Reform Committee, and its goals were rather less advanced than the manhood suffrage and annual parliaments demanded by the PUWC. In Sheffield there was a more co-ordinated campaign and considerable unity, while in London personal and ideological differences made a broad reform alliance impossible. The RRA split after its leaders Cobbett and Hunt quarrelled. Hunt wanted a vigorous popular campaign for parliamentary reform, but Cobbett favoured an extensive programme of political, financial and economic improvements. In March 1830 Hunt and O'Connell founded the

Metropolitan Political Union, which relied on the well established political resources of London's artisan radicals.

Divided by their specific local concerns, reform groups also disagreed on broader questions relating to goals and tactics. Plebeian activists were less restrained in their ideas and conduct than respectable reformers, and there was strong mutual distrust. Nevertheless, there were some common stimuli: the economic situation, political corruption, and parliament's tendency to disregard public opinion. Reformers were compelled to act by continuing evidence of the harmful effects of ineffective and selfish government. Most of them did not regard parliamentary reform as an end in itself, but looked forward to improvements that would come in its wake. These benefits, they assumed, could not be obtained from the unreformed legislature. Reformers envisaged the eventual resolution of a host of outstanding problems concerning corn laws, slavery, factory conditions, the Church, currency, poor relief and public health.

Notwithstanding the division and disagreements, reform agitation was undeniably impressive. Press and platform were skilfully exploited, and the movement rested on a combination of large numbers (which gave reform the backing of mass pressure) and clearly articulated demands. Particularly disturbing for the formal political nation was the activism of propertied, wealthy and intelligent reformers, for they could not simply be ignored. If respectable opinion turned against aristocratic government, it was thought, the future of the established order would be in doubt. Governments had managed to subdue plebeian radicals in the past, but never before had such pressure been exerted by merchants, manufacturers, bankers and lawyers, and by the middle-class liberal press they controlled. The state's ability to contain popular mobilisation, moreover, was now impaired by serious divisions in parliament, executive weakness, and a growing sense of crisis at the centre of power.

The 1830 general election increased the excitement, and parliamentary reform was a key issue in many constituencies. The number of contests was quite small, as usual, but the government's poor showing gave a great fillip to reformers, for it meant that Wellington's ministry would probably be unable to control the new House of Commons. Furthermore, though the new king, William IV, had confirmed the ministers in place, he was generally regarded as more favourable to reform than his brother, George IV, had been, having supported Catholic emancipation. The 1830 election also brought some significant victories for reformers, notably Brougham, who was successful in Yorkshire though he had no previous association with the county. Brougham was determined to make himself the popular champion of parliamentary reform in the Whig party. Meanwhile Hunt stood as a candidate in Preston, a relatively open borough with a wide pot-walloper suffrage. Though he was unsuccessful at the general election, Hunt won a Preston by-election in December 1830. Commotion increased during the summer of 1830 because of an uprising in Paris, which brought down the reactionary French king Charles X and established a new, constitutional monarchy. This fundamental yet peaceful change encouraged the reform movement at home. Then further revolutions in Belgium and Poland were taken to mark the dawning of a new era of reform across Europe. There were enthusiastic meetings in many towns, and detailed press reports covering events in Europe. Messages of support were sent to Paris from reform groups in Britain. Norman Gash argues that news of developments in Paris at the end of July arrived too late to influence the result of the 1830 general election, but Roland Quinault suggests that the issue of reform, and interest in the French political crisis, may have been more significant in Britain than is often supposed.[12]

Unrest continued. As well as strikes and disorders in industrial towns, there were 'Captain Swing' disturbances in the rural south and east of England (so named because of the signature on threatening letters sent to landowners and magistrates). The arson, cattle-maiming and assaults in southern and eastern counties were prompted by poverty and unemployment in the countryside, which had long been suffering the effects of population increase, the decline of rural industries, enclosures, and the mechanisation of farming. Elie Halevy argues that a political consciousness lay behind the 'Swing' outrages, and that the smiths, joiners and artisans who participated in the violence admired the revolutionaries of Paris and Brussels. On the other hand, John Stevenson notes that rural labourers generally lacked the literacy, ideology and organisation to pose a serious threat to the state.[13]

173

When the Wellington ministry fell at the end of 1830, not only was there turmoil in high politics, but a very alarming situation had developed out of doors owing to the determined and organised reform movement, industrial protest, and serious rural disorder. The new administration, led by Grey, had to provide competent and confident government in order to promote political stability and calm popular agitation.

The Whigs, the people and parliamentary reform

Grey's cabinet included members of all the groups which had combined to overthrow Wellington, though its personnel and parliamentary support were predominantly Whig. There were initially nine Whigs in the ministry, including Grey, Lansdowne, Holland, Lambton (now Lord Durham), Althorp (who assumed the leadership of the Commons) and Brougham. They were joined by three Canningites (Palmerston, Goderich and Grant) and one ultra Tory (the Duke of Richmond). To the cabinet of thirteen were added two more Whigs, Russell and E. G. Stanley, in June 1831. One result of the negotiations attending the formation of this government was that Brougham had to leave the Commons and allow others to determine the ministry's policy on parliamentary reform. Senior Whigs disliked Brougham. They were determined to prevent him from domi-nating reform discussions, but he was too dangerous to leave out of the cabinet, and the solution was to raise him to the peerage and bring him in as lord chancellor. Brougham did not want reform to be taken out of his hands. He was warned by Althorp and others, however, that if he made trouble he would wreck Grey's efforts to form a ministry. This would deprive the Whigs of their first taste of office as a party in over twenty years.

The new government was committed to peace, fiscal retrench-ment and reform. The last was the outstanding requirement and received most attention. Ministers realised that it would not be easy to frame a parliamentary reform bill that would mollify public opinion without damaging established structures of government and representation. As they struggled with this task, chancellor of the exchequer Althorp found many of his budget proposals rejected by an unruly House of Commons.

This created financial difficulty and indicated that ministers would not be able to manage parliament. Grey and his allies had complained about the ineffective government of Wellington, which they thought had undermined the reputation of public men generally, but it seemed that they might not be able to do any better. Meanwhile violence and disorder in depressed urban and rural areas continued, prompting special commissions, executions, and hundreds of transportations. Home secretary Lord Melbourne dealt severely with rioters, and the Grey government proved to be no more liberal-minded in this respect than the most reactionary Tories.

Parliamentary reform was the priority for Grey and the Whigs not because they considered it inevitable, nor because they wished to act upon previous pledges. Reform was appropriate primarily because of the needs and opportunities of the moment. Parliamentary and public opinion had shifted decisively in favour of reform during the late 1820s, and the circumstances surrounding the fall of Wellington and appointment of Grey made it a question that simply had to be settled. Deciding on the precise extent and details of any reform bill, however, presented Grey with some disagreeable prospects. The Whig connection included progressive, moderate and conservative elements, and Grey could not afford to alienate any of them. The bill also had to secure the approval of everyone in the cabinet, since any disunity would be fatal, but some ministers were rather more advanced in their political ideas than others. Indeed, Melbourne, Palmerston, Lansdowne and Richmond saw themselves as restraining influences, and they were unlikely to accept an extensive measure. Grey wanted to prevent thorough change, but he persistently argued that too mild a reform would fail to provide a lasting settlement. In dealing with cabinet colleagues and with William IV he emphasised the urgency of the situation. The piecemeal proposals of the 1820s would no longer be enough, Grey affirmed. A bold measure was needed, but one that would modify and improve the electoral system rather than refashion it completely.

Grey was worried by popular unrest. He wanted to put an end to it while protecting aristocratic government. Reform was the only method available, and there was no time to lose because confusion in high politics, economic distress, radical mobilisation, and the excitement created by recent events (notably the July Revolution in France and Wellington's speech against reform) placed established institutions in grave danger. A measured concession to pressure from without was necessary. By passing a reform bill Grey and his associates expected to improve the Whig party's electoral performances, check agitation, attach the propertied middle classes to the established order, and thereby strengthen resistance to further change. A settlement would also demonstrate the competence of the patrician elite, and remove any doubts about its ability and right to govern.[14]

The details of the government's reform bill were worked out by a committee of four: Durham, Sir James Graham, Lord Duncannon and Russell. Durham and Graham were cabinet ministers, while Duncannon had been a Whig party whip for several years. He was a moderate, Graham was more conservative, Durham was the most advanced reformer of the four, and Russell was the Whigs' acknowledged expert on parliamentary reform. The committee therefore represented a spectrum of opinion. Brougham's exclusion aroused much comment, but it accorded with the Whig grandees' wish to limit his influence. In addition, Grey did not care for Brougham's close association with prominent journalists and wanted to prevent details of the committee's deliberations from leaking out. Russell also thought this essential. The reform plan would have much greater impact if it remained confidential up to the time of its introduction in the Commons, Russell argued, and anti-reformers would be deprived of the information they needed to prepare their defences.

Grey directed that the committee should prepare a reform bill 'of such a scope and description as to satisfy all reasonable demands and remove at once, and for ever, all rational grounds for complaint from the minds of the intelligent and independent portion of the community'.[15] As altered by the cabinet (which ruled out the ballot and shorter parliaments) and approved by William IV (though he maintained that the demand for extensive reform was not as strong as it seemed), the main features of the reform bill were as follows. Sixty boroughs with populations below two thousand would be completely disfranchised (schedule A), and one seat would be taken from each of forty-seven boroughs with populations between two and four thousand (schedule B). Not all of these seats would be redistributed, for ministers had decided to reduce the total number of members in the Commons. England was to receive ninety-seven of the redistributed seats, and Scotland, Ireland and Wales would receive five, three and one, respectively. Seven large English towns, including Manchester, Sheffield, Leeds and Birmingham, were to have two seats each, as were four new London constituencies (schedule C). Twenty smaller towns would have one seat each (schedule D). Two seats would be added to Yorkshire's county representation, making six in all, and twenty-six other counties would have their representation doubled (schedule E). The county franchise was to be extended to £10 copyholders and some £50 leaseholders, and a uniform borough franchise would be introduced: ownership or occupancy of property worth £10 a year.

The Tory opposition was at a serious disadvantage in the weeks leading up to Russell's introduction of the reform bill on 1 March 1831. Unaware of the precise details of the measure, Tories assumed that it would be moderate and could not believe that Grey would attempt greatly to alter the electoral system. They doubted that the bill would go much further than Russell's previous reform proposals. But Tories were divided on tactics. Some thought that a moderate bill should be accepted. It could not be defeated, they reasoned, and it would undermine radical influence. Others counselled resistance no matter how mild the government's bill proved to be, because they found parliamentary reform objectionable in principle and feared that the bill would set a dangerous precedent. Continuing resentment against Wellington and Peel added to opposition disunity at this time. Many Tory MPs were also worried that too hasty a rejection of the reform bill would mean a dissolution and general election. They knew they would probably lose their seats if voters were presented with a stark choice between reform and no reform. Late in February 1831 most Tory MPs and peers decided not to block the reform bill at the outset, but to wait until it had been properly discussed.

The reform bill was a compromise. Durham favoured the ballot and shorter parliaments, and the committee's original scheme had included these proposals, balancing them with a

£20 borough qualification. But it soon became clear that the £20 franchise would not greatly increase the size of the electorate, and Grey and others in the cabinet opposed the ballot on the grounds that voting was a public trust and should be open. They also thought that the ballot would weaken landlord power where it was most important, in counties and small boroughs. Therefore the ballot and shorter parliaments were given up, and the uniform £10 borough franchise was approved. This was what Russell had wanted all along. He and Althorp used fear of the ballot to persuade cabinet and king to accept a lower voting qualification in boroughs. Grey also used this tactic in discussions with Lansdowne, who was persuaded to accept the reform bill despite strong reservations. Brougham objected to the disfranchisement clauses, which he considered excessive (and therefore a gift to the opposition), but he was easily overruled. Eventually the cabinet agreed that the final bill went far enough to satisfy opinion out of doors, and would provide a lasting settlement of the reform question.

Most contemporaries had no idea that the reform bill would be so broad and comprehensive in nature. Opposition members in the Commons laughed in disbelief when Russell named the condemned boroughs, and there was general surprise at the uniform borough franchise. Yet Russell maintained that the government's plan, though much larger than previous reform proposals, respected the established order. The redistribution of seats was determined by property and interest, not population, and Russell spoke less about the enfranchisement of large towns than about the need to save the constitution by removing its anomalies. Althorp argued that the electoral system had to be rendered less exclusive, but that quality mattered more than numbers. The bill would preserve and enhance the influence of property. Government supporters were assured that if the £10 franchise greatly increased the size of some borough electorates, it would be the wealth and respectability of new centres of population that really gained representation. The £10 qualification was a yardstick of good character, and would confine the vote to those who could safely be entrusted with it.

Whig MPs rallied behind the government's bill. Tory spokesmen accused ministers of rousing the people and creating expectations that would inevitably be disappointed, but Whigs insisted that reform had become urgently necessary, and that obstruction would stimulate such violence that the institutions and values which Tories claimed to cherish might be completely crushed. Peel objected strongly to the bill and rejected the arguments offered in its defence. He accepted that some reform was necessary, but maintained that the government's proposals were too extreme. Peel also denounced the Whigs for attempting to coerce parliament. Whigs had stressed that the king approved of the reform bill, that there would be a dissolution if the Commons rejected it, and that civil disorder would follow. But Peel argued that MPs must look to their own consciences when casting their votes, and he refused to take any blame for popular agitation. Ministers who proposed sweeping change at a time of unrest, said Peel, were solely responsible for the consequences. Peel reminded MPs of Russell's former remarks about parliamentary reform (in 1819 Russell had discountenanced an entire reconstruction of the House of Commons), and pointed out that reform had never been seriously considered as an antidote for disorder. He criticised the government's bill in detail. The uniform borough suffrage would replace older and in some cases wider franchises, abolish long-established rights, and exclude the lower ranks from direct representation. By disfranchising rotten boroughs, Peel continued, the bill would destroy an essential and advantageous part of the electoral system, for these boroughs had always provided seats in the Commons for veteran statesmen and young men of talent. The reform bill had little to recommend it, Peel concluded. It offered no lasting settlement, would overturn the old constitution, and promised to weaken executive influence at a time when the nation was in desperate need of effective administration.

Peel consistently opposed the reform bill, but he did so on his own terms. Still uncomfortable about Catholic emancipation and the fall of Wellington's government, Peel was determined to uphold his public character and did not wish to co-operate closely with unenlightened Tories who had caused so much trouble for the cabinets of which he had been a member. Peel's temperament and training fitted him for government, not opposition, and this strengthened his reluctance to engage in a factious, unthinking resistance to reform. Peel respected the unreformed system. In his opinion it worked well and maintained an appropriate balance between legislature and electorate, and he saw no need to give the latter more control over the former. Though Peel realised by the end of 1830 that reform had to be conceded, he wanted it to address specific anomalies rather than alter the whole representative system. Peel also maintained that in view of their values and history, Tories could not honourably take up reform. Their task was to defeat the government's bill, or render it less harmful, by debate and division. Though other Tories shared some of these opinions, they resented Peel's aloof manner and repeatedly complained that his opposition to the reform bill was too selfish and independent.

Through March 1831 there was mounting speculation about the likely outcome of the Commons division on the bill's second reading. Ministers informed William IV that they would have to recommend a dissolution if the bill was defeated. The king was reluctant to dissolve parliament at a time of such unrest, however, and considered an election on a single issue, the fate of the reform bill, entirely irregular. Grey and Durham were annoyed to find that news of the king's objections leaked out, for it encouraged Tory MPs to persist with their resistance. On 23 March the bill passed its second reading by the narrowest of margins, 302 to 301 votes. Disappointed Tories blamed Peel for not moving a vote against ministers when the bill was introduced on 1 March, but as John Prest points out, it is by no means clear that this vote would have been carried.[16] In fact, Peel was highly satisfied by the division of 23 March: there would now be weeks of debate in the committee stages, and many opportunities for the opposition to alter the bill and break the ministry's spirit. On 19 April ministers were defeated on the Tory Isaac Gascoyne's motion that the number of MPs for England and Wales should not be reduced. This result indicated the power now being exercised in the Commons by moderate backbenchers who were not firmly committed to either government or opposition. As M. O'Neill and G. Martin have shown, these men of the centre had sided with ministers on 23 March, but subsequently voted for the Gascoyne amendment.[17] Meanwhile Grey's cabinet had already decided that defeat on Gascoyne's motion would be tantamount to a rejection of the reform bill, and that there would have to be a general election to give ministers a secure majority in the lower house.

The success of Gascoyne's motion created a wave of fury and frustration out of doors. From late 1830 reform meetings regularly took place in many large towns. Radical associations, assemblies, marches, banners and symbols reminded contemporaries of the force of the postwar mobilisation, and there was growing fear about what would happen if reform was not granted. Radical leaders exerted themselves to convince parliament that the only way to calm the nation was to pass a substantial measure of reform. In particular, Bentham's circle in London and its provincial middle-class allies were determined to push Grey's ministry forward and prevent it from retreating now that it had taken up reform. Political unions were multiplying and growing in influence. This intensified the prevalent sense of crisis, as did local political struggles, for anti-reformers were organising in an effort to block further assaults upon the old constitution. To conservatives the repeal of the Test and Corporation Acts and granting of Catholic emancipation had done enough damage already, and there was an urgent need to protect what was left of the established order in Church and state.

Pressure from the political unions had increased early in 1831, as reformers waited impatiently for the government's reform plan to be unveiled. Radical newspapers in London and the provinces inspired and informed the movement, Cobbett's influence grew, and William Carpenter's unstamped open letters to leading politicians achieved circulation figures of about 20,000 per issue. Hunt's career took off again after his electoral victory in Preston. His supporters staged a triumphal entry into London in January 1831, and Hunt's ambitions increased quickly as he tried to recreate the mass platform of former times. There were more demonstrations, and intimidatory language prompted by continuing economic distress. Though they disliked Hunt and his followers, some middle-class reformers were convinced that mass agitation was essential. Parliament would rather grant reform, it was assumed, than provoke a violent uprising.

Once Russell had outlined the reform bill in the Commons, it met with general approval out of doors because it went much further than expected. Advanced radicals rejected it, however, as a Whig attempt to deceive the people. Hunt declared that the government's measure was not the democratic reform the masses wanted and deserved. It granted them no political influence because it did not provide for manhood suffrage. The reform bill in fact deprived the people of the means to make sure that parliament would attend to their needs, said Hunt, and it would strengthen rather than change the established order. Grey's ministry clearly intended to win over the middle classes so that the ruling elite could retain its power and privileges intact. Some metropolitan radicals, notably Henry Hetherington of the *Poor Man's Guardian*, uttered similar objections to the reform bill: it excluded and offered nothing to the working classes.

Plebeian leaders and publicists were already angered by the government's harsh response to urban and rural suffering. Some involved themselves more actively in trade unionism. If they could not have political rights, they decided, they would campaign for economic rights. There were efforts to form general workers' combinations, extending beyond single regions and trades. Meanwhile the NUWC in London merged economic with political questions. In April 1831 the NUWC issued a manifesto for full economic and political equality, which entailed agitation for something more than the ministry's reform bill (annual parliaments, manhood suffrage, the ballot and abolition of property qualifications for MPs).

Though there were some dissentient voices, most radicals were prepared to accept the reform bill as a first instalment. They expected it to make possible further changes in the future, and trusted that government would henceforth be more responsive to public opinion. Francis Place organised agitation in favour of the bill, Cobbett approved it and condemned the Huntite position, and O'Connell, Joseph Hume and other radical MPs warmly commended the government's measure. Respectable middle-class reformers were enthusiastic supporters of the reform bill (they stood to gain most from it) (see Document 10). Their organisation and campaigning were extended, and their newspapers explained how the ministers' reform proposals would facilitate future progress on a range of political, financial, economic, municipal and religious matters. In Manchester, Leeds, Birmingham, Newcastle, Sheffield and other industrial centres there were strong middle-class reform lobbies, and campaigners were sure that the reform bill would mean better representation for their towns and economic interests. The bill would check disorder, they believed, and erect a barrier against democracy. Respectable reformers used the rhetoric of rights, public opinion and popular pressure, but they were steadfastly opposed to mass voting and contended that the vote should go only to men of property and education. As had always been the case, respectable and plebeian groups did not view reform in the same way. The stark social divisions in large towns during the reform struggle of 1830 to 1832 ensured that there could be no united reform campaign.

Differing responses to the reform bill, in parliament as well as the nation, arose partly because it contained both radical and conservative provisions. People could focus on those parts that were most agreeable to them specifically. Depending on the audience, ministers could present their bill as a drastic or a moderate measure, and thereby attract the greatest possible support. The reform bill's ambiguity was one of its most important attributes.

Majority mainstream opinion wanted reform, and there was great disappointment out of doors when the Gascoyne motion was passed in April 1831. Grey was angered by this Tory success (he had not expected it). The prime minister and his colleagues pressed the king to dissolve parliament. Though the activity of political unions was to be regretted, Grey argued, their goal of reform was a legitimate one, and if there was a dissolution popular pressure would probably assist the government. Certainly it would be dangerous if the popular movement took the contrary direction. William IV hated the idea of a dissolution in such circumstances, but he agreed to accept his ministers' advice. The king decided that he could not dismiss them so soon after the previous change of administration and at a time when stability was essential, and he was outraged to hear that some opposition MPs were contesting his right of dissolution. William IV attended parliament in person to announce the dissolution on 22 April 1831. Relations between cabinet and king began to deteriorate, however, because William IV thought that Grey, Durham and others were out to deceive and dominate him. The king directed that the reform bill be modified in order to appease Tory moderates.

The 1831 general election was remarkably successful for the Grey ministry. There were countless demonstrations in favour of the reform bill and candidates who supported it. Newspapers, pamphlets, electoral posters and other printed material discussed nothing else, and voters and non-voters alike were caught up in the excitement. Place and some of the Benthamites helped to form a Parliamentary Candidate Society to promote the return of reformers to the Commons. Many Tory MPs who had voted for the Gascoyne amendment were either forced to retire (as in Lancashire) or defeated at the polls (as in Devon). Gascoyne himself, a Liverpool MP for over thirty years, lost his seat. The Tories did poorly even in their traditional stronghold, the English counties, and most opposition MPs in the new parliament sat for boroughs which were to be wholly or partially disfranchised by the reform bill. Though the number of contests in 1831 was slightly lower than in 1830, and over five hundred members of the previous Commons retained their seats, there were 148 new MPs. The 1831 election took place in a period of widespread agitation, and many successful candidates would in other circumstances have had little chance. Wellington complained that there were twice as many changes as usual. He and other Tory leaders had been incensed by the dissolution, and they now had to accept that the election result, which gave the government a large majority, represented a clear mandate for reform.

A slightly amended reform bill was presented to the Commons by Russell on 24 June 1831. Tories did all they could to delay its progress, and the contest dragged on through the summer. Political unions and the reform press complained about the endless argument. Tension increased, and thoughts turned to the likely reception of the bill in the Lords, since its eventual passage through the Commons was assured. Tory lords were determined to resist dictation from outside, and reformers began to advocate a creation of pro-reform peers to ensure that the government's bill would not be defeated in the upper house. The cabinet balked at this idea: the king would probably refuse to create peers, and in any case it was not clear how many would be needed, and at what stage in the bill's progress. Pressure on the cabinet began to tell, and some ministers recommended significant changes to the reform bill. As Grey told the king, however, too many alterations would render the bill useless. More rather than less instability would result because the people would accuse ministers of going back on their promises. Reformers in the cabinet insisted that there must be no retreat.

There was one important amendment to the bill in the Commons, however, when ultra Tory Lord Chandos carried a motion on 18 August 1831 to extend the county franchise to £50 tenants-at-will. Ministers had arranged that £50 leaseholders would qualify for the vote only after seven years' tenancy, but tenants-at-will could qualify after only one year. The Chandos amendment was designed to increase landlord influence, and it pleased Tories who had long been complaining that the reform bill favoured manufacturing regions at the expense of the landed interests. Whig landowners joined with Tories in passing the amendment, and radical MPs also deserted the government on this matter because they thought that any extension of the franchise should be supported.

After Peel had again argued forcefully against the government's bill, questioning the motives behind it and the benefits it purportedly offered, the Commons passed the measure on its third reading by a majority of 109 on 22 September. There were celebrations all over the country, but the cabinet's mood grew sombre as the Lords made ready to debate reform. Mass meetings continued. Political unions issued threats to Tory peers, while opposition newspapers urged them not to forget their duty to protect the constitution. There was much discussion about a possible creation of peers, though Grey sought to postpone a decision on this for as long as possible. Tory leaders assumed that ministers would rather modify their bill than have it rejected. Tories also thought that many people were bored by the reform struggle. Of the seven by-elections held since the 1831 general election, anti-reformers had won six. Opinion was shifting against the government as interest in reform declined, Tories claimed. The king would never agree to create peers, they added, and nor would Grey subvert the aristocratic order to which he belonged. The ministers' difficulties increased as reform agitation narrowed their options. The reform bill intact was the very least that most reformers would accept, while plebeian radicals had already declared themselves against the bill on the grounds that it was inadequate.

The Lords rejected the bill on 8 October by 199 to 158 votes, provoking indignant outbursts in most large towns. Newspapers appeared with black mourning borders, and protest meetings in London and Birmingham attracted huge audiences. As the 'Swing' disturbances continued in the rural south, there was serious rioting in Nottingham, Derby and Bristol. Alarm spread, and the government's misgivings about the influence of political unions grew as the council of the BPU advocated the establishment of paramilitary bodies comprising a national guard to defend property and deter any conservative reaction against the reform campaign. Althorp expected the ministry to fall. Grey thought of resigning in the hope that Wellington, forced to respond to the mounting crisis, would be better able to carry some reform through the Lords. But as doubts about the cabinet's resolve increased, and rumours abounded that the reform bill would be altered before ministers tried again in the Lords, Grey announced that he would not identify himself with any measure that differed fundamentally from the one the peers had thrown out.

King and ministry were unnerved by the violence of these weeks, and Joseph Hamburger has suggested that much of the disorder was orchestrated by middle-class reformers as an 'art of revolution'. They tried to extort concessions by convincing the ruling elite that the established order was in danger, and that it would be better for the elite to deal with them than further to antagonise the turbulent masses. John Belchem has called this 'the middle-class version of bargaining by riot', and though the control exercised by leaders of the political unions was exaggerated for effect, they did influence the reform struggle at decisive moments. Geoffrey Finlayson, however, denies that reform leaders such as Joseph Parkes in Birmingham acted upon some master strategy. They were opportunists. They may have exerted pressure on the government, but sometimes they acted on the government's behalf. Parkes was in close communication with Althorp, for example, and when BPU leaders considered establishing a military organisation, Parkes persuaded them to abandon the plan. This was what the government wanted.[18]

The reform movement splintered in the aftermath of the Lords vote of 8 October. In London, Manchester and elsewhere rival radical bodies competed for influence, and plebeian activists continued to demand something more than what Grey's government was offering. Attwood stressed the need for disciplined action guided by political unions under respectable leadership, and argued that the serious disturbances in Bristol might never have occurred had the local union been stronger. Attwood and Parkes in Birmingham, Place in London, Prentice in Manchester, John Fife in Newcastle, Baines in Leeds, and similar middle-class spokesmen in other towns sought to forestall a conservative backlash while preventing the reform campaign from being taken over by extremists.

Ministers tried to reassert their authority by banning certain forms of extra-parliamentary organisation (to check the political unions), and by arranging for the reform bill to be reintroduced before Christmas. But the cabinet was now deeply divided. Durham, Brougham and Holland wanted to force the Lords to give way, and argued for a creation of peers. Grey, Richmond, Melbourne, Palmerston and Lansdowne objected. William IV complained about the continuing unrest out of doors, and though he assured ministers that they still had his confidence, the king would not hear of a creation of peers. He pressed again for the reform bill to be modified. Grey saw that a large creation (the Lords majority against the bill on 8 October had been forty-one) would demean the peerage and contradict the spirit of the reform bill, which was meant to safeguard aristocratic government. As the king continued to make difficulties, it was decided that the bill would be altered in some minor details. Negotiations began with moderate Tory peers Harrowby and Wharncliffe, who spoke for an as yet unknown number of waverers in the Lords. Grey was willing to remove certain boroughs from schedule B if waverers approved of added representation for large towns, but schedule A and the £10 borough franchise were not to be given up. Ministers argued about these points (Palmerston and Melbourne wanted to offer the waverers much more), and Wellington and Peel took the negotiations as a sign of government weakness. Though nothing could be agreed with Harrowby and Wharncliffe, Grey found that several bishops who had previously voted against the reform bill in the Lords now intended to vote for its second reading, thereby accepting the principle of reform.

The bill was altered to take account of recent census returns and new information about property values and the taxes paid in particular towns. Fifty-six boroughs were now to be completely disfranchised, and thirty would each lose one of their two seats. Twenty-two new boroughs would return two members each, and twenty would each return one member. The total number of MPs was not to be reduced. Some restrictions on the £10 borough franchise were relaxed (those relating to continuous occupancy, for example, and the payment of local rates), and the voting rights of resident freemen were to be unaffected.

This third version of the reform bill was introduced in the Commons on 12 December 1831. There was further contact with wavering peers and bishops, and Grey assured the king that ministers were still prepared to make alterations that would not undermine the bill's integrity and efficiency. Durham, however, urged Grey to request a creation of peers rather than discuss modifications. In January 1832 Grey told William IV that the bill would almost certainly be defeated in the Lords, and that the effect on the people would be disastrous. The king again rejected the idea of a creation of peers, but he finally agreed to consider (not accept) ministerial advice on this matter if submitted in writing. Suggested promotions to the upper house, he added, should be confined to the eldest sons and collateral heirs of existing peers, and Scottish and Irish peers. This would ensure that the character of the House of Lords would not be permanently affected, and that the hereditary principle would survive intact. William IV maintained that the best way for the ministry to end the reform crisis was to make yet more changes to the bill, but Grey did not entirely trust the Tory waverers. The prime minister was offended by their reluctance to vote for the second reading in the Lords when only the principle of reform was at stake.

As the bill made its way through the Commons, Peel moved several amendments which, though unsuccessful, were intended to prepare the way for a second Lords rejection. When Harrowby suggested that a Tory reform bill might be introduced when the Lords came to debate the government's measure, Peel advised against this. Unwilling to assume responsibility for reform, he thought it would be better for opposition peers to amend the existing bill rather than propose an alternative. The government's bill passed its third reading in the Commons on 23

March 1832. Ministers were doubtful about its prospects in the Lords, however, and did not feel able to make the further concessions required by waverers. Some of Grey's weary and irritable colleagues preferred not to confront the Lords once again, and wanted to resign, but he persuaded them to remain in place. Meanwhile pressure was building up out of doors for ministers to break the deadlock and overcome resistance in the Lords with a bold use of the royal prerogative. William IV told Grey that he should not be asked to create peers until ministers knew precisely how many they needed. The *Westminster Review* advocated a creation even if the reform bill could be carried without it: progressive peers would be useful in the future, and liberal policies could no longer be obstructed if the conservative majority, a legacy of fifty years of Pittite and Tory rule, was balanced by new promotions. Grey, however, continued to seek some other solution, and he appeared to have found it when moderate Tory peers agreed to vote for the bill's second reading if the idea of creation was given up.

Waverers had decided that a bargain on reform would be less harmful than a creation of peers, but Peel found their position reprehensible. He accused ministers of trying to overturn the independence of the House of Lords, joined with other Tories in declaring the government's conduct unconstitutional, and urged Tory peers not to give up their resistance. Peel wanted the Lords to force the government formally to request a creation of peers, a course so drastic and controversial that no future cabinet could undertake another such outrage against the constitution. After William IV again urged Grey to respect the waverers' objections to the reform bill, and alter it accordingly, the ministers decided on 3 April that if a creation of peers became necessary to pass the bill as it stood, they would consider themselves bound to recommend one. The reform bill passed its second reading in the Lords on 14 April by a margin of only nine votes. There would have been no majority without waverer support, but Grey was painfully aware that Harrowby and Wharncliffe had given no promises about amendments in committee. In fact, they now consorted with Wellington and other opponents of the bill to delay and amend it, a development welcomed by Peel. Grey was furious because he thought that his previous negotiation with waverers entitled him to be kept informed of their intentions.

On 7 May ministers were defeated on Lord Lyndhurst's motion to postpone discussion of the disfranchisement clauses until the rest of the bill had been approved. Grey refused to treat this as a matter of procedure, and he immediately rejected the alternative reform plan now proposed by Tory peers (this included retention of the scot and lot franchise, fewer disfranchisements than were provided for in the government's schedule A, abandonment of schedules B and D, and the redistribution of 113 seats).

Now Grey was ready to recommend a creation of peers, and all members of the cabinet apart from Richmond backed his decision. They insisted that their reform bill must be passed intact, and informed William IV that they would resign if he decided not to follow their advice. The king was not willing to go above twenty peers, a figure mentioned during previous discussions, but Grey asked for fifty. On 9 May the ministers resigned. They were even more relieved to be free of the vexations of office than the king was to be rid of them (he never forgave them for failing to shield him from pressure and embarrassment), yet Grey and his allies were back in office within days. Wellington was unable to form a ministry because Peel refused to serve, and relations between the two deteriorated again as in 1830. Though Peel agreed that a reform bill had to be passed, he repeated his earlier opinion that it should not be passed by a Tory government. Peel preferred to have nothing to do with any reform settlement. This would give him freedom in the future to accept or condemn the consequences of reform as he found appropriate. Meanwhile the Commons had resolved that the king should only appoint ministers who were willing to carry a reform bill of the same character as the one previously passed by the lower house. William IV grudgingly recalled Grey, who himself was reluctant to return, and the king agreed to create peers if the government could not be sure of carrying the reform bill without them.

This crisis at the centre of power during May 1832 was matched by another wave of violence out of doors. The Grey ministry's resignation prompted demonstrations in many towns. A joint meeting of political unions in Birmingham was said to be the largest assembly in British history (some accounts say over 100,000 people were present), and prominent reform spokesmen, fearing for property and order as agitation reached its climax, demanded that Grey should be recalled and the reform bill passed without further delay. In an effort to prevent Wellington from taking office, mass petitions called for supplies to be stopped (the Manchester petition gained 25,000 signatures in just a few hours), and there was a call for taxpayers to withhold contributions. Place raised the cry 'To stop the duke, go for gold', hoping that a run on the banks would make court and Lords give way. Radical organisers, caricaturists, journalists and demagogues attacked particular peers and members of the royal family for their resistance to reform. The BPU council warned that if the reform bill was not passed, the people would press for a more extensive measure, and in London and Manchester there was a momentary truce between respectable and plebeian leaders. Many political unions threatened to take control of local government in their districts, there was more talk of forming a civil guard, and the *Poor Man's Guardian* issued instructions about street-fighting and self-defence. Some prominent Whigs, including Durham and Althorp, kept middle-class reformers informed of high political developments and implicitly encouraged the general protest. This wave of agitation disturbed trade and business, and the widespread unease was exacerbated by continuing economic hardship and the recent cholera epidemic. As in previous months, various complaints and aspirations found their focus in the fate of the reform bill.

Tory inability to take office, and growing excitement in the nation, combined to bring about Grey's rapid return to the premiership. He and his colleagues secured (and made known) the king's agreement that there would be a creation of peers if this proved necessary to pass the reform bill without amendment. With considerable annoyance and ill-humour, and solely to avoid the extremity of a creation, some opponents of the bill decided to abstain or stay away from subsequent divisions in the Lords. The reform bill was finally passed on its third reading in a poorly attended upper house on 4 June. In a final show of displeasure, William IV refused to give the royal assent in person, but this made little difference. Ministers had won a momentous victory, to the relief and satisfaction of most interested people out of doors.

The Great Reform Act

There will probably never be a consensus of opinion about what happened in 1832. Many different interpretations have been advanced, some of which are impossible to harmonise. Historians often focus on particular aspects of the reform struggle in order to make sense of the whole. For E. A. Smith, the ministry's success in carrying reform owed much to the talent and influence of Grey. The prime minister held together a divided cabinet through very difficult times, and he managed to retain control over the reform process so that the final measure was substantially the one he wanted.[19] But it can also be argued that Grey's mistakes added to the cabinet's discomfort, for at different stages he miscalculated the reactions of the Commons, William IV, and the Lords. Fortunately for the government none of these mistakes proved fatal, and Grey showed enormous strength of character in adhering steadfastly to his basic premises: that the reform bill could not be greatly modified, and that a creation of peers was categorically the last resort, to be considered only when all other options had been tested. The crises which broke out as ministers sought to carry reform through parliament demonstrated above all that their course was uncertain and experimental. G. Williams and J. Ramsden have pointed out that there was no previous experience on which to draw, nor much agreement on the likely effects of specific parts of the bill. Perhaps the vital point is that important decisions were made early on: a public commitment to reform, the appointment of the committee of four, and cabinet approval of a draft measure.[20]

The propertied middle classes accepted the reform bill and were thereby attached to the established order. Advanced radicals were foiled. This was what ministers wanted, and they were probably right to believe that anything less than their bill would have failed to commend aristocratic government to influential groups in society. Reform was electorally useful for Whigs in the early 1830s, moreover, and not just because the issue had direct appeal. Reform abolished rotten boroughs, and Tory patrons controlled three times as many of these as did Whigs. But if the reform of 1832 turned the propertied classes away from radicalism and increased their respect for established institutions – 'once they had their rightful position', writes Michael Brock, 'they did not favour further adventures'[21] – it also failed to provide a final settlement. Plebeian radicals denounced 1832 as a middle-class betrayal of the common people. Reform would have been impossible without mass agitation, yet workers gained nothing for their exertions. Social and political friction increased, radicals rejected Whig finality, and Chartism was to confirm the continuing vitality of independent popular politics.

The importance of popular pressure between 1830 and 1832, and the potential for revolution at this time, have attracted a great deal of comment. Asa Briggs states that reform removed the danger of revolution, but George Rude discerns no genuine revolutionary threat, and Jonathan Clark insists that reform owed most not to popular agitation but to high political conflict and a confusion of parties brought on by Catholic emancipation.[22] No explanation of the reform crisis, however, would be complete without at least some reference to popular pressure. Indeed, there were times when this pressure had an important effect on the reform struggle, most notably when the Lords rejected the bill in October 1831, and in May 1832, when Grey's cabinet resigned. During and after May 1832, reformers had no doubt that their agitation prevented Wellington from forming an administration, and that it promoted the return of Grey. While Eric Evans admits that this unrest was serious, he doubts that it really altered the course of events. Wellington's failure and Grey's return resulted from decisions made by William IV and prominent Tories. Michael Brock points out that leading politicians may not have believed or been very alarmed by reports of violence, and John Cannon asserts that pressure from below had far less impact than decisions taken at the top.[23]

But it hardly seems likely that elite politicians felt themselves able to disregard unrest out of doors. Grey, Durham, Russell and their colleagues, and William IV for that matter, sensed that external pressure was dangerously rising through 1831 and 1832. Such was the agitation in May 1832 that Grey would return to the premiership only if the king consented to a creation of peers. Yet it is by no means clear that there could have been a rising had Wellington taken office at this time. John Stevenson points out that the necessary leadership and organisation were lacking. In addition, the riots of October 1831, the most serious of the period, were unplanned, unconnected, and easily put down. To Stevenson this does not suggest that reform had to be passed at any cost. Rather, it shows that the state could deal even with the very worst manifestations of popular impatience and anger.[24] In any case, most reformers eschewed violence and confined themselves to peaceful agitation, even if they used threatening language. There was no strong commitment to unconstitutional methods. Warnings about a resort to physical force were often made, but these were meant to intimidate the political elite and weaken resistance to reform. The threat of revolution was not as serious as some contemporaries claimed.[25] Many feigned alarm in order to move others. Promoters and supporters of the reform bill, inside as well as outside parliament, asserted that reform was the only way to stave off revolution. For all those who said this because they would have said anything to make their opponents give way, however, there were others who genuinely believed it.

The situation was particularly difficult for Grey and the ministry because of a disturbing new development. Popular pressure had been given more focus and weight by the rise of the political unions. Grey and the king both complained at length about the power of these bodies and the trouble it took to restrain them, yet the political unions paradoxically assisted the government in negotiations with court and parliamentary opposition, for Grey was able to maintain that the only way to break their influence was to pass the reform bill. Perhaps there would have been no reform without them.[26]

Early twentieth-century studies of the nature and significance of the Great Reform Act tended to treat it as a concession to popular pressure and a means of weakening the Tories and assisting the Whigs electorally.[27] But D. C. Moore has since argued that reform was intended as a cure rather than a concession. Moore contends that the Grey government's real aim was to reinforce deference. This was to be achieved by denying influence to those who lacked property, by clearly separating borough from county constituencies and minimising the middle-class vote in the latter, and by enhancing landlord power by giving more seats to the counties.[28] The deference thesis has been questioned by Eric Evans, Norman Gash, Frank O'Gorman,

Norman McCord, E. P. Hennock and R. W. Davis. They point out that ministers did not have the time or expertise needed to draft a reform bill that would do what Moore suggests, and that general concerns (cabinet and party divisions on reform, the need to remove electoral anomalies while reserving political influence for property, the problems that would arise if middle-class reformers were driven to unite with the masses) mattered more than some supposed master plan. The reform bill was a clumsy rather than logical device, a useful rather than efficient tool. It was not meant to reorganise the electoral system entirely, and its authors were more interested in continuity than in change.[29]

The idea of reform as a concession has been advanced by J. Milton-Smith, who thinks that when ministers spoke of a final settlement, what they really meant was that their bill would satisfy existing demands. They accepted that in the future representation might have to be granted to new interests. J. A. Phillips also treats reform as a concession. There was a growing desire for inclusion in the political process, he explains, and the reform bill met this demand. Extra-parliamentary politics had expanded remarkably since the 1780s, and reform in 1832 gave the vote to many men who had been politically active for years. Phillips may be confusing effects with intentions, however, and Derek Beales has argued that Grey's ministry considered a redistribution of seats far more important than an expansion of the electorate.[30]

Nevertheless, Phillips is right to fit 1832 into a longer-term perspective. John Derry also considers that the timing and nature of reform were partly determined by political developments during and after the ascendancy of Pitt. Pitt raised the reputation of the unreformed order, and his determination to provide effective and trustworthy government was later taken up by Liverpool. Together they ensured that serious debate about parliamentary reform, when it came, would proceed within parameters they had defined. The old order was not exhausted by 1832, writes Derry, but vital, and basic tenets about property, liberty and rights survived unaltered from the 1780s through to the 1830s.[31] Reflections of this kind make a valuable contribution to current analysis of the Great Reform Act, and though a rigid teleology is best avoided, it would be

impossible to understand what happened in 1832 without paying attention to preceding events. In one of the most interesting
studies of the reform bill, Leslie Mitchell places it within the
context of the old Whig struggle against the crown. Fox had
always maintained that liberty and property were mutually
dependent. To increase the influence of men of property, therefore, would be to protect liberty and check royal tyranny. The
Whigs of 1832 remembered the politics of the 1780s and 1790s,
and since rotten boroughs no longer gave property enough
authority, the solution was to redistribute seats and alter the
borough franchise.[32] If Mitchell is right, Whig methods were
adaptable while their aims remained unchanged, another reminder of the essential continuity underlying the achievements
of 1832.

Conclusion

Wellington's fall made possible the Whigs' return to office after
more than twenty years in opposition, and the sensation caused
by the duke's speech against parliamentary reform in November
1830 helped to ensure that a reform settlement would be the
Grey ministry's chief priority. Wellington later maintained that
his speech was not the primary cause of his government's final
collapse. He considered Catholic emancipation and the July
Revolution in France of far greater importance. But at the time
Wellington saw how quickly reform sentiment was growing,
and he was glad he could resign on some measure other than
reform. Wellington doubted the Whigs' ability to establish a
lasting administration. They would have no choice but to
introduce a reform bill, and he expected Tories to unite and
defeat it. Once the ultras had rejoined followers of Wellington
and Peel, they would easily bring Grey's government down.

As events were soon to prove, on most of these points
Wellington was mistaken. Indeed, historians have even suggested that the duke was wrong about the reasons why he was
forced to vacate the premiership. Carlos Flick discounts the
French Revolution and popular pressure, and emphasises high
political machination. The key development was a union of
opposition groups. The civil list vote on 15 November 1830
finally brought about a combination of forces against Wellington's

ministry, five months after the 1830 general election. Apparently the duke had not seen it coming. Norman Gash maintains that Wellington did not have the personal manner or necessary political skills to be a successful prime minister in the circumstances of the late 1820s. Gash considers the government's main failing to have been its indecisive approach to economic problems.[33]

The change of ministers at the end of 1830 has broader significance. A cabinet had not been forced to resign by a hostile vote in the Commons since 1804, and Wellington's fall led to the first complete change of personnel since the dismissal of the Talents in 1807. Wellington and Peel realised that the dismemberment of Liverpool's conservative alliance in 1827 made the task of re-establishing a stable Tory administration very difficult. They had to make the attempt, but their effort to repair the alliance failed. Liverpool's ministry had tried to follow moderate and uncontroversial courses, kept Catholic emancipation an open question, and depended on the support of mainstream conservative opinion in parliament and the nation. But it was able to last mainly because difficult decisions had been postponed. After Liverpool's stroke it was not so easy to put off these decisions, and Toryism fell apart. In 1829 the Catholic question had to be settled. Not only did emancipation fail to pacify Ireland, however, but it proved politically damaging. Ultras turned against Wellington and Peel. Moderates had been alienated by the Canningite resignations of May 1828, and any hope of winning them back was destroyed by Wellington's speech against reform in November 1830. The duke's cabinet was already divided. In particular, there was growing animosity between Wellington, who had more courage than wisdom, and Peel, whose faith in the duke's political judgement had been all but destroyed.

Wellington's clumsy endeavour to push parliamentary reform off the political agenda actually encouraged more Whigs to declare themselves unequivocally for reform. Previously Whig leaders had found it impossible to have a party commitment to reform and maintain party unity at the same time. Now the situation was changing. E. A. Wasson and Austin Mitchell have noted a trend towards firmer Whig attachment to parliamentary reform from the fall of the Talents onwards,[34] and this was certainly accelerated in the late 1820s. The appointment of the

Grey ministry at the end of 1830 elevated reform to the status of an explicit government policy, though the ensuing reform struggle was not shaped solely by high political battles. Extra-parliamentary agitation was decisive. The reform struggle also demonstrated the decline in royal power. William IV was happy to get rid of the Grey cabinet in May 1832, but the crown was no longer able to make and unmake ministries, and the king was forced by events to take Grey and his colleagues back. The viability of governments owed less to royal approval than to prevalent political circumstances.

One should not underestimate the role of chance in bringing on the reform struggle. Key events could not be predicted: Liverpool's stroke; Canning's death; the death of George IV, which necessitated a general election; the reaction to Wellington's anti-reform speech. Reform was not inevitable, though political developments over the preceding decades made it likely. Liverpool's government, and the nature of Toryism after Pitt, prevented gradual parliamentary reform, which meant that pressure for more substantial change would build up. By 1831 it seemed that only an extensive reform bill could settle the question and bring the electoral system into line with contemporary needs. The outcome of the reform struggle between 1830 and 1832 was never a foregone conclusion, of course, and there was no single, cumulative, inexorable thread of ideas or events leading from the political changes of the 1780s through to 1832. Nevertheless, what happened in 1832 has to be interpreted in the light of the problems and contests of preceding years. Any valid explanation of the Great Reform Act must include a just recognition of general and particular causes, long-term and short-term developments: the gradual growth of resentment against the established order, salient political needs and opportunities, instability in high politics, and the maturation of extra-parliamentary radicalism.

Notes

1 See for example R. W. Davis, 'Tories, Whigs and Catholic emancipation 1827–9', *EHR*, 97, 1982, pp. 89–98; G. I. T. Machin, 'Canning, Wellington and the Catholic question', *EHR*, 109, 1984, pp. 94–100.

2 E. A. Wasson, 'The coalitions of 1827 and the crisis of Whig leadership', *HJ*, 20, 1977, pp. 587–606.

3 M. Bentley, *Politics without Democracy 1815–1914*, London, 1984, p. 61; D. Beales, 'Parliamentary parties and the "independent" Member, 1810–60', in R. Robson (ed.), *Ideas and Institutions of Victorian Britain*, London, 1967, pp. 1–19; D. Large, 'The decline of the "party of the crown" and the rise of parties in the House of Lords 1783–1837', *EHR*, 78, 1963, pp. 669–95; A. Aspinall, 'English party organisation in the early nineteenth century', *EHR*, 41, 1926, pp. 389–411, 'The last of the Canningites', *EHR*, 50, 1935, pp. 639–69, and introduction in A. Aspinall (ed.), *The Formation of Canning's Ministry*, London, 1937.

4 G. I. T. Machin, 'Resistance to repeal of the Test and Corporation Acts 1828', *HJ*, 22, 1979, pp. 111–39.

5 K. A. Noyce, 'The Duke of Wellington and the Catholic question', in N. Gash (ed.), *Wellington. Studies in the Military and Political Career of the First Duke of Wellington*, Manchester, 1990, pp. 139–58.

6 A. Aspinall, 'The Canningite Party', *TRHS*, 4th series, 17, 1934, pp. 177–226.

7 J. C. D. Clark, *English Society 1688–1832: Ideology, Social Structure and Political Practice during the Ancien Regime*, Cambridge, 1985, pp. 401–2; A. Briggs, *The Age of Improvement 1783–1867*, rev. edn, London, 1979, p. 234; E. J. Evans, *The Forging of the Modern State 1783–1870*, 2nd edn, London, 1996, pp. 215, 218–19, and *Britain before the Reform Act: Politics and Society 1815–32*, London, 1995, p. 74; E. Halevy, *The Triumph of Reform*, London, 1961, pp. 10–11; J. Cannon, *Parliamentary Reform 1640–1832*, Cambridge, 1973, pp. 201–3; N. Gash, *Mr Secretary Peel*, London, 1961, pp. 646–7.

8 J. J. Sack, 'Wellington and the Tory press', in Gash, *Wellington*, pp. 159–69.

9 See for example M. J. Turner, *Reform and Respectability. The Making of a Middle-Class Liberalism in Early Nineteenth-Century Manchester*, Manchester, 1995, pp. 242–7, 278–89.

10 J. E. Crimmins, 'Jeremy Bentham and Daniel O'Connell: their correspondence and radical alliance 1828–31', *HJ*, 40, 1997, pp. 359–87.

11 A. Briggs, 'The background of the parliamentary reform movement in three English cities', in vol. I of his *Collected Essays*, Brighton, 1985, pp. 180–200.

12 N. Gash, 'English reform and the French revolution in the general election of 1830', in R. Pares and A. J. P. Taylor (eds), *Essays Presented to Sir Lewis Namier*, London, 1956, pp. 258–88; R. Quinault, 'The French Revolution of 1830 and parliamentary reform', *History*, 79, 1994, pp. 377–93.

13 Halevy, *Triumph of Reform*, p. 8; J. Stevenson, *Popular Disturbances in England 1700–1832*, 2nd edn, London, 1992, pp. 266, 269.

14 As has often been noted, the Grey ministry was the most aristocratic of the whole nineteenth century. E. L. Woodward, *The Age of Reform 1815–70*, 2nd edn, Oxford, 1961, p. 79; Halevy, *Triumph of Reform*, p. 14; E. A. Smith, *Lord Grey 1761–1845*, Stroud, 1996, pp. 259–60; E. A. Wasson, *Whig Renaissance: Lord Althorp and the Whig Party 1782–1845*, New York, 1987, pp. 189–90.

15 'Report on Reform', in H. Grey (ed.), *Correspondence of the Late Earl Grey with King William IV*, London, 1867, vol. I, Appendix A, p. 461.

16 J. Prest, *Lord John Russell*, London, 1972, p. 46.

17 M. O'Neill and G. Martin, 'A backbencher on parliamentary reform 1831–32', *HJ*, 23, 1980, pp. 539–63.

18 J. Hamburger, *James Mill and the Art of Revolution*, New Haven, 1963, ch. 4; J. Belchem, *Popular Radicalism in Nineteenth Century Britain*, Basingstoke, 1996, p. 61; G. Finlayson, 'Joseph Parkes of Birmingham, 1796–1865: a study in philosophic radicalism', *HR*, 46, 1973, pp. 186–201.

19 Smith, *Lord Grey*, p. 261.

20 G. Williams and J. Ramsden, *Ruling Britannia. A Political History of Britain 1688–1988*, London, 1990, p. 198.

21 M. Brock, *The Great Reform Act*, London, 1973, p. 319.

22 Briggs, *Age of Improvement*, p. 259; G. Rude, 'English rural and urban disturbances on the eve of the First Reform Bill, 1830–31', *P&P*, 37, 1967, pp. 87–102; Clark, *English Society*, p. 402.

23 Evans, *Britain before the Reform Act*, pp. 92–3; Brock, *Great Reform Act*, pp. 305, 307–9; Cannon, *Parliamentary Reform*, pp. 238–40.

24 Stevenson, *Popular Disturbances*, pp. 293, 296.

25 E. P. Thompson, *The Making of the English Working Class*, rev. edn, London, 1980, pp. 887–903; Hamburger, *James Mill and the Art of Revolution*, ch. 4; M. Thomis and P. Holt, *Threats of Revolution in Britain 1789–1848*, London, 1977, ch. 4; D. G. Wright, *Popular Radicalism. The Working-Class Experience 1780–1880*, London, 1988, pp. 89–95.

26 N. Lopatin, 'Political unions and the Great Reform Act', *PH*, 10, 1991, pp. 105–23; H. Ferguson, 'The Birmingham Political Union and the government 1831–32', *VS*, 3, 1960, pp. 261–76.

27 J. R. M. Butler, *The Passing of the Reform Bill*, London, 1914; G. M. Trevelyan, *Lord Grey of the Reform Bill*, London, 1920; O. F. Christie, *The Transition from Aristocracy*, London, 1927.

28 D. C. Moore, 'Concession or cure: the sociological premises of the First Reform Act', *HJ*, 9, 1966, pp. 39–59, and *The Politics of Deference*, Hassocks, 1974.

29 Evans, *Britain before the Reform Act*, pp. 93–4; N. Gash, *Aristocracy and People. Britain 1815–65*, London, 1979, pp. 150–2; F. O'Gorman, 'Electoral deference in unreformed England, 1760–1832', *JMH*, 56, 1984, pp. 391–429; N. McCord, 'Some difficulties of parliamentary reform', *HJ*, 10, 1967, pp. 376–90; E. P. Hennock, 'The sociological premises of the First Reform Act: a critical note', *VS*, 14, 1971, pp. 321–7, and see Moore's reply on pp. 328–37; R. W. Davis, 'Deference and aristocracy in the time of the Great Reform Act', *AmHR*, 81, 1976, pp. 532–9.

30 J. Milton-Smith, 'Earl Grey's cabinet and the objects of parliamentary reform', *HJ*, 15, 1972, pp. 55–74; J. A. Phillips, 'Popular politics in unreformed England', *JMH*, 52, 1980, pp. 624–5; D. Beales, 'The electorate before and after 1832: the right to vote, and the opportunity', *PH*, 11, 1992, pp. 139–50, and reply by F. O'Gorman, *PH*, 12, 1993, pp. 171–83.

31 J. Derry, *Politics in the Age of Fox, Pitt and Liverpool*, Basingstoke, 1990, pp. 195–7.

32 L. G. Mitchell, 'Foxite politics and the Great Reform Bill', *EHR*, 108, 1993, pp. 338–64.

33 C. Flick, 'The fall of Wellington's government', *JMH*, 37, 1965, pp. 62–71; N. Gash, 'Wellington and the prime ministership', in Gash, *Wellington*, p. 136.

34 E. A. Wasson, 'The great Whigs and parliamentary reform 1809–30', *JBS*, 24, 1985, pp. 434–64; A. Mitchell, 'The Whigs and parliamentary reform before 1830', *HSANZ*, 12, 1965, pp. 22–42.

Conclusion

In seeking to understand British politics between the early years
of George III's reign and the passing of the Great Reform Act,
one is presented with essential features for analysis. None of
these can be contemplated in isolation, for they all relate to each
other. The most important have been discussed at length in the
foregoing chapters: the political role of the crown; changing
relationships between crown and politicians; the formation of
party and party ideology; the expansion of popular participation in politics and the points of contact between politicians
and people; new difficulties in attending to urgent public issues,
and how these affected or were affected by developments in
high and low politics.

There were slow but monumental changes in the respective
positions of crown and politicians, the role of the cabinet, and
the nature of the office of prime minister. These changes were
promoted by the incapacity of George III, the laziness and errors
of George IV, the increasing complexity of government business,
continual pressure for administrative and financial reforms
(which weakened patronage), increasing co-ordination of ministerial activity under a recognised head, a growing sense of
shared commitments and responsibilities in cabinet, and the rise
of party, which meant that politicians had less need for royal
favour. The result was a gradual transformation of executive
power from the power of the monarch to power exercised in his
name by ministers. Quite simply, ministers became more independent of the crown.

Conclusion

Many contemporaries realised that this was happening, of course, and their arguments for and against change added to the conflicts which so characterised late eighteenth-century and early nineteenth-century British politics. The most significant source of contention was the programme of George III. Perhaps the king had no fixed ideas or goals, but his manner of proceeding allowed his opponents to claim otherwise. Opposition to the crown was bolstered by the notion, one that Foxites made their own, that the final decision on men and measures should be made by the House of Commons. By 1832 it was widely accepted that, in order to survive, a ministry had to have a secure majority in parliament, and that the preferences of MPs normally mattered more than those of the reigning monarch. To forfeit parliamentary confidence, it was thought, was to risk being forced out of office.

Though this situation did not make cabinets powerless, much depended on the debating and administrative expertise of leading ministers, and on prevalent circumstances in parliament and the nation. When opinion turned against ministers, they could get their way by employing skilful argument, bargains, superior information, and even threats of resignation. A majority of MPs might vote against the government on a particular issue, but this did not usually indicate a wish to bring it down. The income tax division of March 1816 illustrates the point. The civil list vote of November 1830, however, was a notable reminder to politicians that they ignored changing circumstances at their peril.

A long period of relatively stable government under Pitt between 1784 and 1801 was notable for the sympathetic understanding between an efficient and confident prime minister and a king who at last had a chief adviser on whom he could fully rely. Pitt was able to build up a strong personal influence in cabinet and in parliament, and he respected the crown's political functions. Though Pitt did not attend energetically to party formation, political developments during his period of ascendancy promoted the rise of party sentiment and behaviour. The Foxites were already an identifiable group, with their own particular goals and methods, before 1801. Then Foxite association with the Grenvillites between 1804 and 1817 accentuated Whig party spirit. Meanwhile Pitt's allies and successors had cohered more effectively as a party, and the conservative alliance built up under Liverpool after 1812 dominated British politics for fifteen years.

Politicians and parties operated within an agreed framework, that established by the Glorious Revolution of 1688. But unresolved conflicts affected their interpretation of the revolution, and there were disagreements about the work it left undone, the rights it had established, and conventions which had since arisen. Through the eighteenth century it was repeatedly claimed that Tories, long condemned as enemies of the revolution settlement, still disliked its central features, especially limitations on the power of the crown and toleration for Dissenters. Party names were less meaningful during the long Whig ascendancy under George I and George II, but party principles and terminology became more influential in the late eighteenth century under George III. Some contemporaries pointed to a revived Toryism after 1760 as George III and his allies tried to increase royal power by (allegedly) breaking with established constitutional practice. In the early nineteenth century some Tory publicists found it necessary to reiterate their acceptance of the Glorious Revolution and to acknowledge the legitimacy of the political order it had established, but the revolutionary settlement remained contested ground. One of the causes of the controversy inspired by Price, Burke and Paine in the 1790s was a clash of opinion about the evolution of the British constitution and whether it was more appropriate to emphasise its conservative or libertarian aspects.

Clearly, the role of ideology in political change and party formation should not be underestimated. But changing political circumstances and opportunities, and the need to respond to difficult problems, old and new, were also important. By 1815 the two-party division involved distinctive positions on the leading issues of the time, notably Catholic emancipation, the royal prerogative and parliamentary reform. Specific events, George III's dismissal of the Talents administration in 1807 for example, had also reinforced opinions and allegiances. Whigs stood for civil and religious liberty, and wanted to limit the influence of the crown, while Tories sought to defend the established order in Church and state.

Elite politicians could no longer think and act in a detached, self-referential manner. One of the most significant features of late eighteenth-century and early nineteenth-century politics was the growth of popular political participation and consciousness. This created many points of contact between governors and governed, and extra-parliamentary protest became increasingly influential. Wilkes during the 1760s and 1770s, and Wyvill in the 1780s, emerged as important figureheads. They and their followers involved themselves principally in agitation for parliamentary and economical reform, responding to such stimuli as poor harvests, high taxes, political corruption and failure in the American war of independence. The French Revolution and British involvement in the subsequent wars polarised opinion and led to intense and protracted political struggles. All sections of society were moved. The political activity of respectable middle-class merchants and manufacturers, and of unenfranchised and propertyless labouring people, expanded as never before. Committed radicals established new organisations, ideas, methods and aims. Reforms were demanded, especially parliamentary reform, for it seemed that political, economic and social improvements would be impossible unless government and legislation became more representative. Full use was made of the press, petition and mass meeting. Most reformers avoided violence, but a revolutionary fringe developed and its insurrectionary ideology was passed on to extremists who attached themselves to postwar radical campaigns.

Radical commitments survived wartime and postwar repression, though extra-parliamentary agitation would decline during the relatively prosperous 1820s. New leaders arose in the early nineteenth century, notably the veteran Cartwright, the wealthy Burdett and the ambitious Hunt, while the vigorous journalism of Cobbett focused the people's attention ever more clearly upon political and economic injustice. Mobilisation for reforms changed political attitudes and expectations. Grievances were more effectively presented. Outdoor protest developed quickly, premised upon shared interests, firm intellectual convictions, and the general resentment created by hunger and hardship. Responses were thoughtful as well as emotional. But radicalism was continually divided. There were disagreements on aims and tactics, personality clashes among leaders, and a lack of unity and co-operation. Reformers from respectable and plebeian backgrounds tended not to act together. Another obstacle to the radical advance was the fact that popular political participation could take conservative rather than anti-establishment forms. This trend was seen during the war and afterwards, as loyalist associations, volunteer units, Pitt Clubs, committees in aid of the civil power, and efforts to prosecute radical writers and booksellers forced many reformers into temporary retreat.

Changes in high and low politics affected the manner in which urgent public issues were addressed. Administrative and financial reforms limited executive influence and deflected some of the accusations about corruption and incompetence in government. These reforms were demanded from below, but they were also conceived and implemented from above, by elite politicians. Catholic emancipation was secured at a time of violent agitation in Ireland and ministerial vulnerability in parliament. Parliamentary reform became possible in 1832 for many reasons, and it can be explained only with reference to needs and circumstances which prevailed in both elite and extra-parliamentary arenas.

There is no consensus among historians about many of the developments outlined in this book, and it is not possible to be utterly precise about the timing and extent of those political changes that took place in Britain between the 1780s and 1830s. It is clear, however, that a gradual and cumulative process of transformation continued throughout the late eighteenth and early nineteenth centuries, and that Britain's political complexion after 1832 was quite unlike what it had been in the early years of George III's reign. This was truly an age of reform. Alongside an increase in the political knowledge and consciousness of the masses came the rise of a respectable middle-class radicalism. There was ample proof of the ability and readiness of committed radicals to galvanise and to lead their less active friends and neighbours. Meanwhile the balance between crown and ministers shifted irreversibly in favour of the latter, and many problems pertaining to the powers of the cabinet, shared ministerial responsibility, the office of prime minister and relations between ministry and parliament began to be resolved in new ways. The Whig revival under Grey, Tory realignment after the retirement of Liverpool, and the unprecedented influence of extra-parliamentary opinion led many contemporaries to believe that post-1832 British politics would involve degrees of reorganisation, adaptation, representation and inclusiveness which had never been known before.

Selected documents

Document 1

Party cohesion developed slowly and unevenly during the late eighteenth and early nineteenth centuries. Indeed, particular policies, events or crises often had unpredictable consequences in parliament: they might strengthen party allegiances, but could easily promote greater instability and confusion. It was dangerous for political leaders to take supporters for granted, and difficult to calculate the likely result of controversial divisions in parliament (especially in the House of Commons). Conflict and faction were highly pronounced during the political battles of 1782 to 1784. In a letter of August 1782, included in W. T. Laprade (ed.), *Parliamentary Papers of John Robinson 1774–84*, London, 1922, pp. 42–8, secretary to the treasury John Robinson, the government whip and patronage manager, informed prime minister the Earl of Shelburne that it was almost impossible to determine the ministry's strength in the Commons.

> In a stable, permanent government to whom gentlemen have professed friendship, with whom they have in general acted, and from whom they have received favours, conjectures may be formed with a tolerable certainty of the opinions which gentlemen will entertain on particular questions, but in a state so rent as this has lately been, torn by intestine divisions, and split into different parties, with an administration to be established after one has been overturned and another divided, it is the hardest task that can be to class them.

Document 2

A defining moment in Foxite politics was George III's dismissal of the Fox–North coalition ministry in December 1783. This was followed by Pitt's appointment as prime minister, and from then on Fox never ceased to question the constitutional propriety of what had happened, nor to impugn the goals and motives of the king and Pitt. The struggles of 1783 and 1784 strengthened the old Rockingham legend about excessive royal power, and Fox brought unresolved political issues into sharper focus with his speech to the Commons on 16 January 1784. The following extract is taken from A. Aspinall and E. A. Smith (eds), *English Historical Documents 1783–1832*, London, 1959, p. 140. Fox upheld the authority of the House of Commons. He argued that though the king had the right to appoint ministers, it was vital also to consider:

> how far it may be prudent, wise and politic in a monarch to continue them in power and support them in office when they are declared by that House to have been elevated to their station by means unconstitutional, and such as to have rendered them unworthy of confidence. It has been asserted that the influence of the Crown in this House is diminished. Still, however, is it not great and extensive? Does not the dismissal of the late ministry, and adoption of the present, exhibit its magnitude?

Document 3

The French Revolution encouraged politicians and the public alike to scrutinise the British political system, and heated disputes arose concerning the historical development of the constitution, the nature of rights and meaning of liberty, and the conduct of monarchs and governments. One of the most significant contributions to the revolution debate was Edmund Burke's *Reflections on the Revolution in France* (1790), and among Burke's chief concerns was the manner in which French ideas and events were being interpreted by reformers at home. Burke was incensed by the 'Discourse on the Love of our Country', given by radical Dissenting minister Richard Price to the Revolution Society at the Old Jewry, London, on 4 November 1789. Price compared the French Revolution to Britain's Glorious

Selected documents

Revolution of 1688, but Burke insisted that the two cases were entirely antagonistic. While 1688 had marked the beginning of gradual, conserving, propitious political transition, the French Revolution was essentially violent and innovatory. Burke also rejected Price's statement of the rights established in 1688. The following extracts are taken from B. W. Hill (ed.), *Edmund Burke on Government, Politics and Society*, London, 1975, pp. 279–96.

So far is it from being true that we acquired a right by the Revolution to elect our kings, that, if we had possessed it before, the English nation did at that time most solemnly renounce and abdicate it, for themselves, and for all their posterity forever ... the succession of the crown has always been what it now is, an hereditary succession by law.... When such an unwarrantable maxim is once established, that no throne is lawful but the elective, no one act of the princes who preceded this era of fictitious election can be valid. But the course of succession is the healthy habit of the British Constitution. A few years ago I should be ashamed to overload a matter so capable of supporting itself by the then unnecessary support of any argument; but this seditious, unconstitutional doctrine is now publicly taught, avowed, and printed.... The people of England will not ape the fashions they have never tried, nor go back to those which they have found mischievous on trial. They look upon the legal hereditary succession of their crown as among their rights.

... The second claim of the Revolution Society is 'a right of cashiering their governors for misconduct'.... No government could stand for a moment, if it could be blown down with anything so loose and indefinite as an opinion of 'misconduct'.

... The third head of right asserted by the pulpit of the Old Jewry, namely the 'right to form a government for ourselves', has, at least, as little countenance from anything done at the Revolution, either in precedent or principle, as the first two of their claims. The Revolution was made to preserve our *ancient* indisputable laws and liberties, and that *ancient* constitution of government which is our only security for law and liberty. If you are desirous of knowing the spirit of our constitution, and the policy which predominated in that great period which has secured it to this hour, pray look for both in our histories, in our records, in our acts and journals of Parliament, and not in the sermons of the Old Jewry, and the after-dinner toasts of the Revolution Society.... We wished at the period of the Revolution and do now wish, to derive all we possess as an inheritance from our forefathers.

Document 4

Burke's arguments about the evolution of the British constitution, and his adulation of the hereditary principle and suspicion
of the French Revolution, drew forth a truculent response from
the radical thinker Thomas Paine. A well known international
revolutionary, Paine criticised the notion that decisions made
and governments formed by one generation had prescriptive
force on later generations, and he could not accept that political
rights should be framed to preserve the established order rather
than to reform it. The following extracts are taken from Thomas
Paine, *Rights of Man* (1791–2), ed. Henry Collins, London, 1969,
pp. 63–4, 105, 229–30.

There never did, there never will, and there never can exist a
parliament, or any description of men, or any generation of men,
in any country, possessed of the right or the power of binding and
controlling posterity to the end of time, or of commanding for
ever how the world shall be governed, or who shall govern it; and
therefore all such clauses, acts or declarations, by which the
makers of them attempt to do what they have neither the right
nor the power to do, nor the power to execute, are in themselves
null and void. Every age and generation must be as free to act for
itself, *in all cases*, as the ages and generations which preceded it.
The vanity and presumption of governing beyond the grave, is
the most ridiculous and insolent of all tyrannies.

... the idea of hereditary legislation is as inconsistent as that of
hereditary judges, or hereditary juries; and as absurd as an
hereditary mathematician, or an hereditary wise man; and as
ridiculous as an hereditary poet-laureate.

... Government is but now beginning to be known. Hitherto it
has been the mere exercise of power, which forbade all effectual
inquiry into rights, and grounded itself wholly on possession.
While the enemy of liberty was its judge, the progress of its
principles must have been small indeed.

The constitutions of America, and also that of France, have
either affixed a period for their revision, or laid down the mode
by which improvements shall be made. It is perhaps impossible to
establish anything that combines principles with opinions and
practice, which the progress of circumstances, through a length of
years, will not in some measure derange, or render inconsistent;
and, therefore, to prevent inconveniences accumulating, till they
discourage reformations or provoke revolutions, it is best to

provide the means for regulating them as they occur. The Rights of Man are the rights of all generations of men, and cannot be monopolised by any. That which is worth following, will be followed for the sake of its worth; and it is in this that its security lies, and not in any conditions with which it may be encumbered. When a man leaves property to his heirs, he does not connect it with an obligation that they shall accept it. Why then should we do otherwise with respect to constitutions?

Document 5

Though Pitt had proposed moderate parliamentary reform during the mid-1780s, new political circumstances created by revolution and war forced him not only to abandon reform but to become its decided opponent. In the Commons in May 1797, responding to Charles Grey's motion for parliamentary reform, Pitt warned of the danger posed by reformers who were influenced by French revolutionary principles, and discussed the ways in which his own thinking on reform had developed in recent times. The following sections of his address are taken from volume II of *Speeches of the Right Honourable William Pitt*, London, 1808, pp. 299–312.

The question is not merely, whether some alteration might or might not be attended with advantage; but it is the degree of advantage which that alteration is likely to effect in the shape in which it is introduced; the mischief which may be occasioned from not adopting the measure, and the chance, on the other hand, of producing by the alteration an effect upon those to whom you give way, very different from that which had induced you to hazard the experiment.

... we must consider the danger of introducing an evil of a much greater magnitude than that we are now desirous to repair; and how far it is prudent to give an opening for those principles which aim at nothing less than the total annihilation of the constitution.

... From the period when the new and alarming era of the French Revolution broke in upon the world, and the doctrines which it ushered into light laid hold of the minds of men, I found that the grounds upon which the question rested were essentially and fundamentally altered. Whatever may have been my former opinion, am I now to be told that I am inconsistent, if I feel that it is expedient to forego the advantage which any alteration may be calculated to produce, rather than afford an inlet to principles with which no compromise can be made; rather than hazard the utter annihilation of a system under which this country has flourished in its prosperity, by which it has been supported in its adversity, and by the energy and vigour of which it has been enabled to recover from the difficulties and distresses with which it has had to contend?

Document 6

The upsurge in popular agitation after 1815 was assisted by new radical organisations and vigorous recruitment, mobilisation and propaganda. Particularly important was the reform press. Lancashire weaver Samuel Bamford, who became secretary of the Middleton Hampden Club in 1816, noted the influence of William Cobbett's publications, which educated plebeian reformers and helped to create an environment within which mass political activity became possible in the immediate postwar period. Bamford's retrospective account of postwar radicalism was first published as *Passages in the Life of a Radical* in 1844. The following extract concerning the impact of Cobbett's work is taken from volume II of Bamford's *Autobiography*, ed. W. H. Chaloner, London, 1967, p. 7.

> At this time the writings of William Cobbett suddenly became of great authority; they were read on nearly every cottage hearth in the manufacturing districts of south Lancashire, in those of Leicester, Derby and Nottingham; also in many of the Scottish manufacturing towns. Their influence was speedily visible; he directed his readers to the true cause of their sufferings – misgovernment, and to its proper corrective – parliamentary reform. Riots soon became scarce, and from that time they have never obtained their ancient vogue with the labourers of this country.

Document 7

Popular agitation after the war disturbed middle-class reformers. They mistrusted independent working-class political activity, disliked the methods and goals of the plebeian leadership, and feared that the latter's lack of restraint would hinder rather than advance the cause of reform. Respectable reformers wanted to encourage and control a peaceful, honourable, principled campaign for constitutional improvement, but they found that plebeian assertiveness inhibited men of property and influence who might in other circumstances have been willing to participate. The middle-class liberal position was clearly expressed by the *Manchester Gazette* of 19 June 1819.

> It is impossible to regard without deep commiseration the sufferings of our manufacturing population, arising from the inadequate wages and the scarcity of labour; and our pity for them is augmented by perceiving that they are pursuing measures which will infallibly aggravate their distress. It must be obvious to anyone who can reason at all, that the interference of the labouring classes in political matters has almost invariably an effect contrary to that which is intended. Harsh as it may appear, we must say that poverty incapacitates for public usefulness, for the poor man has no influence otherwise than by the exertion of physical strength, to which it would be absurd as well as treasonable to have recourse.... We can account for the apathy of the rich in the cause of reform, which it is most palpably *their own interest* to obtain, no otherwise than by supposing that it originates in an undefined fear of the designs of the poor.

Document 8

The Peterloo meeting of 16 August 1819 represents a climax to the mass mobilisation of the postwar years. It was followed by repressive legislation (the 'Six Acts'), which seriously weakened plebeian radicalism. An improving economic situation in the early 1820s also weakened the reform movement, for material prosperity robbed radical leaders and organisers of their mass following. There was no suspension of political activity and discussion, however, at either middle-class or plebeian levels. A period of relative stability altered public campaigns, bringing them into line with prevalent conditions. This tendency was welcomed by Archibald Prentice, a leader of Manchester's respectable reformers, who edited the *Manchester Gazette* from 1824 to 1828. Prentice recorded in his *Historical Sketches and Personal Recollections of Manchester* (1851), new edn, London,

1970, pp. 178, 200, that radicalism was not extinguished, but became more thoughtful and deliberative after the Six Acts.

> They had the effect of repressing the wilder and more violent of the radical orators; but in so doing, they allowed the principles of reform to be more quietly and more calmly considered by men who would otherwise have been frightened by the fierce front of an intolerant radicalism.
>
> ... Instead of great meetings, where noisy braggarts usurped the place due to the intelligent and thoughtful men who represented the better part of the industrious classes, there were the little congregations of the workshop and at the fireside, at which the principles of representation were calmly discussed, and comparatively sound opinions formed, as to what ought to be the real objects of government.

Document 9

Following Lord Liverpool's stroke in February 1827, the dominant Tory alliance in parliament fell apart and the long period of Pittite-Tory ascendancy in government came to an end. Tension rose and there was a period of political flux. The Duke of Wellington became prime minister early in 1828, but he was unable to unite the Tories, not least because of controversies surrounding the repeal of the Test and Corporation Acts in 1828 and the granting of Catholic emancipation in 1829. The Wellington ministry's problems increased and Whig fortunes improved, while the return of economic hardship offered new opportunities for committed radicals out of doors. Wellington tried to take control of the situation by stating his unequivocal opposition to parliamentary reform, which he thought would bring about Tory reunion and thereby improve his government's position in parliament. He was also determined to thwart the popular reform movement. In fact his anti-reform speech in the House of Lords on 2 November 1830 brought none of the advantages for which Wellington had hoped, and his ministry resigned only days later. The following report of what was an astoundingly insensitive speech is taken from *Hansard Parliamentary Debates*, 3rd series, 1, 1831, 52–3.

> He had never read or heard of any measure ... which could in any degree satisfy his mind that the state of the representation could

be improved, or be rendered more satisfactory to the country at large.... He was fully convinced that the country possessed at the present moment a Legislature which answered all the good purposes of legislation, and this to a greater degree than any Legislature ever had answered in any country whatever. He would go further and say, that the Legislature and system of representation possessed the full and entire confidence of the country.

Document 10

The parliamentary reform bill introduced by Earl Grey's Whig-dominated administration in March 1831 surprised many contemporaries, for they had not expected the measure to be so thorough and wide-ranging. Conservatives were alarmed by what they took to be a dangerous and drastic set of proposals, while some advanced reformers rejected the bill because they found it too moderate. Respectable liberal opinion was firmly behind the Grey government, however, and at local as well as national level prominent middle-class reformers did all they could to promote the bill's passage. The early enthusiasm inspired by the government's measure is clear from remarks made at the time by Edward Baines, founder editor of the *Leeds Mercury*. The following section of a letter he wrote to his son on 6 March 1831, five days after the reform bill's introduction, is taken from Edward Baines Jr, *The Life of Edward Baines, by his Son Edward Baines*, London, 1851, pp. 153–4.

All real Reformers are highly gratified by it, and Ministers are considered to have more than redeemed their pledges. I hope they will stand firm upon the ground, and the country will beyond doubt support them. To make this support efficient, it must be prompt and decided. From the best information I can collect, the numbers in the House of Commons are likely to be nearly balanced – 300, or thereabouts, on each side, and the nation must be the arbitrators.

Bibliographical essay

The following bibliographical essay provides suggestions for further reading. It is not exhaustive, but refers solely to published sources that are of special relevance to the 'age of reform' (and those that were particularly useful in the writing of this book). All works were published in London unless otherwise stated.

The best general accounts of British politics in this period are to be found in A. Briggs, *The Age of Improvement 1783–1867*, rev. edn, 1979; E. J. Evans, *The Forging of the Modern State 1783–1870*, 2nd edn, 1996; J. B. Owen, *The Eighteenth Century 1714–1815*, 1974; N. Gash, *Aristocracy and People. Britain 1815–65*, 1979; J. S. Watson, *The Reign of George III*, Oxford, 1960; E. L. Woodward, *The Age of Reform 1815–70*, 2nd edn, Oxford, 1961; G. Williams and J. Ramsden, *Ruling Britannia. A Political History of Britain 1688–1988*, 1990; E. Halevy, *The Liberal Awakening 1815–30*, rev. edn, 1961, and *The Triumph of Reform*, 1961. J. Derry, *Politics in the Age of Fox, Pitt and Liverpool*, Basingstoke, 1990, and J. R. Dinwiddy, *From Luddism to the First Reform Bill*, Oxford, 1986, offer brief but perceptive surveys. J. O. Baylen and N. J. Gossman (eds), *Biographical Dictionary of Modern British Radicals*, 2 vols, 1979 and 1984, is a helpful reference tool. A highly significant theme in British politics between the 1780s and 1830s is examined in P. Harling, *The Waning of 'Old Corruption'. The Politics of Economical Reform in Britain 1779–1846*, Oxford, 1996.

One of the easiest and most enjoyable ways to familiarise oneself with public affairs in late eighteenth- and early nineteenth-century Britain is to sample the modern biographies of leading politicians, some of which are excellent. The best works on Pitt and Fox are J. Ehrman, *The Younger Pitt*, 3 vols, 1969, 1983 and 1996, and L. G. Mitchell, *Charles James Fox*, Oxford, 1992. N. Gash's *Lord Liverpool*, 1984, *Mr Secretary*

Peel, 1961, and *Sir Robert Peel*, 2nd edn, 1986, and E. A. Smith's *Lord Grey 1761–1845*, 2nd edn, Stroud, 1996, are all superb, but see also J. Brooke, *King George III*, 1972; P. Jupp, *Lord Grenville 1759–1834*, Oxford, 1985; P. Ziegler, *Addington. A Life of Henry Addington, First Viscount Sidmouth*, 1965; W. Hinde, *Castlereagh*, 1981; K. Bourne, *Palmerston. The Early Years 1784–1841*, 1982; C. R. Fay, *Huskisson and His Age*, 1951; N. Gash (ed.), *Wellington. Studies in the Military and Political Career of the First Duke of Wellington*, Manchester, 1990; R. Stewart, *Henry Brougham. His Public Career*, 1985; J. Prest, *Lord John Russell*, 1972.

Intellectual, religious, emotional, cultural and other influences shaping contemporary political conduct and discourse have been the subject of some extremely stimulating and often controversial books. The most important are J. C. D. Clark, *English Society 1688–1832: Ideology, Social Structure and Political Practice During the Ancien Regime*, Cambridge, 1985; R. Hole, *Pulpits, Politics and Public Order in England 1760–1832*, Cambridge, 1989; L. Colley, *Britons. Forging the Nation*, 1992; J. J. Sack, *From Jacobite to Conservative: Reaction and Orthodoxy in Britain 1760–1832*, Cambridge, 1993; J. Vernon, *Politics and the People. A Study in English Political Culture c. 1815–67*, Cambridge, 1993. See also H. T. Dickinson, 'The eighteenth-century debate on the Glorious Revolution', *History*, 61, 1976, pp. 28–45, and *Liberty and Property. Political Ideology in Eighteenth Century Britain*, 1977.

Among the many works on high and low politics in the early decades of George III's reign, there is none better than J. Brewer, *Party Ideology and Popular Politics at the Accession of George III*, Cambridge, 1976, and I. R. Christie, *Myth and Reality in Late Eighteenth-Century British Politics, and Other Papers*, 1970, both of which have stood the test of time (and been supplemented by a steady stream of essays and articles from these two distinguished scholars). For a penetrating examination of how the political system worked in the mid-eighteenth century, see L. B. Namier, *The Structure of Politics at the Accession of George III*, 2nd edn, 1963. Personalities rather than structures feature prominently in R. Pares, *George III and the Politicians*, Oxford, 1953. An informative article on a relatively neglected topic is M. W. McCahill, 'Peerage creations and the changing character of the British nobility 1750–1850', *EHR*, 96, 1981, pp. 259–84. See also J. J. Sack, 'The House of Lords and parliamentary patronage in Great Britain 1802–32', *HJ*, 23, 1980, pp. 913–37.

Pitt's premiership is outlined in D. G. Barnes, *George III and William Pitt 1783–1806*, New York, 1965, and there are some interesting articles on Pitt in *History*, 83, 1998, including M. Duffy, 'The Younger Pitt and the House of Commons', pp. 217–24; P. O'Brien, 'Political biography and Pitt the Younger as chancellor of the exchequer', pp. 225–33;

J. Mori, 'The political theory of William Pitt the Younger', pp. 234–48; D. Wilkinson, 'The Pitt–Portland coalition of 1794 and the origins of the "Tory" party', pp. 249–64. A. Aspinall, 'The cabinet council 1783–1835', *Proceedings of the British Academy*, 38, 1952, pp. 145–252, is a detailed study of the changing relations between cabinet, crown and parliament. On these matters see also A. S. Foord, 'The waning of "the influence of the crown"', *EHR*, 62, 1947, pp. 484–507.

Extra-parliamentary politics in the period before the French Revolution are analysed in I. R. Christie, *Wilkes, Wyvill and Reform*, 1962; P. D. G. Thomas, *John Wilkes. A Friend to Liberty*, Oxford, 1996; J. Saintsbury, 'John Wilkes, debt, and patriotism', *JBS*, 34, 1995, pp. 165–95; H. Butterfield, 'The Yorkshire Association and the crisis of 1779–80', *TRHS*, 4th series, 29, 1947, pp. 69–91; N. C. Phillips, 'Edmund Burke and the county movement 1779–80', *EHR*, 76, 1961, pp. 254–78.

Political change out of doors is also examined in E. C. Black, *The Association. British Extra-Parliamentary Political Organisation 1769–93*, Cambridge, Mass., 1963; M. Thale, 'London debating societies in the 1790s', *HJ*, 32, 1989, pp. 57–86. Some enlightening discussions of the role of the press in the expansion of popular politics during the late eighteenth century can be found in H. Barker, 'Catering for provincial tastes? Newspapers, readership and profit in late eighteenth-century England', *HR*, 69, 1996, pp. 42–61; E. Nicholson, 'Consumers and spectators: the public of the political print in eighteenth-century England', *History*, 81, 1996, pp. 5–21. On the continuing expansion of political consciousness and participation, see J. A. Phillips, 'Popular politics in unreformed England', *JMH*, 52, 1980, pp. 599–625, and *Electoral Behaviour in Unreformed England: Plumpers, Splitters and Straights*, Princeton, 1982; F. O'Gorman, *Voters, Patrons, and Parties. The Unreformed Electoral System of Hanoverian England 1734–1832*, Oxford, 1989, and 'Campaign rituals and ceremonies: the social meaning of elections in England 1780–1860', *P&P*, 135, 1992, pp. 79–115.

British wartime politics are examined in A. D. Harvey, *Britain in the Early Nineteenth Century*, 1978; C. Emsley, *British Society and the French Wars 1793–1815*, 1979; I. R. Christie, *Stress and Stability in Late Eighteenth-Century Britain. Reflections on the British Avoidance of Revolution*, Oxford, 1984. J. J. Sack, *The Grenvillites 1801–29. Party Politics and Factionalism in the Age of Pitt and Liverpool*, Chicago, 1979, focuses on one of the most influential political connections of the period. J. Beckett, 'Responses to war: Nottingham in the French Revolutionary and Napoleonic Wars 1793–1815', *Midland History*, 22, 1997, pp. 71–84, is an informative local study.

Political conflicts in the period of the French Revolution and subsequent wars have been investigated in G. Claeys, 'The French

Bibliographical essay

Revolution debate and British political thought', *History of Political Thought*, 11, 1990, pp. 59–80; A. Goodwin, *The Friends of Liberty. The English Democratic Movement in the Age of the French Revolution*, 1979; G. A. Williams, *Artisans and Sans-Culottes. Popular Movements in France and England during the French Revolution*, 1968; R. R. Dozier, *For King, Constitution and Country. The English Loyalists and the French Revolution*, Lexington, 1983; C. B. Cone, *The English Jacobins. Reformers in Late Eighteenth-Century England*, New York, 1968; H. T. Dickinson, *British Radicalism and the French Revolution 1789–1815*, Oxford, 1985; R. Wells, *Insurrection: The British Experience 1795–1803*, Gloucester, 1983; A. Wharam, *The Treason Trials 1794*, Leicester, 1992. Three collections of essays are essential reading: M. Philp (ed.), *The French Revolution and British Popular Politics*, Cambridge, 1991; H. T. Dickinson (ed.), *Britain and the French Revolution 1789–1815*, Basingstoke, 1989; C. Jones (ed.), *Britain and Revolutionary France: Conflict, Subversion and Propaganda*, Exeter, 1983.

Developments in Ireland, and issues relating to the 'Irish question' in British politics, are discussed in J. Kelly, *Prelude to Union: Anglo-Irish Politics in the 1780s*, Cork, 1992; A. T. Q. Stewart, *A Deeper Silence: The Hidden Origins of the United Irishmen*, 1993; J. Smyth, *The Men of No Property: Irish Radicals and Popular Politics in the Late Eighteenth Century*, 1992; K. T. Hoppen, *Ireland since 1800: Conflict and Conformity*, 1989.

On early nineteenth-century radicalism generally, E. P. Thompson's sensitive treatment of popular political ideas, activity and aspirations in *The Making of the English Working Class*, rev. edn, 1980, is of pivotal importance. C. Calhoun, *The Question of Class Struggle. Social Foundations of Popular Radicalism during the Industrial Revolution*, Oxford, 1982, is also essential reading. Some of J. R. Dinwiddy's influential articles have been collected together in his *Radicalism and Reform in Britain 1780–1850*, 1992, and another useful collection is J. Epstein, *Radical Expression: Political Language, Ritual and Symbol in England 1790–1850*, New York, 1994. J. Belchem has provided a succinct overview in his *Popular Radicalism in Nineteenth Century Britain*, Basingstoke, 1996, and the career of postwar Britain's leading radical figurehead is discussed in Belchem's *'Orator' Hunt. Henry Hunt and English Working-Class Radicalism*, Oxford, 1985. Other prominent radicals are the subjects of M. Philp, *Paine*, Oxford, 1989; I. Dyck (ed.), *Citizen of the World. Essays on Thomas Paine*, 1987; J. R. Dinwiddy, *Christopher Wyvill and Reform 1790–1820*, York, 1971; F. Knight, *The Strange Case of Thomas Walker. Ten Years in the Life of a Manchester Radical*, 1957; D. Miles, *Francis Place 1771–1854*, Brighton, 1988; N. C. Miller, 'John Cartwright and radical parliamentary reform 1808–19', *EHR*, 83, 1968, pp. 705–28; I. Dyck, *William Cobbett and Rural*

Political Culture, Cambridge, 1992; K. Schweizer and J. Osborne, *Cobbett in His Times*, Leicester, 1990; T. R. Knox, 'Thomas Spence: the trumpet of jubilee', *P&P*, 76, 1977, pp. 75–98; V. Chancellor, *The Political Life of Joseph Hume 1777–1855*, 1986; R. G. Kirby and A. E. Musson, *The Voice of the People: John Doherty 1785–1854*, Manchester, 1975.

Other aspects of extra-parliamentary political activity are considered in P. Brett, 'Political dinners in early nineteenth-century Britain: platform, meeting place and battleground', *History*, 81, 1996, pp. 527–52; P. Fraser, 'Public petitioning and parliament before 1832', *History*, 46, 1961, pp. 195–211; M. Chase, *The People's Farm. English Radical Agrarianism 1775–1840*, Oxford, 1988; N. Thompson, *The People's Science: The Popular Political Economy of Exploitation and Crisis 1816–34*, Cambridge, 1984; G. Claeys, 'The triumph of class-conscious reformism in British radicalism 1790–1860', *HJ*, 26, 1983, pp. 969–85; T. M. Parsinnen, 'Association, convention and anti-parliament in British radical politics 1771–1848', *EHR*, 88, 1973, pp. 504–33; M. I. Thomis and P. Holt, *Threats of Revolution in Britain 1789–1848*, 1977; S. Maccoby, *English Radicalism 1786–1832*, 1955; E. Royle and J. Walvin, *English Radicals and Reformers 1760–1848*, Hassocks, 1982; P. E. Spence, *The Birth of Romantic Radicalism: War, Popular Politics and English Radical Reformism 1800–15*, Aldershot, 1996; J. T. Ward (ed.), *Popular Movements 1830–50*, 1970; D. G. Wright, *Popular Radicalism. The Working-Class Experience 1780–1880*, 1988; R. J. Morris, *Class and Class Consciousness in the Industrial Revolution 1780–1850*, 1979; R. Glen, *Urban Workers in the Early Industrial Revolution*, 1984.

There have been some important studies of radicalism in local and regional contexts, notably J. A. Hone, *For the Cause of Truth: Radicalism in London 1796–1821*, Oxford, 1982; J. Stevenson, *Artisans and Democrats. Sheffield in the French Revolution 1789–97*, Sheffield, 1989; J. L. Baxter and F. K. Donnelly, 'Sheffield and the English revolutionary tradition 1790–1820', *IRSH*, 25, 1975, pp. 398–423; J. M. Main, 'Radical Westminster 1807–20', *HSANZ*, 12, 1966, pp. 186–204; T. M. Parsinnen, 'The revolutionary party in London 1816–20', *HR*, 45, 1972, pp. 266–82; D. Read, *Peterloo. The Massacre and its Background*, 2nd edn, 1973; A. Temple Patterson, 'Luddism, Hampden Clubs, and trade unions in Leicestershire 1816–17', *EHR*, 63, 1948, pp. 170–88; A. Prentice, *Historical Sketches and Personal Recollections of Manchester*, 2nd edn, 1970.

J. Bohstedt, *Riots and Community Politics in England and Wales 1790–1810*, 1983, examines the changing nature of popular protest with specific reference to Manchester and Devon, an expanding commercial centre and a predominantly rural county. Luddism is investigated in J. R. Dinwiddy, 'Luddism and politics in the northern counties', *SH*, 4, 1979, pp. 33–63; F. O. Darvall, *Popular Disturbances and Public Order in*

Regency England, 2nd edn, Oxford, 1969; M. I. Thomis, *The Luddites. Machine Breaking in Regency England*, Newton Abbot, 1970. Disorder in the English counties has been analysed in G. Rude and E. Hobsbawm, *Captain Swing*, 1973. J. Stevenson, *Popular Disturbances in England 1700–1832*, 2nd edn, 1992, is the best general account of protest in this period.

On respectable middle-class radicalism see M. J. Turner, *Reform and Respectability. The Making of a Middle-Class Liberalism in Early Nineteenth-Century Manchester*, Manchester, 1995; A. Briggs, 'Middle-class consciousness in English politics 1780–1846', *P&P*, 9, 1956, pp. 65–72; J. E. Cookson, *The Friends of Peace. Anti-War Liberalism in England 1793–1815*, Cambridge, 1982; R. G. Cowherd, *The Politics of English Dissent*, 1959; R. E. Richey, 'The origins of English radicalism: the changing rationale for Dissent', *Eighteenth Century Studies*, 7, 1973–4, pp. 179–92; J. Seed, 'Gentlemen Dissenters. The social and political meanings of rational Dissent in the 1770s and 1780s', *HJ*, 28, 1985, pp. 299–325; R. J. Morris, 'The middle class and British towns and cities of the industrial revolution 1780–1870', in D. Fraser and A. Sutcliffe (eds), *The Pursuit of Urban History*, 1983, pp. 286–306, and 'Voluntary societies and British urban elites 1780–1850. An analysis', *HJ*, 26, 1983, pp. 95–111; J. Hamburger, *James Mill and the Art of Revolution*, New Haven, 1963; W. Thomas, *The Philosophic Radicals. Nine Studies in Theory and Practice 1817–41*, Oxford, 1979; G. Finlayson, 'Joseph Parkes of Birmingham, 1796–1865: a study in philosophic radicalism', *HR*, 46, 1973, pp. 186–201; D. Nicholls, 'The English middle class and the ideological significance of radicalism 1760–1886', *JBS*, 24, 1985, pp. 415–33.

Two important books on the government of Lord Liverpool are J. E. Cookson, *Lord Liverpool's Administration: The Crucial Years 1815–22*, Edinburgh, 1975, and A. J. B. Hilton, *Corn, Cash and Commerce. The Economic Policies of the Tory Governments 1815–30*, Oxford, 1977. See also Hilton's 'Lord Liverpool: the art of politics and the practice of government', *TRHS*, 5th series, 38, 1988, pp. 147–70; N. Gash, 'After Waterloo: British society and the legacy of the Napoleonic Wars', *TRHS*, 5th series, 28, 1978, pp. 145–57; B. Gordon, *Political Economy in Parliament 1819–23*, 1976, and *Economic Doctrine and Tory Liberalism 1824–30*, 1979. The nature of post-Pitt Toryism is analysed in J. J. Sack, 'The memory of Burke and Pitt: English Conservatism confronts its past 1806–29', *HJ*, 30, 1987, pp. 623–40.

Vital developments in high politics after the time of Pitt and Fox are examined in four articles by A. Aspinall: 'The Canningite party', *TRHS*, 4th series, 17, 1934, pp. 177–226; 'The coalition ministries of 1827', *EHR*, 42, 1927, pp. 201–26, 533–59; 'English party organisation in the early nineteenth century', *EHR*, 41, 1926, pp. 389–411; 'The last of the Canningites', *EHR*, 50, 1935, pp. 639–69. Party formation is also among the themes taken up in B. W. Hill, *British Parliamentary Parties 1742–1832*, 1985; E. J. Evans, *Political Parties in Britain 1783–1867*, 1985; F. O'Gorman, *The Emergence of the British Two-Party System, 1760–1832*, 1982, and 'Party politics in the early nineteenth century, 1812–32', *EHR*, 102, 1987, pp. 63–88; P. Fraser, 'Party voting in the House of Commons 1812–27', *EHR*, 98, 1983, pp. 763–84; D. Large, 'The decline of the "party of the crown" and the rise of parties in the House of Lords 1783–1837', *EHR*, 78, 1963, pp. 669–95; D. Beales, 'Parliamentary parties and the "independent" Member 1810–60', in R. Robson (ed.), *Ideas and Institutions of Victorian Britain*, 1967, pp. 1–19; J. A. W. Gunn, 'Influence, parties and the constitution: changing attitudes 1783–1832', *HJ*, 17, 1974, pp. 301–28; B. W. Hill, 'Executive monarchy and the challenge of the parties 1689–1832: two concepts of government and two historiographical interpretations', *HJ*, 13, 1970, pp. 379–401; J. C. D. Clark, 'A general theory of party, opposition and government, 1688–1832', *HJ*, 23, 1980, pp. 295–325.

Whigs and Whiggism are studied in S. Farrell, 'Division lists and the nature of the Rockingham Whig party in the House of Lords 1760–85', *PH*, 13, 1994, pp. 170–89; B. W. Hill, 'Fox and Burke: the Whig party and the question of principles 1784–9', *EHR*, 89, 1974, pp. 1–24; R. W. Davis, 'Whigs in the age of Fox and Grey', *PH*, 12, 1993, pp. 201–8; A. D. Kriegel, 'Liberty and Whiggery in early nineteenth-century England', *JMH*, 52, 1980, pp. 253–78; E. A. Smith, *Whig Principles and Party Politics. Earl Fitzwilliam and the Whig Party 1748–1833*, Manchester, 1975; M. Roberts, *The Whig Party 1807–12*, 2nd edn, 1965; D. Rapp, 'The left-wing Whigs: Whitbread, the Mountain and reform 1809–15', *JBS*, 21, 1982, pp. 35–66; E. A. Wasson, 'The coalitions of 1827 and the crisis of Whig leadership', *HJ*, 20, 1977, pp. 587–606, and 'The great Whigs and parliamentary reform 1809–30', *JBS*, 24, 1985, pp. 434–64; A. Mitchell, 'The Whigs and parliamentary reform before 1830', *HSANZ*, 12, 1965, pp. 22–42, and *The Whigs in Opposition 1815–30*, Oxford, 1967; E. A. Wasson, *Whig Renaissance: Lord Althorp and the Whig Party 1782–1845*, New York, 1987.

There have been many studies of the specific issues which divided politicians and public in late eighteenth- and early nineteenth-century Britain. On the corn laws see D. G. Groves, *A History of the English Corn Laws from 1660 to 1846*, 2nd edn, 1961; T. L. Crosby, *English Farmers and the Politics of Protection 1815–52*, Hassocks, 1977; C. R. Fay, *Corn Laws and Social England*, Cambridge, 1932; S. Fairlie, 'The corn laws and British wheat production 1829–76', *EcHR*, 22, 1969, pp. 88–116, and 'The nineteenth-century corn law reconsidered', *EcHR*, 18, 1965, pp. 563–74; M. J. Turner, 'Before the Manchester School: economic ideas in early nineteenth-century Manchester', *History*, 79, 1994, pp. 216–41. The Catholic question is the focus of G. I. T. Machin, *The Catholic Question in English Politics 1820–30*, Oxford, 1964, and 'Canning, Wellington and the Catholic question', *EHR*, 109, 1984, pp. 94–100; G. Best, 'The Protestant constitution and its supporters 1800–29', *TRHS*, 5th series, 8, 1958, pp. 105–27; R. W. Davis, 'Tories, Whigs and Catholic emancipation 1827–9', *EHR*, 97, 1982, pp. 89–98. See also U. Henriques, *Religious Toleration in England 1787–1833*, 1961. Agitation against the slave trade is among the topics covered in D. Turley, *The Culture of English Antislavery 1780–1860*, 1991; M. J. Turner, 'The limits of abolition: government, Saints and the "African question" 1780–1820', *EHR*, 112, 1997, pp. 319–57; S. Drescher, 'Whose abolition? Popular pressure and the ending of the British slave trade', *P&P*, 143, 1994, pp. 136–66; R. J. Hind, 'William Wilberforce and the perceptions of the British people', *HR*, 60, 1987, pp. 321–35; A. D. Kriegel, 'A convergence of ethics: Saints and Whigs in British antislavery', *JBS*, 26, 1987, pp. 423–50; R. Blackburn, *The Overthrow of Colonial Slavery 1776–1848*, 1988.

On those influences and events that eventually led to parliamentary reform in 1832, J. Cannon, *Parliamentary Reform 1640–1832*, Cambridge, 1973, is a full and informative study, but there are also some useful articles, notably G. M. Ditchfield, 'The House of Lords and parliamentary reform in the 1790s', *HR*, 54, 1981, pp. 207–25; W. Thomas, 'James Mill's politics. The "Essay on Government" and the movement for reform', *HJ*, 12, 1969, pp. 249–84, and debate between Thomas and W. R. Carr in the same journal, 14, 1971, pp. 553–80, 735–50, and 15, 1972, pp. 315–20; M. J. Turner, 'Manchester reformers and the Penryn seats 1827–28', *NH*, 30, 1994, pp. 139–60. On the reform of 1832, M. Brock, *The Great Reform Act*, 1973, is the standard account. See also M. O'Neill and G. Martin, 'A backbencher on parliamentary reform 1831–32', *HJ*, 23, 1980, pp. 539–63; J. A. Phillips, 'The many faces of reform: the reform bill and the electorate', *PH*, 1, 1982, pp. 115–35; N. McCord, 'Some difficulties of parliamentary reform', *HJ*, 10, 1967, pp. 376–90; D. C. Moore, 'Concession or cure: the sociological premises of the First Reform Act', *HJ*, 9, 1966, pp. 39–59; R. W. Davis, 'Deference and aristocracy in the time of the Great Reform Act', *AmHR*, 81, 1976, pp. 532–9, and 'Toryism to Tamworth: the triumph of reform 1827–35', *Albion*, 12, 1980, pp. 132–46; J. Milton-Smith, 'Earl Grey's cabinet and the objects of parliamentary reform', *HJ*, 15, 1972, pp. 55–74; E. P. Hennock, 'The sociological premises of the First Reform Act: a critical note', *VS*, 14, 1971, pp. 321–7; F. O'Gorman, 'The electorate before and after 1832', *PH*, 12, 1993, pp. 171–83; L. G. Mitchell, 'Foxite politics and the Great Reform Bill', *EHR*, 108, 1993, pp. 338–64.

Bibliographical essay

Extra-parliamentary forces promoting the reform of 1832 have been discussed in A. Briggs, 'The background of the parliamentary reform movement in three English cities', in the first volume (of three) of his *Collected Essays*, Brighton, 1985, pp. 180–200; R. Quinault, 'The French Revolution of 1830 and parliamentary reform', *History*, 79, 1994, pp. 377–93; P. Brett, 'John Fife and Tyneside radicalism in the 1830s', *NH*, 33, 1997, pp. 184–217; H. Ferguson, 'The Birmingham Political Union and the government 1831–32', *VS*, 3, 1960, pp. 261–76; N. Lopatin, 'Political unions and the Great Reform Act', *PH*, 10, 1991, pp. 105–23; J. E. Crimmins, 'Jeremy Bentham and Daniel O'Connell: their correspondence and radical alliance 1828–31', *HJ*, 40, 1997, pp. 359–87; G. Rude, 'English rural and urban disturbances on the eve of the First Reform Bill, 1830–31', *P&P*, 37, 1967, pp. 87–102.

Index

Index

Index

Sheridan, Richard Brinsley 43, 62, 71
Sidmouth, Henry Addington, 1st Viscount 44–7, 74–81, 117, 124, 126
sinking fund 34–5, 74, 107, 131, 143
'Six Acts' (1819) 118–19, 121, 126, 135, 214–15
slavery and the slave trade 8, 41, 64, 78–9, 86, 91, 100–1, 172
Smith, Adam 35
Society for Constitutional Information (SCI) 84–5
Society for the Diffusion of Useful Knowledge 122
Society of the Friends of the People 64–5, 85, 89
specie payments
  suspension (1797) 73, 129
  resumption (1819) 129, 131, 171
Spenceans 113, 119
Stamp Act (1765) 14
stamp duty 111
Stanley, Edward George 174
Stevenson, John 87, 173, 193–4

Temple, George Nugent Temple Grenville, 3rd Earl 30
Test and Corporation Acts 7, 62, 64, 86, 159–60, 169, 181, 215
Thelwall, John 89
Thistlewood, Arthur 119
Thompson, E. P. 2, 5–6, 9, 85, 90–1, 94, 149
Thurlow, Edward, 1st Baron 29–30, 41
Tierney, George 64–5, 71, 74, 76, 127, 132–4, 155, 158
Tooke, John Horne 89
Tories and Toryism 5, 8–9, 48–9, 81–2, 109, 125, 127–8, 140–9, 153–8, 160, 162–9, 174–5, 177–80, 183–5, 187–94, 196–8, 203–4, 206, 215
Treasonable Practices Act (1795) 69, 89, 91, 98

Union Societies 112
United Englishmen 90

United Irishmen 90
United States of America 92, 111, 118
University College, London 122

volunteer movement 99–100, 206

Wahrman, Dror 86, 93
Walker, Thomas 89
Wasson, E. A. 155, 197
Wellington, Arthur Wellesley, 1st Duke of 124, 141, 153–4, 156–69, 172, 174–7, 179, 184, 186–7, 189–91, 193, 196–8, 215
Westminster 21, 37, 95, 115
Westminster Committee 95, 115
West Riding 35, 90, 135
Wharncliffe, James Archibald Stuart-Wortley-Mackenzie, 1st Baron 187, 189
Whigs and Whiggism 2–5, 11–13, 17–18, 33, 42–3, 45–6, 48–9, 51–2, 56, 58, 61–8, 70–1, 74, 78, 80–5, 95, 101, 106, 109–10, 115, 120, 123–5, 127, 129, 131–41, 146, 149, 153–61, 163–70, 173–6, 178–9, 182, 185, 191–4, 196–7, 203–4, 206, 209, 215–16
Whitbread, Samuel 78, 83, 109
Wilberforce, William 79, 91
Wilkes, John 12–14, 84, 89, 205
William IV 172, 175–6, 178–80, 183–94, 198
Winchilsea, George William Finch-Hatton, 10th Earl of 163
Windham, William 62–3, 67, 69, 77, 79–80
Wood, Matthew 120
Wooler, Thomas Jonathan 111, 115, 118
Wynn, Charles 133, 146
Wyvill, Christopher 14, 19, 22, 25, 37, 63, 85, 87, 95, 115, 205

York, Prince Frederick, Duke of 91
Yorke, Henry 89
Yorkshire 126, 137, 173, 177
Yorkshire Association 14

Printed in the United Kingdom by
Lightning Source UK Ltd., Milton Keynes
142298UK00001B/20/A